Psychoanalytic therapy in the hospital setting

Though the impetus for psychoanalytic and group-analytic inpatient psychotherapy largely came from Britain, it is in Germany that this work has been supported, developed and researched to a greater extent than elsewhere.

Psychoanalytic Therapy in the Hospital Setting describes this development and the different models which have been tried and evaluated, and Paul Janssen explains his integrative model in detail, illustrating it with vivid clinical vignettes.

This German experience has not previously been made known to English-speaking readers and will stimulate and encourage workers in this area, especially as changes in health delivery militate against this approach.

Paul Janssen has a unique knowledge of the British and German scene and has clearly and lucidly described them both.

Psychoanalytic Therapy in the Hospital Setting will be invaluable reading for psychiatrists, psychotherapists, nurses, social workers and anyone working in health care.

Paul Janssen is Chair of Psychosomatic Medicine and Psychotherapy at the University of Bochum and Director of the Psychiatric Hospital of Dortmund.

The International Library of Group Psychotherapy and Group Process

General Editor

Dr Malcolm Pines
Institute of Group-Analysis, London, and formerly of the Tavistock Clinic, London

The International Library of Group Psychotherapy and Group Process is published in association with the Institute of Group-Analysis (London) and is devoted to the systematic study and exploration of group psychotherapy.

Psychoanalytic therapy in the hospital setting

Paul Janssen

Translated by Dinah Cannell

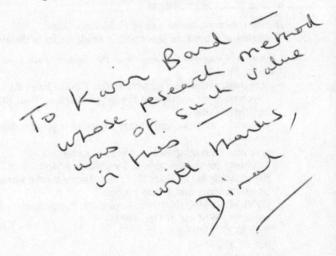

To Karin Bond —
whose research method
was of such value
in this —
with thanks,
Dinah

London and New York

First published by Ernst Klett Verlag für Wissen und Bildung GmbH, Stuttgart

© Ernst Klett Verlag für Wissen und Bildung GmbH, Stuttgart 1987

English-language edition first published 1994
by Routledge
11 New Fetter Lane, London EC4P 4EE

Simultaneously published in the USA and Canada
by Routledge
29 West 35th Street, New York, NY 10001

© English translation: Dinah Cannell 1994

Typeset in Times by Florencetype Ltd, Kewstoke, Avon
Printed and bound in Great Britain by Mackays of Chatham PLC,
Chatham, Kent

British Library Cataloguing in Publication Data
A catalogue record for this book is available from the British Library.

Library of Congress Cataloging in Publication Data
Janssen, Paul L.
   [Psychoanalytische Therapie in der Klinik. English]
   Psychoanalytic therapy in the hospital setting/Paul Janssen; translated
   by Dinah Cannell.
   p. cm. – (International library of group psychotherapy and group
   process)
   Includes bibliographical references and index.
   1. Group psychotherapy. 2. Psychiatric hospital care. 3. Group
   psychoanalysis. I. Title. II. Series: International library of group
   psychotherapy and group process.
   [DNLM: 1. Models, Psychological. 2. Psychoanalytic Therapy–
   methods. WM 460.6 J35p 1993]
   RC488.J3713 1993
   616.89′152–dc20
   DNLM/DLC
   for Library of Congress   93–20497
                                                                      CIP

ISBN 0-415-07295-6 (hbk)
ISBN 0-415-07296-4 (pbk)

Contents

Illustrations

As you know, we have never prided ourselves on the completeness and finality of our knowledge and capacity. We are just as ready now as we were earlier to admit the imperfections of our understanding, to learn new things and to alter our methods in any way that can improve them.

It is very probable, too, that the large-scale application of our therapy will compel us to alloy the pure gold of analysis freely with the copper of direct suggestion; . . . But, whatever form this psychotherapy for the people may take, whatever the elements out of which it is compounded, its most effective and most important ingredients will assuredly remain those borrowed from strict and untendentious psychoanalysis.

Sigmund Freud 'Lines of Advance in Psycho-Analytic Therapy'

Foreword

This book on inpatient group therapy is of great interest and value to the English-speaking world. Professor Janssen gives us a unique opportunity to share his wide and deep experience of inpatient group psychotherapy in Germany over the past thirty years, of which little is yet translated into English. His extensive bibliography which is mostly of German-language articles attests to this. Yet the reader will soon recognize that the work is of great value to all psychotherapists working in this area.

In England and North America inpatient group psychotherapy has received neither the support from the health services nor the attention of the academic world that is exemplified in this book, and our loss is evident. Janssen and his colleagues have had the opportunity to try different models of inpatient group therapy and to research their effects. The outcome results are 'good enough' to encourage further work and development of this field and it is opportune that this translation is available at a time of great change in mental health delivery services, particularly in Britain. Psychotherapy, both out- and inpatient, is under threat; financial support is difficult to obtain and maintain; audits and efficiency drives challenge therapists to prove their worth; short-term treatments with biological methods have the ascendance. Yet therapists know from long experience that the large number of people with personality disorders, the borderline states, the 'ego-structural' problems described by Janssen, do need and do respond to skilled inpatient group therapy. Ironically, as Janssen describes, the approach originated in Britain, and his stay at the Cassel Hospital, then directed by T.F. Main, gave him firsthand experience of this pioneer centre of excellence, and this has influenced his own work. Main's work originated in the wartime experience of British psychiatry, particularly at Northfield Hospital where he and Foulkes were colleagues. I am happy to have been able to help Professor Janssen to make that visit to the Cassel Hospital and to have arranged for this publication.

Many therapists will both admire and envy the facilities that the German health services provide through the support both of the state and of the insurance schemes. The skilled teams combine the resources of psychoanalysts, psychotherapists, nurses, art and music therapists, and how well these resources are used is exemplified in the vivid clinical vignettes that Janssen describes. I am particularly impressed by the work of the music therapists; perhaps the deep and strong musical tradition of the German-speaking countries has been its source.

Inpatient group therapy has a strong position in the Netherlands, in Belgium and some parts of Scandinavia and North America. The health authorities of these countries, predominantly Germany, have recognized that such patients are not to be treated only as nuisances, as not ill in any acceptable psychiatric diagnosis, but as disturbed people who will continue in their morbid conditions until effectively treated. This book clearly demonstrates that effective treatment is achievable and should bring much needed stimulation and encouragement to its readers.

Malcolm Pines

Chapter 1

Introduction

The type of therapy I shall be discussing in this book takes place at the junction where psychoanalysis and the hospital meet. My aim is to show how theories about the genesis of psychic illness become analytic practice in the clinical setting. The demands of the inpatient environment have challenged analysts to revise their concepts and design new models. Theory is driven by need, and practice generated by theory, in a process of reciprocal influence. As ideas are tested, untrodden avenues are opened up and theoretical underpinning is given to experimental techniques. I shall be taking the reader through this process as it has unfolded in German hospitals committed to psychosomatic medicine and the provision of inpatient psychotherapy. In so doing, I hope to contribute to general thinking on the place of psychoanalytic theory and practice in hospitals everywhere.

My immediate focus will be on mental health structures in western Germany. I am aware that there has been work done in the same field in North America (see Yalom 1983; Rice and Rutan 1987), in England, especially, as documented in the present book, at the Cassel Hospital, as well as in the Netherlands, in Belgium and in other countries. My intention here is not to compare these approaches – such a comparison may well be the subject of a future book by myself or others – but to focus on work done in western Germany in the last thirty years. As the field is so rich in experiments of different kinds, let me begin with a little orientation.

The first attempt to introduce analytic principles into inpatient psychic care was made by Simmel (1928). This venture did not last long (cf. Schulz and Hermanns 1987), although Simmel's ideas were taken up and developed in America (Menninger 1936). It was not until after the war that any further progress took place in

Germany itself. In 1948, a residential centre for the treatment of psychogenic disorders was opened in Berlin (Wiegmann 1968).[1] A similar move followed in 1949 at Tiefenbrunn, near Göttingen. In 1950, a unit was set up for the treatment of psychosomatic disorders in Heidelberg. Headed by Alexander Mitscherlich, it was equipped with its own inpatient ward. The University of Freiburg's Department of Medicine established a psychosomatic ward in a country house at Umkirch in 1959. All of these pioneering clinical approaches to the treatment of neurotic and psychosomatic disorders were grounded in psychoanalytic theory.

As the years went by, more beds became available for patients needing residential care for psychic and psychosomatic ailments. Recent surveys (Lachauer *et al.* 1992; Meyer *et al.* 1991) speak of around 100 units and a total of 8,000 to 10,000 beds. The main thrust of therapeutic work is analytic, although other methods are employed: behavioural, person-centred, Gestalt, psychodrama. Most models incorporate a creative and active component: art, music, dance movement therapies, autogenic training, etc. Milieu therapy is frequently offered on the ward.

While inpatient capacity has been constantly growing since 1950, the same cannot be said of enthusiasm on the part of psychoanalysts (cf. Strotzka 1975) and psychiatrists (cf. Häfner 1975). The general sentiment has been that inpatient psychotherapy fails to cater for adequate working through of unconscious material. One explanation for this scepticism is that inpatient psychotherapy has usually been seen as outpatient treatment in an inpatient environment, with no concern for the impact of the hospital setting on therapeutic processes. Inpatient and outpatient practitioners alike have been the losers.

Given all the criticism – not only from psychiatrists, but also from fellow psychotherapists and analysts not involved in hospital work – I decided to subject the inpatient enterprise to some rigorous interrogation. What are the indications for inpatient psychotherapy? How is residential treatment organized and administered? Which methods have proved most successful? The answers to these questions are of scholarly as well as practical interest. The type of inpatient therapy I shall be championing draws on the insights of traditional psychoanalysis, as well as

[1] *Translator's note.* Since clinical structures in different countries seldom match perfectly, the English renderings of German hospital terms given here are necessarily approximations.

looking to subsequent developments, in particular object relations theory. I am assuming a readership with some background knowledge of analytic thinking. Where more specialist issues are touched upon, references are given to the literature.

Chapter 2 offers a brief history of psychoanalysis, enabling newcomers to the field to appreciate what is at stake when applying analytic principles in a hospital setting. In a second section, I comment on the modifications in technique necessitated by transposition to an inpatient environment.

At this introductory stage, I can but hint at the issues surrounding the question: when is inpatient psychotherapy indicated? Each individual case has to be considered on its own merits and assessed in the light of a commonly agreed set of criteria (cf. Janssen 1981b). Inpatient treatment is generally indicated where:

- the patient's symptoms preclude him[2] from pursuing outpatient therapy, e.g. cases of severe agoraphobia, anxiety neurosis, obsessional neurosis;
- internal medical diagnosis and care are required, e.g. psychosomatic patients with acute physical symptoms;
- the individual concerned is incapable of engaging in, and sustaining, an oupatient therapeutic relationship, e.g. patients with pronounced ego weakness;
- crisis intervention is required to deal with acute decompensation;
- the patient needs to be taken out of a milieu which appears to be shoring up his pathogenic psychodynamics;
- regional shortages of outpatient psychotherapists make hospital admission the only option.

The underlying question running like a red thread through this book is: how can we design an inpatient setting which truly harnesses and exploits all the elements present in a hospital environment (Fürstenau 1974, 1977c)? Over the years, psychoanalysts with a commitment to residential therapy have been battling to find the answer. They have tackled problems of organization, administration, staff relations, lack of premises, hospital timetables, etc. In order to obtain as complete a picture as possible, I

---

[2] *Translator's note.* Where the sex of therapist or patient is not defined by the particular circumstance described, he or she is referred to, for convenience, in the masculine gender throughout this book; such references should be taken to imply male or female.

undertook to find out how different clinicians had coped in different situations with different patient groups. The results of this investigation will be found in Chapter 3.

Chapter 4 is devoted to my own attempts to put analytic theory into institutional practice. I was determined to carry out a running evaluation of the validity of my chosen method; details of assessment and outcome studies are duly provided. Finally, Chapter 5 offers a *theory of practice*, backed by extracts from case histories and scenes from ward life.

My hope is that I will succeed in convincing the doubters of the credentials of inpatient analytic psychotherapy. It is, I believe, a bona fide form of psychoanalytic practice – tailored to meet the needs of patients who are beyond the therapeutic reach of outpatient care.

The ideas I shall be presenting have grown out of personal clinical experience and hours of fruitful discussion with colleagues and co-workers from all fields of therapy. My gratitude goes out to them for their cooperation and commitment. Thanks also to Dinah Cannell, the translator, and to Edwina Welham of Routledge, who took charge of the English-language edition. Finally, I am grateful to the Breuninger Foundation for assistance with the costs of translation.

Chapter 2

The psychoanalytic method
Basic principles

All varieties of psychoanalytic therapy concern themselves with causality in that they look to those parts of the personality which are infantile, unperceived and pathogenic, seeking to bring them into consciousness. Once individuals can acknowledge this hidden dimension, they are better able to live an integrated inner life. Fürstenau (1977b) has described the mission of psychoanalysis as 'the rendering conscious of residual infantile patterns, liable to keep people unconsciously tied to parents or parent representatives'. The psychoanalyst is not an operator with a patented technique to apply; he is implicated in the analytic process as an ordinary person with ordinary affective responses (Morgenthaler 1978). We are not talking about a rationally-driven, cognitive approach to the problems of childhood, but rather an exploration of infantile patterns of relating. Unconsciously, past constellations take shape afresh in new relationships. The analytic situation allows these workings to be observed in action and talked through (Fürstenau 1977b).

Early experiments in psychoanalysis led to the development of the *classical technique*, characterized by a one-to-one, highly personal, relationship between patient and analyst. This original dyad has left its imprint on all subsequent forms of psychoanalytic therapy. Attempts to treat more severe psychical disorders admittedly led to technical adjustments; alternative settings were envisaged and new therapeutic goals pursued. The dyadic setting has none the less remained a constant in analytic psychotherapy (cf. Blanck and Blanck 1974, 1979; Kernberg 1975a, 1981; Kutter 1977) and in dynamic psychotherapy (Dührssen 1972).

One-to-one is also the norm in brief or focal psychotherapy (cf. Balint *et al.* 1972; Malan 1963; Beck 1974; Bellak and Small 1965).

Where psychic problems appear to be clearly circumscribed, agreement is reached at the outset to focus in therapy on particular elements of neurotic conflict only; ancillary material is not interpreted, whereas it would be under a classical approach.

Nowadays analysts also work on relationships within couples (cf. Richter 1970; Willi 1975, 1978), families (cf. Richter 1970; Stierlin 1975) and inside groups. The first two permutations need not concern us here, but no one with a commitment to inpatient therapy can afford to ignore the significance of group experience. Multipersonal configurations are part and parcel of the hospital setting – which explains why so much attention will be paid in the pages that follow to group-analytic psychotherapy.

THE CLASSICAL TECHNIQUE

Once Freud (1914) had put the finishing touches to his writings on technique, exposition of the psychoanalytic method was virtually complete (Greenson 1967; Sandler *et al*. 1973). In terms of the structural theory of the mind, the aim of psychoanalysis was to bring to the level of consciousness *unconscious infantile drive-defence conflicts* (i.e the intersystemic rivalry between ego, superego/ego ideal and id). This was to be achieved by working through and interpreting the *transference neurosis* generated by the analytic situation. Cremerius (1977a) took his lead from Rangell in describing psychoanalysis as:

> a therapeutic method which favours the development of transference neurosis. The past is recreated in the present and neurosis (transference and infantile) can then be combated via a concerted interpretative assault on resistance. The aim throughout is to promote structural modification of the psychical apparatus, enabling it to adjust optimally to the world around.

An intact ego and reasonably sound reality-testing faculties were among the prerequisites if patients were to benefit from analysis of this kind. The ego had to be capable of sustaining a split into an experiencing and an observing part; the individual entered into a pact with the analysing ego of the analyst. Psychoanalysis accordingly held out the greatest promise for those patients who had reached the oedipal phase of drive and ego development. Interpretation by the analyst granted them insight into possible oedipal complications, incest wishes and castration anxieties (cf. Tyson and Sandler 1974).

Let us now consider the *basic model of psychoanalysis* and how the goals just outlined are achieved. (Detailed surveys of method can be found in the literature, e.g. Fenichel 1941; Greenson 1967; Sandler *et al.* 1973.) The process begins with an initial interview or a trial therapy session. The psychic pain beset-ting the potential analysand provides him with the motivation to seek psychoanalytic help. The next step is the actual decision to engage in a working alliance with the analyst. This threshold will be crossed if the patient's first contact with the therapist touches off a desire for self-exploration and encounter. The analyst's decision as to whether or not to enter into a therapeutic pact with the patient is less clear-cut. Countertransference reactions and diagnostic ability play their part, as do practical considerations: how much money the patient can afford to pay, where he lives, how much of his time he is willing to invest, the likely duration of treatment etc.

Once agreement to go ahead has been reached (Freud 1913), the future analysand is told what the therapeutic process will entail: *free association* (the patient 'tells everything' that passes through his mind); the *setting* or 'ceremonial' (the patient lies on a couch, with the analyst sitting out of sight at the head end); punctuality (sessions start and finish at a fixed time); a regular pattern of attendance (four to five times a week); the investment of time and money; agreed holiday period; discretion.

The key elements of the analysis from the patient's point of view are: free association, transference, resistance, the working alliance and working through. It is vital that patients comply with the *basic* or *fundamental rule*, i.e. they must report everything that comes into their mind. Greenson rightly pointed to free association as the doorway to the unconscious, 'the basic and unique method of communication for patients in psychoanalytic treatment' (1967: 10). The dynamics of the therapeutic process are sustained by the fact that the personal and private concerns of the analyst are kept out of the process (rule of abstinence), while the patient agrees theoretically to be as open as possible. *Resistance* to the unveiling of embarrassing thoughts and feelings inevitably develops, pulling him back from the brink of disclosure. This must be overcome, since analysis hinges on uncovering and illuminating unconscious defences, drives and infantile patterns of relating. Resistance is structurally anchored within the personality; its workings can be detected in all areas of behaviour, although a strong defence reaction is the the most common manifestation. *Transference* refers to the process whereby the analysand's feelings, desires and imaginings – both positive and negative – are directed towards the analyst. The inappropriateness of these feelings is the clearest indicator that transference is involved.

Work on transference is at the heart of psychoanalytic therapy. An actual *transference neurosis* is induced and lived out. 'Transference reactions are essentially repetitions of a past object relationship', said Greenson (1967: 153). Unconscious conflicts leave their imprint in infancy and are transferred to the therapist in analysis. As Greenson noted: 'The transference reaction is unsuitable in its current context; but it was once an appropriate reaction to a past situation' (ibid.: 152). Defences and drives come to the fore as forgotten scenes from the past are relived in the present. Some of these have a libidinal, others an aggressive hue. Through the medium of the analyst past experience is re-actualized. It can be observed and elucidated, interpreted and processed; no longer does it stand in the way of growth. The developing transference neurosis makes way for dramatization in the present of bygone infantile neurosis; unconscious relationships with primary objects surface. Resolution of transference neurosis through the process of analysis simultaneously brings about resolution of infantile neurosis. Reconstruction of the infantile scene restores to the patient a portion of his forgotten past (cf. Freud 1937; Lorenzer 1970; Greenacre 1976). Transference is not the end of the story, however. The analysand must enter into a proper *working alliance* with the analyst.

> The working alliance is the relatively nonneurotic, rational relationship between patient and analyst which makes it possible for the patient to work purposefully in the analytic situation . . . The alliance is formed between the patient's reasonable ego and the analyst's analyzing ego . . . The significant occurrence is a partial and temporary identification that the patient makes with the analyst's attitude and method of work . . .
> (Greenson 1967: 46)

Since the uncovering of unconscious conflict is impeded by powerful resistance, a repeated and comprehensive processing effort is required, known as *working through*. The very term underscores the difficulty of the enterprise. Resistance is stubborn and structurally embedded in the personality; it stands out firmly against insight and change.

The task of the analyst in the psychoanalytic process is to uphold the parameters of therapy, enabling ego functions to operate and keeping the patient 'analysable'. Unconscious, newly actualized patterns of relating take shape in the particular constellation of transference and resistance (cf. Fürstenau 1977b). This is the raw material the therapist is called upon to process. Interpretation has generally been viewed as the prime analytic task (cf. Sandler *et al.* 1973), so let us now consider how this becomes possible, i.e. how the analyst proceeds towards 'concept-oriented perception and the assimilation and processing of that perception' (Fürstenau 1977b).

Freud wrote in 1923:

> Experience soon showed that the attitude which the analytic physician could most advantageously adopt was to surrender himself to his own unconscious mental activity, in a state of *evenly suspended attention*, to avoid as far as possible reflection and the construction of conscious expectations, not to try to fix anything that he heard particularly in his memory, and by these means to catch the drift of the patient's unconscious with his own unconscious. (Freud 1923: 239)

Through *identification* (Freud 1921) – also known as empathy – the analyst stood a chance of understanding what was going on inside his patient. Only then was interpretation possible. Loch (1965b) described empathy as 'a quality enabling us to identify on a temporary basis' with the analysand; without this capability all that remained was 'dead knowledge, devoid of any dynamic effect'.

Lorenzer (1970) pinpointed three types of analytic understanding: the logical, the psychological and the 'scene-aware'. Logical understanding involves comprehending meanings and connections which can be expressed in words. Psychological understanding affords insight into the workings of the person using those words. *Scene-aware* understanding entails grasping the whole of a situation, i.e. the current transference position plus the infantile scene. The scene-aware analyst notes those patterns of interaction and object-relating which signal the fulfilment, consciously or unconsciously, of instinctual desires.

Greenson (1967) called the ability to get inside a patient *empathy*.

> Empathy is a method of establishing close contact in terms of emotions and impulses . . . [it] leads to feelings and pictures . . . Empathy is a function of the experiencing ego . . . it consists of an emotional involvement and requires the capacity for controlled and reversible regressions. (Greenson 1967: 369)

Like Greenson, Spitz (1956/7) stressed that 'a large part of the analyst's insight is based on brief and temporary identification with the patient, i.e. on ego-guided regression by the analyst himself' (cf. Lampl-De Groot 1967; Kemper 1969). Lorenzer (1970) spoke of how the therapist shares in the patient's current life experience by means of 'functional regression'. Yet the analyst must be able to switch back from identificatory to registering and ordering mode. The full range of his clinical and theoretical knowledge must be available for deployment at any time. It behoves him to remain in a position where he can usefully form hypotheses, encourage verbalization and offer interpretation.

Understood in its broadest sense, the term *countertransference* could be said to cover this process of psychoanalytic *tuning in*. Freud (1912) described countertransference as the analyst's unconscious reactions to the transference of his patient; the therapist himself responded neurotically. Greenson (1967) saw no necessary correlation with the analysand's transference reactions; countertransference was simply the analyst's transference to the patient. The trend today is to widen the range still further; countertransference has come to mean all feelings and reactions experienced by the analyst towards his patient (cf. Heimann 1960; Winnicott 1960b; Loch 1965b; Kuiper 1969; Kernberg 1975a; Möller 1977).

Green (1975) suggested yet another dimension to countertransference. The analyst is imbued with ideas drawn from his reading and absorbed during discussion with fellow practitioners. He does not enter the analytic situation empty-handed, but brings with him a whole theoretical and methodological armoury. He is then well placed to make what Brenner has called *conjectures* (1976). The inner life of his patient becomes truly alive and comprehensible to him. These conjectures are then verified or falsified via a two-way process of interpretation by the analyst and reaction from the patient.

Greenson (1967) distinguished between three types of verbal communication: *confrontation*, *clarification* and *interpretation*. Interpretation is generally regarded as the nub of psychoanalytic activity, involving as it does the transposition to consciousness of unconscious material. The unconscious origin of particular manifestations is sought in the past history and circumstances of the patient. One of the core assumptions of psychoanalysis is that *all* psychical events (e.g. insights, feelings, actions) have both topical and psychogenetic significance in the analytic situation (Brenner 1976).

Confrontation and clarification prepare the ground for interpretation. Drawing the patient's attention to avoidance tactics or contradictions is an example of confrontation. Clarification involves homing in on a particular action, event or insight in a bid to uncover the underlying psychical pattern. Confrontation, clarification and interpretation work in unison; it is not easy to draw lines of demarcation between them. Loch (1965a) argued that, for interpretation to work, the patient needed to be offered: 'a coherent psychological explanation of how seemingly separate and disconnected mental acts and states (thoughts, phantasies, feelings, actions etc.) mesh with one another'.

The ultimate purpose of all psychoanalytic intervention is to enhance the ego's capacity for insight. The knowledge gained is then harnessed to bring about structural change. Sandler *et al.* (1973) have claimed that the success or failure of therapy in bringing about change depends on whether the patient can be offered a frame of reference which matches his subjective sense of himself and the world. Emotional and cognitive insight proves to be just as important as intellectual conviction.

MODIFICATIONS TO TRADITIONAL PSYCHOANALYTIC THERAPEUTIC TECHNIQUE

Over the past thirty years the methods outlined above have undergone further extension and modification. In an effort to sum up the prevailing climate, Cremerius (1979a,b) divided analytical thinking into two, crystallizing a *classical* and a *pre-genital* school. The classicists championed enshrined technique, deeming the major parameters to have been defined once and for all. The others believed in the possibility of broadening the range of indications for analytic therapy to take in pre-genital disturbances. Cremerius drew his distinction on the basis of therapeutic goals: one group was in pursuit of *insight*, the other favoured *emotional experience*. He referred to insight-oriented therapy (which was described in the previous chapter) as 'paternalistic reason-therapy', while the experiential variety was 'maternal love-therapy' (associated among others with the names Balint and Winnicott). Many differences could be detected between the approaches, ranging from the way illness was defined, through the management of regression to the conception of the analyst-patient relationship and the overall approach to transference, resistance and interpretation.

Arguments abound as to the *correct* psychoanalytic attitude and the *proper* method of interpretation. It would take us too far to explore all the permutations here, but I do wish to dwell on three approaches to the treatment of structural ego disorders, since the issues raised are of considerable relevance to inpatient psychotherapy in general (cf. Chapter 5).

Structural ego disorder (Fürstenau 1977a,b) is used here as an umbrella term for the many psychogenetic *disorders of early onset*, where development of the ego or self is disrupted before completion of the phase of individuation and separation (Mahler *et al.* 1975). Unlike neurotics – whose egos do have structure – patients with this defect cannot boast a structurally 'intact' ego or self. Examples of the clinical syndromes encompassed are: borderline personality disorder, antisocial personality disorder, addiction, perversion, psychosomatic disorders and even some neurotic disturbances, e.g. hysterical paralysis or compulsion. A range of therapeutic strategies has been devised to treat such complaints. My interest centres on the ideas of G. and R. Blanck, Otto Kernberg and Donald Winnicott, whose views I now propose to explore – with no claim whatsoever to exhaustiveness.

G. and R. Blanck

Ego psychology was the point of departure for G. and R. Blanck (1974, 1979) in their search for new treatment techniques which would do therapeutic justice to the needs of patients with structural ego disorders. They took a fresh approach to the analysis of resistance, laid more stress on verbalization in analysis and called for positive efforts to strengthen patient autonomy. Their objective was not so much to resolve unconscious conflict by interpreting transference neurosis as to boost patients' strivings towards individuation.

One of the tenets of ego psychology is that both primarily and secondarily autonomous ego functions (i.e. defence mechanisms) are important for adaptive ego performance. In order to avoid the risk of ego decompensation, therapists treating structural ego disorders need firstly to ascertain whether the defence strategies being deployed are adaptive; if so, they deserve support. Classical theory, as we have seen, has always viewed resistance as an obstacle to be removed, whereas the Blancks contended that it needed to be nurtured. They even went so far as to advocate creating resistance if it was not already present, e.g. in cases of structural disorder where past traumatic anxiety returns massively to the surface.

Accordingly, the main purpose when treating such patients was to safeguard and promote autonomy. It was not so much a matter of having a patented technique; what counted was therapeutic attitude. The Blancks' ideal therapist yielded up his monopoly on interpretation and instead encouraged the patient to deploy his own interpretive skills. This strengthened the synthetic capability of the ego and with it the autonomy of the patient. The faculty of symbolization was enhanced and instinctual energy, which might otherwise have been released in motor form (via acting out), or physiologically (through somatization), could be effectively neutralized.

Fostering autonomy also means granting special therapeutic priority to the management of transference-induced regression. The moment of parting from the therapist is highly relevant in this regard. G. and R. Blanck believed in working on the process of individuation in tandem with the consolidation of object relationships. Spitz (1957) put this idea very well when he said that patients must learn to use and value the word 'no'. It allows them to ventilate aggression and gain autonomy, whereas always answering 'yes' keeps them dependent on the therapist. An autonomy-driven approach helps to stall the tendency inherent in any therapeutic relationship towards ever-increasing regression. Under this approach, interpretation is reserved for the management of regressive defence mechanisms; drive development is allowed to take its course. If we take the example of oedipal feelings of love, what will be interpreted is the warding off of desire, not the desire itself. The actual love deserves support and encouragement; only the symbiotic strategies deployed to defend against it need to be subjected to clarification and interpretation.

Therapy of this variety is designed to underpin the fragments of ego formation that do exist; not to interpret and elaborate transference neurosis. Backing the ego means championing the patient in his struggle for individuation and autonomy. The therapist with his diagnostic capability seeks out those areas where ego development has peaked and offers support. Understood in this way, ego support is not a technique for keeping people down; nor is it an instrument for dispensing narcissistic gratification. Essentially it offers a means of promoting the patient's own ego capability.

Otto Kernberg

Kernberg's understanding of borderline personality organization, with its grounding in ego psychology and object relations theory (1975a,b, 1976a, 1981), opened up new avenues for the treatment of certain groups of inpatients (cf. Chapter 5). His therapeutic method was designed around his own model of borderline psychopathology and, although the detailed psychodynamics cannot be examined here, the strategies he advocated are of paramount relevance to the treatment of patients with structural ego disorders, e.g. psychosomatic sufferers. Kernberg found that structurally impaired egos displayed two common features: internalized, pre-oedipal, negative maternal aspects (revealed in feelings of hatred and anger towards maternal objects) and primitive forms of defence organization (resulting in ego weakness). He departed from standard technique in advocating:

- exhaustive and systematic work on manifest and latent negative transference and transference acting out in the 'here and now' (without complete psychogenetic reconstruction);
- thorough confrontation with, and interpretation of, pathological forms of defence (splitting, projective identification, primitive idealization, devaluation, denial).

Patients with structural ego disorders very soon build up negative transference in therapy; their slide into regression is particularly pronounced precisely because their ego functions are so underdeveloped. What is more, frustration thresholds are low where oral-narcissistic needs are high. As regression deepens, primitive self-representations and negative maternal object representations are projected on to the analyst, weakening the patient's ego and further promoting regression. The 'mock' element of transference tends to become forgotten; the therapist is transformed in the patient's mind into Big Brother, a 'bad' object with a will to control. Projected self and object images are foisted on to the therapist, casting him in the role of powerful and manipulating mother, capable only of delivering disappointment and frustration. In extreme instances this may resemble psychosis. Alternatively the patient may over-idealize the therapist; negative aspects of the original maternal bond become split off and acted out in some other relationship. The therapist then has to look to negative relationships outside the transference and interpret these.

As we have seen, projection can lead to distorted perceptions. The task of the therapist in Kernbergian terms is to encourage the patient to distinguish between phantasy and reality. This strengthens the ego, whereas offering psychogenic explanations simply reinforces patients in their disavowal of reality.

Additional steps are required if negative transference is expressed through acting out. Patients may no longer content themselves with purely verbal outbursts of anger and disappointment, but instead take action specifically designed to insult or damage the therapist. Acting out in the transference is one of the main ways in which change is resisted. Given the level of ego weakness in structural patients, Kernberg advocated prevention rather than interpretation. Provided the issue was discussed – to avoid charges of therapist authoritarianism or sadism – a straight 'ban' on acting out in the transference was in his view a feasible option.

Positive measures to safeguard the therapeutic situation and the neutrality of the therapist are therefore to be recommended on occasions. Where acting out involved self-mutilation, Kernberg would ask the patient to refrain from such activity: anger was to be expressed solely in verbal form. If the underlying purpose was blackmail (e.g. in the cases of suicide threats or persistent self-destructive behaviour), prolonged re-structuring of the individual's living environment might be required: inpatient treatment, institutional care, or supervision by a social worker. Measures needed to be taken to prevent the advent of *counter-transference fixation*. The ever-present danger was that 'insoluble transference-countertransference binds' (1975a: 90) would be formed, undermining therapeutic identity and locking both therapist and patient in a vicious circle of transference and countertransference. Pathological modes of object relating would then be repeated ad infinitum.

Kernberg did nevertheless encourage interpretation when faced with early forms of defence such as: splitting, primitive idealization, projective identification, devaluing and denial. Splitting occurs when an attempt is made to keep mutually contradicting introjects separate. The process is a carry-over from early infancy, when objects were perceived as 'all good' or 'all bad', depending on whether the mother was generous or withholding. An emotionally flat or over-idealizing attitude towards the therapist, accompanied outside therapy by its opposite (e.g. destructive or self-destructive behaviour), is a reliable indicator of splitting. Negative aspects of the original maternal relationship are kept separate from the analyst; only the 'good' things are projected on to him (primitive idealization, denial). Projective identification of this kind is one of the most disturbing forms of defence. The patient deprives the therapist of all room for manoeuvre, leaving him with a feeling of total domination. Convinced that he is up against a true enemy, the patient sadistically wields his power and dominion. Any sense of the reality of the analyst as a fellow human being is lost (transference psychosis). In order to halt further psychotic slippage in such situations, Kernberg advocated firm structuring measures and thorough interpretation to lay bare the projective processes involved.

Experience with structural ego disorders led Kernberg to concentrate his interpretation and intervention on primitive forms of defence and negative transference. Positive transference he encouraged, using it to shore up the therapeutic alliance and to facilitate ego splitting. Supportive therapy alone could never suffice, since the therapist ended up playing the part of a real mother. Ego-impaired patients could always be showered with love, protection and concern, satisfying their need for dependency, but this only consolidated pathology. Without proper working through of negative transference, the therapeutic process was doomed to failure – or the patient to lifelong therapy. Insight was acquired in Kernberg's view not so much through reconstruction of the past, but by engaging in direct experience via the medium of the analyst.

> The therapist's availability as a real person, as somebody willing to understand and to help – a good, real object in contrast to the patient's transference distortions – is crucially important in the treatment. In this connection, the patient-therapist unit might be described as a higher-order unit of object-relations: a higher-order self . . . , a higher-order helpful object . . . Only within this conceptualization may treatment be formulated as the

learning of 'managerial skills' in order to understand one's self, one's boundaries, one's internal needs, one's environment, and one's life tasks . . . (Kernberg 1976b: 264–5).

Michael Balint and Donald Winnicott

Object relations analysts have generally been less interested in methodological deviation from the classical line than Kernberg or G. and R. Blanck. The object relations school views the patient's dealings with his new object, i.e. the therapist, as the bedrock of psychoanalytic therapy. The process is experience-driven and practitioners of such *experiential therapy* share an interest in the therapist's maternal countertransference to the patient – which, they believe, precedes the patient's transference to the therapist (cf. Cremerius 1979b). Countertransference is seen as more than just a reverse indicator of patient dynamics. The analyst's attitude in countertransference reflects an endeavour to respond to existentially significant messages from deep within the patient's psyche. Intimations of this approach were already to be found in Spitz (1956/7), who held that the analyst should respond to the anaclitic leanings of his patient as a nurturing mother to her child.

The idea of a facilitating, maternal attitude in countertransference has been formulated in different ways by different analysts. Loch (1974) argued that 'true psychoanalytic therapy is a vehicle for promoting human growth and change, not simply a procedure for uncovering the structures of an already complete psychical apparatus'. His view was that 'the analyst must be able and willing to adopt a nurturing role, positively fostering development'. Here we are close to Winnicott's notion of a *holding*, maternal object, capable of *primary maternal preoccupation*. The analytic setting functions as a container, embodying the symbiotic relationship between analyst and patient. If a patient decides to challenge this setting, he has taken the first step towards moving beyond symbiosis.

Winnicott and Balint were the main proponents of this theoretical approach. *Holding, handling, object presenting* were some of the terms used by Winnicott (1960a, 1962) to describe his vision of therapeutic mothering. The analyst offered the patient a *facilitating environment* in which to exploit the availability of a *good* mother and grow. The analyst as an object to be used is the key in therapy of this kind. In Balint's words, the therapist needed to be 'in tune' with his patient (Balint 1968: 53). He was not there to impose *correct* interpretations from on high. Where treatment of a regressed patient 'reached the area of the basic fault', it was up to the analyst to 'create the object relationship which, in his opinion, is the most suitable for that particular patient; or, in other words, will probably have the best therapeutic effect' (ibid.: 173). Balint in other words placed his faith in the healing and holding power of the object relationship. Interpretation would never of itself bring about change; severely regressed patients often experienced interpretive clarification as a kind of assault. What was required from the therapist was sympathy and support, backed by a sufficient degree of objectivity. This new relationship then mirrored the dyadic relationship between mother and child during the phase of 'primary love' (ibid.: 168). It had to be borne in mind, however, that 'harmony, or being in tune, must include the regressed patient's whole life, not merely his relationship with his analyst' (ibid.: 56). Only then, in the presence of *the unobtrusive analyst*, would wounds be healed and new object relationships forged.

The experiential therapies, with their emphasis on a second chance with a 'better' mother, have breathed new life into the concepts of transference and countertransference. The asymmetry of the transference configuration in classical psychoanalysis gives way to 'psycho-physiological symmetry in the form of a need-satisfying mutual relationship' (Cremerius 1979b). No longer is it simply a matter of interpreting transference and resistance; we are now talking about a fully fledged *maturational process*, generated through the relationship between analyst and patient.

Loch (1974) and Fürstenau (1977a,b) viewed the dynamic interplay of experience and insight as fundamental to the psychoanalytic process. Unconscious and conflictual behaviour patterns became reactivated in transference and resistance. The process of analysis not only allowed such patterns to be worked through; it also promoted 'the building of a new affective and cognitive behavioural model, rooted in the unique relationship established with the analyst' (Fürstenau 1977b). This was the result of experiential acquisition of insight, a process not generally reducible to abstract concepts. Loch (1974) believed that, once neurotic transference had been worked through, the patient was better placed to distinguish between reality and phantasy. The door would then be open to 'mild transference', heralding cure in offering experience of new, undisturbed object relationships. Insight-oriented interpretations alone did not in his view yield adequate therapeutic results; new object relationships need to be forged, both within the analytic situation and outside.

With cases of structural ego disorder, the interplay between insight and experience strengthened *ego integrity* (Fürstenau 1977a, b); the analyst had to wield his perceptive capability on both fronts. He needed to cultivate what Freud called 'free-floating attention', yet a grip had to be gained on the structural defect afflicting the patient. Structural disorder could be gauged in the analytic setting by the patient's failure to respond to confrontation and interpretation with the expected degree of insight and recognition. Fürstenau believed that: 'The analyst's efforts to uncover conflict by means of confrontation and interpretation lead to an increase in tension, triggering ego decompensation, regressive breakdown or psychosomatic crisis' (Fürstenau 1977a).

In order to pre-empt this kind of ego decompensation, Fürstenau expected the analyst to stand in for those ego functions which were deficient or entirely non-operative. Such intervention was supportive in nature and could be described as the proxy or surrogate exercise of ego functions. The therapist performed maternal activities in order to bring about healing (Fürstenau 1977b). One element of this proxy mothering was to provide the patient with safe and reliable treatment parameters, enabling him to overcome the distrust carried over from his real relationship with his mother. Patient-analyst contact would only prove effective in Fürstenau's view if there was some libidinal leaning. The analytic situation offered the patient a 'pilot' experience, helping him little-by-little to structure his ego. By the end of the process he should ideally be capable of healthier relationships with future partners. Classical psychoanalysis operates with notions such as: neutrality, distance, constancy, free-floating attention, holding up a mirror. Here we are dealing with a method which, when the time is right, requires from the therapist a much more pro-active role.

Ego-psychology, self-psychology and object relations theory have opened up new dimensions in psychoanalytic treatment. All these schools have their origins in basic analytic principles and offer clearly differentiated therapeutic techniques with which to probe deeper into the workings of structural ego disorders. I do not wish to comment on the effectiveness of such methods in a non-institutional setting. As a clinician, my impression is that analysts in hospital outpatient departments and inpatient wards are more likely to be faced with structural ego cases than their colleagues in private practice. What really matters to me at this stage, however, is that patients with these disorders should have the chance to enjoy the benefits of therapeutic strategies adumbrated here.

Chapter 3

Designs of inpatient therapy

In all spheres of psychoanalysis the treatment process is governed by the parameters within which it takes place. The climate of classical analysis is not the same as that of focal therapy and so on. It was in an outpatient environment that psychoanalytic techniques were first developed, mainly in private practice. Principles such as the *basic rule* and the *rule of abstinence* were instated. The non-institutional setting perfectly matched the new strategy as it unfolded, offering what de Schwaan (1978) has described as: 'a zero social situation, an experimental area where transference is free to manifest itself as the unadulterated product of psychical forces within the patient'.

Circumstances within the hospital diverge considerably from this ideal of neutrality and the kind of therapeutic relationships generated differ accordingly. The rule of abstinence can never be fully respected in a multipersonal institution. What is more, inpatients are liable to regress more deeply than outpatients. Not to mention the fact that the intimate one-to-one constellation of classical analysis is 'upset' by additional relationships with nurses and other therapists.

We might go so far as to say that admission for inpatient therapy pre-determines the nature of the treatment process (cf. Nerenz 1977). A successful outcome depends on whether the various elements within the setting can be harnessed in a therapeutically effective fashion.

In this chapter I propose to examine the workings of a series of hospitals and units, looking at the kind of therapy on offer and taking account wherever possible of the following factors:

– Institutional parameters; hospital size; influence of the hospital

operators;[1] whether treatment is offered in the psychotherapy department of a general or psychiatric hospital, or in a private clinic.
- Primary function of the institution, e.g. university hospital with pilot unit; hospital specializing in medical care; psychosomatic *Kurklinik*;[2] psychotherapeutic rehabilitation centre.
- Presenting complaint of patients, e.g. severe neurosis; personality disorder; psychosomatic disturbance; internal medical symptoms; psychosis.

As it is not my intention to comment on the treatment of psychotic patients in psychiatric hospitals, I refer the reader to the work of Benedetti (1964), Battegay (1971) and Bister (1977).

My enquiries into the nature of different therapeutic strategies yielded a highly variegated picture (cf. Janssen 1983, 1985, 1986). Not only did institutional circumstances vary, but therapists themselves had diverging conceptions of inpatient treatment. The structures practitioners create obviously depend on the objectives they are pursuing. There is almost infinite potential, but I eventually managed to crystallize six main approaches to analytically oriented psychotherapy (see Figure 1).

---

1 Inpatient psychoanalysis, analytic psychotherapy or group psychotherapy; patients' life on the ward not seen as part of the therapeutic process.
2 Combined inpatient-outpatient group therapy, with or without partial incorporation of ward life.
3 Bipolar strategies distinguishing between analytic work (in psychotherapeutic space) and sociotherapy (in social space), e.g. therapeutic communities.
4 Integrative models, where no such distinction is made: a group of patients is treated by a group of therapists.
5 Analytic approaches to the treatment of medical and psychosomatic conditions.
6 Pragmatically-conceived (eclectic) use of analytic and other psychotherapeutic therapies in hospitals.

Figure 1: Different forms of inpatient psychoanalytic psychotherapy

[1] *Translator's note.* In Germany hospitals are run by a variety of bodies: local authorities, universities, insurance companies, private individuals, workers' compensation schemes, religious orders, charitable organizations etc. Their influence might be compared with that of the regional health authorities in Britain. For convenience, *hospital operators* will be used as an umbrella term.
[2] *Translator's note.* A feature of the German healthcare system, which includes provision of spas, convalescence centres etc. for people to go on 'cures'.

Approaches 1 to 4 related to similar clinical situations, although comparison between them revealed: differing attitudes towards the therapeutic objectives of inpatient treatment; more or less emphasis on the importance of communal life on the ward; varying views on the roles and tasks of members of the professional staff; different perspectives on the management of group-engendered transference and countertransference. Approach 5 covered departments of internal medicine which apply analytic criteria when taking treatment decisions, while the last heading encompassed psychotherapeutically-oriented convalescence centres, *Kurkliniks* etc.

INPATIENT PSYCHOANALYSIS

The first attempt to introduce psychoanalysis into hospitals was undertaken by Simmel (1928) in Berlin. He believed that an inpatient setting would make it feasible to extend psychoanalytic methods to the treatment of psychoses, narcissistic neuroses, severe character disorders and addictions. The residential environment struck him as offering enormous advantages. Acting out could be contained and worked through within the four walls of the hospital, with valuable feedback from the entire treatment team (including nursing staff). Greatly in advance of his time, Simmel went so far as to draw up rules for coordination among analysts and nurses. He envisaged a structured team, functioning as a true family for the patient. The venture would appear to have foundered on financial grounds. Some of the ideas were then picked up and developed by Menninger (1936) when he was devising his own unit (cf. Bartemeier 1978).

The team dimension of Simmel's thinking nevertheless received short shrift at the Menninger Clinic. The account given by Kernberg (1975a) concentrates on the protective role of the inpatient environment; inpatient admission was indicated where standard psychotherapeutic means were no longer deemed sufficient to cope with extreme instances of regressive acting out in the transference, e.g. suicidal acts, gross destructive tendencies, substance abuse or antisocial behaviour. The hospital provided patients with a taste of structured living, but the true process of cure took place outside its parameters – in 'ambulatory' therapy, which continued throughout the patients' inpatient stay.

Kernberg started out believing that a strict line had to be drawn between life on the ward and psychotherapy; the therapist needed to be informed of everything happening in the unit, but should not himself divulge information (*general discretion*). Lateral transference was avoided by keeping analytic activity in the hands of one person only; the inpatient setting did no more than provide protection against acting out. Reading between the lines, one senses that this arrangement brought with it considerable problems. The purpose of the strict dividing line between analytic psychotherapy and inpatient life was to ensure therapist neutrality, which Kernberg viewed as vital. Yet the 'multiple treatment arrangements' (Kernberg 1975a) of the clinical world inevitably hampered this. Kernberg (1976b) began to explore alternative options. Influenced by Main's work with therapeutic communities (1946), as well as Rice's analytically oriented research into how organizations function (1969), his attitude towards inpatient psychoanalytic therapy progressively changed.

Another pioneer of residential analytic therapy was Frieda Fromm-Reichmann (1950). She was particularly interested in the treatment of psychotic patients and it was at Chestnut Lodge – her private clinic in the USA – that Stanton and Schwartz (1954) undertook the first systematic examination of the influence of institutional parameters on therapeutic processes. They discovered that division and conflict among members of the hospital staff increased the mental disorder of psychotic patients. When the results of their research were published, some practitioners began to question whether psychoanalytic therapy was in fact tenable within a traditionally organized psychiatric setting. Fromm-Reichmann (1947) herself was confident that institutionally induced splitting could be overcome, provided more information was collected on how therapeutic processes worked. Undaunted, she continued to proclaim the separation of psychoanalytic therapy and clinical psychiatric treatment. If remaining members of the professional staff suffered loss of self-esteem because patients idealized their analytic therapist, the answer was to ventilate the subject. Meetings and discussions needed to be held, bringing everyone into the therapeutic process. In this way people would learn about the psychodynamics of patients and their anxieties as they passed through the various phases of treatment.

The inpatient strategies described so far were designed to put into practice the classical psychoanalytic belief in 'the primacy of the one-to-one relationship' (Fürstenau 1974). Hospitalization was tolerated in view of the severity of the patient's condition, but the social and therapeutic potential of the institutional environment remained untapped. A similar attitude was taken at the Heidelberg Psychotherapy Centre under Alexander Mitscherlich (cf. de Boor and Künzler 1963). Patients requiring spells of inpatient care were offered psychoanalysis and focal therapy by therapists attached to the unit, but no actual sociotherapeutic use was made of the inpatient setting.

A methodological approach of this kind is logical enough if the paramount concern is to uphold the sanctity of the dyadic relationship between patient and analyst. The web of multipersonal relations that characterizes an institutional environment – the group-dynamic factor – must needs be frozen out.

Research by Danckwardt (1976) and Biermann (1975) proved illuminating in this regard. Where insufficient account was taken of group dynamics in the design of inpatient treatment, psychotherapy demonstrably fell short of its full potential. The authors looked at the situation on a psychotherapeutic ward in the Psychiatric Department of Tübingen's University Hospital. During their inpatient stay, patients were offered focal therapy and group-analytic psychotherapy; they also had access to occupational and creative therapies. Danckwardt's particular interest was focal therapy. On admission, patients came under the influence not only of their own psychotherapist, but equally of fellow patients (the patient subgroup). New object relationships were formed against the backcloth of the group-dynamic processes at work within the unit. The patient's bond with his focal therapist was but one relational possibility among many and Danckwardt noted that very few individuals managed to maintain a stable transference relationship with their focal therapist. '*Basic fault* elements' spilled over into all object choices within the group milieu, casting relations with the focal therapist into a relative light. Danckwardt spoke in this context of 'institutionally-induced distortion of transference patterns'. The emotional pull of the subgroup generally proved stronger than the affective hold of the focal therapist, whose one-to-one contact with the patient was felt to deviate from the communal norm. It grew more and more likely that the patient would start to reject interpretations offered during individual therapy. Group phantasies had by now become stronger and more compelling than anything the poor therapist could deliver – especially if he persisted in passing over the emotional life of the group.

Both Danckwardt (1976) and Biermann (1975) were of course arguing from a specific standpoint: that of psychoanalytically oriented focal therapy. For them the acid test was whether or not a satisfactory one-to-one transference relationship could be established. Biermann spoke bleakly of the 'failure' of focal therapy in the hospital setting; Danckwardt lamented the 'pathogenic conditions' of the inpatient environment – although he conceded that these pathogenic conditions could be overcome if less emphasis were placed on a single *focus*. Things might look better were the therapist to set out 'incorporating the group-dynamic matrix within which conflict is enacted'. Here we glimpse a positive pointer for the development of an integrative inpatient model.

My trajectory led to the design of an integrative approach in which patients' relations with every member of the professional staff were accorded significance; no object choice made within the group matrix was deemed external to the therapeutic process.

PSYCHOANALYTIC THERAPY AND THE THERAPEUTIC COMMUNITY

The therapeutic community movement, one of whose pioneers was T.F. Main (1946), provided new impetus for the institutional treatment of psychic illness (cf. Hilpert *et al.* 1981; Hilpert 1983). The end of the Second World War saw the start of what became known as the Northfield Experiments. A group of psychoanalysts and psychiatrists at the Northfield Hospital (including Bion and Foulkes, as well as Main) began clinical work with soldiers suffering from psychoneuroses and psychosomatic disorders. While Bion and Foulkes concentrated on devising new forms of group analysis, Main was more interested in changing the very nature of 'the hospital'.

He felt that clinical psychotherapy was being too one-sided in focusing on the patient alone and advocated running the entire hospital – patients plus professional staff – as a *therapeutic community* (Main 1946). Every patient deserved to be actively involved in the daily affairs of the institution. Provided the clinical environment was properly structured, it could usefully offer an alternative to patients' previous *pathogenic* worlds. More scope for responsibility, participation and partnership would automatically ensue.

Theoretical underpinning for this new approach was drawn from

Kurt Lewin's concept of group dynamics; the practical impetus came from actual work in group analysis. The group setting was found to illuminate the social dimension of neurosis, which emerged as a group phenomenon (Bion 1961) and not simply a personal problem – as in dyadic analysis. Having once ascertained the part played by social structures in the dynamics of the individual psyche, Main's therapeutic goal was clear. He summed up his new insights as follows:

> The socialization of neurotic drives, their modification by social demands within a real setting, the ego-strengthening, the increased capacity, sincere and easy social relationships, and the socialization of super-ego demands, provide the individual with a capacity and a technique for stable life in a real role in the real world. (Main 1946: 70)

The role of the therapist was not to work through patients' individual problems, but rather to analyse the interpersonal tension engendered by the group situation. Interpretations needed to be directed towards inter-patient relations and the mental picture one patient formed of another. The therapist was there to act as an 'honest commentator', observing group behaviour, identifying emotional problems and helping people to help themselves. The therapeutic community provided hands-on experience of group processes. A *total* culture of enquiry' grew up, 'an atmosphere of respect for *all*' (Main 1977: 211).

The term 'therapeutic community' was coined around the same time by both Main and the socially minded psychiatrist Maxwell Jones (1953). Jones developed a method of *social analysis* which concentrated on conscious emotional interaction in the group situation. His approach rested on a belief that social factors have a determining part to play in the genesis of psychic disturbance. At a societal level, he saw the therapeutic community as a model for new and progressive forms of social organization. This would be reflected in hospitals by a move away from traditional hierarchies towards more democratic structures.

Far-reaching changes did indeed come about in the wake of Jones's activities, particularly in the psychiatric departments of British hospitals (cf. Brown and Pedder 1979; Hinshelwood and Manning 1979). Useful accounts of therapeutic community influence on psychiatric practice in Germany have been given by Ploeger (1972), Kayser (1974), Kayser *et al.* (1973) and Krüger

(1979). All these surveys confirm that Main's psychoanalytic emphasis gradually lost ground to the more sociotherapeutic thrust of Jones. Witness *milieu therapy*, developed in the United States with the underlying goal of bringing about a transformation of society (cf. Cumming and Cumming 1962; Heim 1978).

Therapeutic community principles can be applied in any inpatient context, although they are of particular relevance to the institutional practice of group-analytic psychotherapy. Emphasis nowadays tends to be less on the community as a therapeutic end in itself and more on ways of restructuring the hospital environment. This is the perspective I shall be taking in the following account of the impact on inpatient psychotherapy of therapeutic community concepts (cf. Brown and Pedder 1979; Hilpert and Schwarz 1981). I propose to give particular consideration to: the impact on team structure and leadership; the attitude of the team towards patients; and the therapeutic function of patients for one another.

Viewed as a therapeutic institution, the hospital is an *organic whole*; strict hierarchies and fixed roles only undermine natural processes. The goal is the creation of *horizontal, democratic structures*. Power is decentralized and decision-taking delegated to the appropriate groups, reducing the social distance found in hierarchically organized institutions.

Horizontal structures bring with them the problem of *leadership*. The radical cry for absolute democracy frequently flies in the face of hospital realities; nor are patients necessarily served by the championing of rigid ideological positions (cf. Rapoport 1960). Few today would dispute the need for leadership in a therapeutic community. Morrice (1972) viewed the task of the leader or conductor as one of conflict-minimizing, ensuring that the organization retained its integrity and the team its capacity for interpersonal learning. This conceptualization of leadership means that there is always someone who will keep his sights on the therapeutic goal being pursued. He also sees to it that processes operating within the group are properly elucidated and takes responsibility for inter-institutional relations and contact with the outside world.

Whiteley's notion of 'focal leadership' (1978) equally acknowledged the need for someone to be in overall charge. The leader was there to offer interpretive guidance, enabling the group to overcome conflicts engendered within it. His presence created an atmosphere of openness and imparted a sense of security. Because he was not immersed in the group he was better able to pinpoint areas of tension and clarify problems. Focal leadership also involved a transference relationship. The constant availability of the group leader provided a degree of protection for members of the therapeutic staff; this facilitated the working through of conflict and kept people in touch with reality. Focal leadership took on its true meaning as individuals began to see the leader as a role model, with whom they might identify. This prepared them to exercise a similar style of leadership in their relations with patients.

Ample scope for acting out was built into Whiteley's model. He saw the therapeutic community as a *large group*, which would by definition generate regressive processes – or, in Bion's terms, *basic assumptions* (cf. Pines 1975). In any such scenario, the task of the group leader is to maintain the viability of the *work group*. He as an individual offers himself as a stable parental figure against whom conflict can be played out in transference. Groups that have become demoralized – the regressive group, the depressive group, the hopeless group – find a figure with whom they can identify. Spurred on by interpretation and confrontation, they move forward to new forms of therapeutic activity. Any such leader should therefore be fully acquainted himself with the nature of group-analytic processes.

Another fundamental tenet of the therapeutic community approach is that all members of the staff team have a therapeutic function and all, as individuals, are equal. This holds good from both psychoanalytic and sociological points of view (cf. Janssen 1979) and is paramount if personal and professional identity are to be sustained in group work. Equal status does not mean that everyone does the same thing; different actors have different roles to play, depending also on their stage of professional development (Morrice 1972). The notion of differentiation within parity is one of the central contributions of therapeutic community thinking to the theory and practice of teamwork in hospitals.

Further principles of team interaction drawn by hospital practitioners from the therapeutic community movement include: uninhibited communication among members of the staff team; an open exchange of feelings and information, i.e. no repression; controlled manifestation of emotion, rather than attempts at affective neutrality; regular discussion of group processes (cf. Hilpert and Schwarz 1981). If these standards can be met there is a strong chance that patients will enjoy a *good enough* therapeutic environment.

Champions of the fully fledged therapeutic community go one step further, entrusting patients themselves with social, therapeutic and organizational tasks in a bid to stimulate activity and promote autonomy. Sociotherapeutic communities, where high priority is given to social learning, favour such an approach. I am not myself convinced that this is appropriate in a psychoanalytically oriented setting. Whilst accepting the need for tolerance towards the behaviour of patients and team members alike – emotional growth would not otherwise be possible – I believe that the notion of parity between therapist and patient is fruitful only if envisaged in terms of the therapeutic process. There comes a time when both parties move of their own accord in the direction of a relationship built on equality. This however is a signal that the end of treatment is nigh; the patient is ready to prepare to take leave of the clinical environment. Strict adherence to a corpus of therapeutic community rules leads to the enshrining of a hospital subculture – a brave new world of isolation where regression is not faced and reality is denied. The result is *institutionalization* in another packaging (cf. Rapoport 1960; Krüger 1979).

An analytically oriented clinical unit must needs focus primarily on psychotherapeutic processes, according only second place to the more educational dimension of therapeutic community living. Hilpert and Schwarz (1981) spoke of 'a mixture of democratic and hierarchical elements; of symmetric and asymmetric relational patterns; of functional and personal areas of responsibility'. Psychoanalytic therapy is necessarily based on *non-equality*, since the whole purpose is to elucidate and work through reactivated infantile conflicts. The inpatient setting allows primitive modes of object relating to become externalized (Bion 1961; Kernberg 1976b; Kreeger 1975; Heising *et al*. 1982). The particular advantage for analytic psychotherapy of the therapeutic community approach is that these primitive object relationships are acted out and clarified in an unrestrained *holding environment* (cf. Chapter 5). Looking back, I believe that we can fairly say that therapeutic community thinking has provided major intellectual input for those who seek to create a nurturing climate within hospitals for the practice of inpatient psychoanalytic therapy.

The penetration of therapeutic community culture eventually led Kernberg (1976b) to abandon his initial conception of how analytic psychotherapy should be organized in hospitals (see pp. 23–6). He switched his theoretical gaze to devising a way of embedding group strategies in an integrated inpatient treatment model. Hilpert (in Hilpert *et al.* 1981) has described how Kernberg once told him that the main inspiration for this new thrust came from watching a therapeutic community grow – at the Menninger Clinic, over the period 1969 to 1973. Object relations theory had always been the mainspring of Kernberg's work and he could not fail to notice that primitive levels of psychic functioning (e.g. as found in borderline cases) seldom become reactivated in classical or analytically oriented dyadic settings, whereas in a group situation these buried structures did resurface. The inpatient milieu turned out to be both a diagnostic tool and a potential therapeutic medium, for it facilitated the externalization of primitive object relationships and provided a locus for therapeutic elaboration. Particularly in the case of borderline patients, group interaction brought to light object relationships which had not before been sufficiently integrated.

Kernberg knew however that reactivation alone was not therapy; there had to be a clear strategy. He therefore advocated group-analytic psychotherapy plus 'hospital therapy'. A *hospital therapist* was delegated to undertake systematic and interpretive study of relations and interaction within the unit (patient-patient, patient-staff, staff-staff etc.). This entailed much gathering of personal observations. Frank and uninhibited exchange of information was vital – which explains why Kernberg came to abandon the principle of general discretion (cf. pp. 23–6).

Underpinning the Kernbergian concept of clinical therapy was a theory of organization based on psychoanalysis and systems theory (Rice 1965, 1969). Independently of Kernberg, Rice's work on institutional dynamics has greatly influenced my vision too of how an inpatient psychotherapeutic setting should ideally be designed (cf. Chapters 4 and 5).

Rice saw the potential for integrating systems theory with the structural theory of psychic organization. He envisaged individuals, groups and institutions as open systems, each with tasks to perform within a climate of constant interchange. At any one time a system is faced with a *primary task*, clearly demarcated from the tasks of other systems. A degree of control is a necessary corollary of satisfactory performance; systems therefore require a regulating agency. In an individual, this agency is the ego. In a group, control functions are performed by the group leader; in a big organization, by the manager. Where there is breakdown in control or leadership, primary task orientation is lost.

Clinical examples abound at an individual level of the collapse of ego function – or the faculty to manage reality. If inner needs grow so strong as to overpower the ego, decompensation inevitably follows; the ego is no longer able to sustain its reality-oriented course and neurotic, psychosomatic or psychotic symptoms develop. In terms of open-system theory, calling on the services of a psychoanalytic therapist equates with bringing in a consultant or adviser; the therapist as *regulating agency* diagnoses the nature of the breakdown and helps the patient to redraw the boundaries within his psyche. The individual is then in position to fulfil his *primary task*, which is to recognize and reconcile the demands of his inner self with the world outside. According to Rice, the group therapist in a group-analytic setting has a similar function to the manager of a large organization; the analyst looks at the reactivation of primitive object relationships and defence mechanisms, while the manager analyses deficiencies in his organization's primary task performance.

Kernberg took up these ideas when designing his own clinical setting. He believed that the tasks of therapists and hospital management could usefully be considered in the light of Rice's organizational model. The common goal was to uncover inner needs and strengthen or restore the regulatory functions of the ego. Therapeutic arrangements (therapists plus therapeutic community) were such that object relating and ego functioning could be dealt with simultaneously when clarifying and interpreting material. Kernberg saw that: 'the hospital as a social system may provide various therapeutic structures which activate in different proportions the patient's control function and internal world of object relations' (1976b: 264). Referring to 'the human, personal element in the therapeutic process', he went on to say that: 'one crucial aspect of the patient's learning process in treatment (managerial skill) is the development of concern for himself' (ibid.). In this way he would come to understand his internal needs, his place within the world and his overall purpose in life.

Since the therapeutic goal was to enhance ego capacity, Kernberg realized that the therapeutic community must operate as an up-and-running social system, with a clear task orientation. If the process were allowed to lapse into no more than an exercise in group dynamics, manipulative manoeuvres would flourish on all fronts. Everyone would finish up in a melting pot and lines of demarcation would disappear. Kernberg's theoretical reminder is crucial for anyone seeking to marry the therapeutic community model with a psychoanalytic approach towards residential therapy.

The Cassel Hospital in Richmond is perhaps the longest-standing example of how psychoanalytically oriented treatment may be provided in a therapeutic community setting (Main 1957, 1977; Plojé 1977; Hilpert 1979; Muir 1980; Denford *et al*. 1983; James 1984). It was my privilege to be able to spend some time familiarizing myself with the arrangements there.[3]

At the Cassel patients live together in an environment shaped along true therapeutic community lines; individual psychoanalytic therapy sessions are offered twice a week. Responsibility for maintaining 'therapeutic culture' (Main 1977) lies largely with the nurses, who uphold the social structure of the community. Their tasks are *reality-oriented*: sorting out everyday problems of coexistence and seeing to it that the house rules are respected etc. They encourage patients to become involved in the general running of the community, urging them to take on part-time duties etc. As to interpersonal learning, the nurses serve as role models for the enhancement of social and communications skills. They instil enthusiasm and set an example, confronting patients with instances of unacceptable behaviour and endeavouring to induce more appropriate conduct. Where morale-boosting is required, it is given. The expectation is that patients will take on tasks and carve out a proper social role for themselves, e.g. a nurse may suggest that someone take charge of a newcomer. Patients are consulted on menus etc. and, in return, the nurses offer advice on leisure activities etc. The functions of the nursing staff are mainly performed in task-oriented large- and small-group settings (cf. Chapman 1984).

Analysts responsible for individual therapy have *psychotherapeutic* tasks only; their domain is clearly demarcated from that of the nurses, although both professional groupings enjoy equal status. Role-definition is clear from the start and the triadic configuration of *doctor–patient–nurses* (Hilpert 1979) is the foundation upon which therapy is built. The nurses perform reality-oriented (or social) tasks, which are swiftly delegated to patients wherever

[3] I should like to thank the Breuninger Foundation for the financial support that made this stay possible.

possible; psychoanalysts hold sway in the analytic realm. As we can see, practice at the Cassel Hospital has gradually moved away from the integrative approach initially espoused by Main (1946) – where the emphasis was on organizational dynamics – towards a bipolar constellation, with a clear dividing line between analytic and social space, i.e. between therapists and nurses.

Plojé (1977) has given a persuasive illustration of the problems engendered by the Cassel's bipolar strategy. From the patient's point of view, the split between psychotherapeutic and sociotherapeutic tasks obscures the fact that therapist and nurses are working together. With this example in front of them, patients themselves develop a tendency to divide things up, projecting their negative self or object aspects on to the nurses and reserving the 'all good' parts for the therapists. This is a classical example of what Kernberg (1975a) termed *splitting of the transference*. Plojé's argument is that splits of this kind, once engendered, can no longer be 'repaired' through interpretation; the process is by then on an escalation course. Negative transference reactions lead to early discharge from the hospital and the whole therapy team is left with a sense of guilt and inadequacy.

Bearing these factors in mind, Plojé set about formulating a new logistical approach. He was determined to find an arrangement where, if splitting did occur, it could at least be reversed. He had learnt that *interpreting-only* therapists – who refrain from entering into the spirit of ward life – are taken advantage of by patients. Unwillingness to take on a parental role for the duration of therapy is perceived as a sign of weakness and indifference. Patients feel entitled to ignore the relational matrix formed by the therapy team, restricting their focus to individual therapy sessions. Plojé wanted therapists working in a residential context to cooperate with the nurses on the wards for all to see, demonstrating to patients that doctors plus nurses formed a true therapeutic partnership. When given the opportunity to put these ideas into practice, he found that the need for individual analytic sessions lessened and the average duration of therapy fell from two years to ten months. Meetings were convened by those in charge of the wards, removing the temptation for therapists to shield regressed patients within the womb of the consulting room.

Hilpert (1979) also spent some considerable time at the Cassel and he too spoke of polarization, transference splitting and high levels of tension and mistrust among the staff team. He sensed that

the highly charged professional climate was inducing psychotherapists to glorify outpatient treatment – especially if they felt envious
of the nurses' predominant role in the group sphere.

It took the Cassel Hospital quite a while to venture the first
tentative steps towards an integrative treatment design (cf. Muir
1980; James 1984). Conceptually, the bipolar approach is retained,
but there is more correlation between therapeutic and social space
(i.e. therapists and nurses). What is more, group therapy sessions
now take place in the presence of both psychoanalytic and sociotherapeutic representatives (Christie 1984).

Looking back over the history of therapeutic communities, we
can fairly surmise that many of the difficulties experienced with the
introduction of psychoanalytic therapy stem from the inbuilt suppositions of the analysts themselves. Training takes place in a one-
to-one, highly personalized setting; it virtually runs counter to an
analyst's sense of professional dignity to be asked to deal with the
affairs of a residential environment: admission procedures, discharge dates, problems of drug withdrawal, scenes of acting out
etc. Considerable personal adjustments are necessary if he is to fit
in with the clinical and community parameters of inpatient treatment. He must be capable of fostering a relationship of equals with
the nurses and other members of the professional staff (i.e. non-
analysts) and willing to bow to team decisions. Where difficulties
arise with patient relations, he has to accommodate himself to the
idea that priority will be given to resolving the matter at team
level.

TRADITIONAL BIPOLAR MODELS:
PSYCHOTHERAPEUTIC AND SOCIOTHERAPEUTIC
SPACE

Psychoanalytic therapists in Germany have tended towards caution in their dealings with therapeutic community concepts (cf.
Beese 1971b; Bräutigam 1974). The bipolar notion of two types of
clinical space – therapeutic and social – did however touch a chord
in some analytically oriented independent hospitals and clinics (cf.
Enke et al. 1964; Enke 1965, 1968).

While ruling out the possibility of practising classical psychoanalysis in hospitals, Enke for one favoured experimentation with
a group-analytic approach. The clinical setting seemed to him
perfect for the re-actualization and working through of infantile

conflict. Anxious as he was to avoid mixing therapy and ward life, he introduced the concept of 'bipolar psychotherapy'. Social issues would be dealt with in 'house groups', saving therapy proper for group-analytic sessions. These ideas were implemented at the Umkirch psychotherapy unit. The result was a form of residential care comprising treatment in a 'therapy community' and life in a 'social community'.

Enke's model exerted a decisive influence on inpatient psychotherapy in Germany and further elaboration of his thinking has since been undertaken by Hau (1969, 1970, 1973) and by Arnds and Studt (1973). Hau's assumption was that the structure and size of a psychotherapeutic institution dictated the nature of treatment. Analytic therapy required a relatively neutral field and it was easier for a therapist to maintain neutrality in a big hospital than a smaller unit, where he might also have to wear the hat of Head of Department, Consultant Psychiatrist, Registrar or whatever. Potential for transference lay all around in a residential environment and Hau (1969) saw the inpatient unit with its professional staff as an 'archetypal community', driven by its own special group dynamics. Not that he advocated a system in which everyday interaction with the staff would be put to therapeutic use; to each task its appropriate 'attitude'. At one end of the spectrum he envisaged an analyst conducting a therapy session; at the other, a nurse routinely reminding a patient of the house rules (Figure 2). Residential psychotherapy found its place in the force-field between the poles of analysis and daily life. Some activities leaned towards the analytic pole, e.g. psychodrama, dance movement therapy, art therapy; others had a more everyday feel: physiotherapy, medical checks etc. Notwithstanding his location in therapeutic space, it behoved the analyst to monitor how his patients made out in social mode (Hau 1970, 1973).

Hau's view was that the 'archetypal' nature of the hospital community could benefit psychoanalytic therapy provided intragroup dynamics and team countertransference were taken on board. The group setting offered an excellent 'sounding box' for examining neurotic patterns of interrelating. Ward life engendered material to be worked on in individual therapy (cf. Arnds and Studt 1973). We are reminded of Kernberg (1976b) and his 'hospital therapist' (see p. 31), whose remit was to analyse social interaction on the ward.

The bipolar approach has proved especially popular in the larger

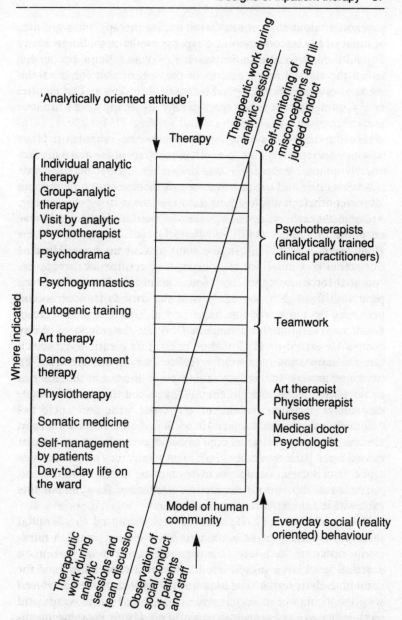

Figure 2 The clinical environment as it relates to psychotherapy, showing the various therapeutic 'attitudes', from the 'analytically oriented' to the 'reality oriented'
Source: Hau 1968

psychotherapeutic centres in Germany. Beese (1977) has given an account of the introduction of a bipolar model at the Sonnenberg Psychotherapy Centre in Stuttgart. König and Neun (1979) surveyed the clinical arrangements in the special unit for the treatment of psychogenic and psychosomatic disorders at Tiefenbrunn near Göttingen, where two types of psychotherapy were practised: focal and group. A. Heigl-Evers and F. Heigl (1973b, 1975, 1976) designed a three-tier system for the groupwork component. There was an interactional plane, a depth psychology plane and a psychoanalytic plane. A clear line was drawn throughout between psychotherapeutic and social space, one of the reasons being that not all patients referred to the hospital were suited to psychotherapy.

Detailed methodological accounts of the Göttingen model can be found in Zauner (1972, 1978), Heigl and Nerenz (1975) and Heigl-Evers *et al.* (1976). In line with Enke's recommendations, a distinction was made for the purposes of residential therapy between therapeutic space and social space. Social learning was promoted through group analysis of the sociodynamic processes occurring on the ward; this happened in 'theme groups' (Heigl-Evers and Heigl 1973a), modelled on the 'interactional theme groups' described by R.C. Cohn (1975). Life on the ward constituted a 'simulation of everyday reality' (König and Neun 1979); working through the events taking place there enhanced social competence. Heigl and Nerenz (1975) placed the social learning element of inpatient treatment on a par with the 'corrective emotional experience' acquired in focal and group psychotherapy. On the interpersonal level, the concept of social space encompassed inter-patient relations, plus the whole area of contact with registrars, nurses, occupational therapists, social workers etc. Activities in the various democratic decision-making bodies that exist within a therapeutic community also belonged in social space.

Heigl and Nerenz (1975) were deeply committed to upholding the everyday social plane in the interest of therapy itself. A minor infringement of the house rules was relevant at more than just a practical level; true insight could be gained from addressing the issue in analytic terms. The idea was for patients to be confronted with their conduct in social space; then asked to delve into the hidden causes in therapeutic space. The difference between the two planes needed to be actively experienced if a true working alliance was to develop. Heigl and Nerenz were effectively advocating *therapeutic ego splitting*. The patient was entitled to know

where the social goalposts stood; he would consequently appreciate the need to cooperate with members of the clinical staff and
feel confident enough in the social sphere to allow his feelings and
phantasies to float freely in the therapeutic sphere.

Underlying the theoretical preference for separation between
therapeutic and social space was a belief that the presence of two
poles facilitated the management of transference reactions and
reduced the intensity of regression. The paramount aim was to
prevent the advent of *transference splitting*, which occurs whenever
there is scope for forming multiple relationships (cf. Heigl and
Nerenz 1975; König 1974, 1975; Beese 1977). Contrary to what I
shall be arguing below (cf. Chapter 5), the advocates of a bipolar
approach saw transference splitting as a solely negative by-product
of the multipersonal environment. One way of impeding its development was to ensure that information passed freely between
therapeutic and social realms. König (1974, 1975) spoke of the need
for 'sound lines of communication' between members of the professional staff. The group therapist should be in possession of a
maximum of information; nurses, occupational therapists, social
workers, activity therapists were all expected to report back to him.
He himself divulged details of patients' behaviour to the Registrar
only. Any tension arising from the divide between therapeutic and
social space was attributed by Heigl and Nerenz (1975) to poorly
defined organizational structures and 'inadequate role-definition'.
What was required was clear task description; yet they provided no
real evidence of whether circumscribing tasks and sustaining the
notion of discrete social space did in fact forestall or minimize
transference to people operating in non-therapeutic mode. My
experience suggests that we ignore such reactions at our peril; they
will occur whether we like it or not (cf. pp. 70–4).

Zauner (1978) too believed that the concept of social space was
vital in a residential environment if regressive tendencies were to
be kept in check. *Malign* regression worried him most of all.
Patients experiencing frustration or hurt in such a state could
easily become aggressive or suicidal. With their diminished ego
functioning, they risked losing touch with reality. Any alteration
to a familiar object relationship would be apprehended as object
loss. Life without the clinical environment and its objects was by
now inconceivable. Unlike Beese (1977), Zauner saw no therapeutic role for regression of this kind and recommended strengthening
the reality link by demarcating a clear social realm. Only intact

areas of the ego should be addressed on the wards. Socio-therapeutic activities were to be encouraged: sport, occupational therapy etc. Actual psychotherapeutic processes would be kept within clear boundaries (focal or group therapy), reducing the potential for regression. Zauner also advocated placing a limit on the amount of time devoted to therapy (e.g. twenty-four group therapy sessions – König and Sachsse 1981).

All these theses and counter-theses revolve around one essential question: to what degree can therapeutic use be made of the community situation obtaining in the protective environment of the hospital? A whole panoply of transference reactions and regressive processes occurs precisely because of the multipersonal configuration and the availability of an entire therapy team. Most psychoanalysts operating in bipolar settings endeavour to control the situation by setting up reality-oriented 'house groups', promoting outside activities, arranging for patients to attend occupational therapy and social rehabilitation sessions etc. Their avowed aim is to pre-empt regression, especially in its malign varieties, e.g. oral-passive attitudes, ocnophilic attachment behaviour, aggressive and sado-masochistic acting out (cf. Ziese 1978). In my view they are misguided. So long as there are adequate mechanisms for keeping countertransference in check, regressive processes can be profitably worked on in the here-and-now (cf. Chapter 5). Admittedly members of the therapy team may contract 'countertransference sickness' (Ziese 1978). This is a risk to be reckoned with; the course of any process of inpatient therapy ultimately hinges on whether regression can be successfully harnessed and utilized.

The core assumptions underpinning bipolar models are summarized in Figure 3. Hands-on experience has inevitably meant that more account is taken nowadays of the social, institutional and staffing dimensions of inpatient psychotherapy.

Psychoanalysts working in hospitals used to ignore the group-dynamic element of clinical life, taking a highly restrictive view of their therapeutic remit (cf. pp. 21–6). This is no longer feasible; they must needs take on board social processes and accept that other professionals have a role to play. There are growing numbers of inpatient analysts willing to concede the artificial nature of the divide between therapeutic and social space. Every day they are confronted with the interweaving patterns of hospital life; little by little the idea is penetrating that ward life and analysis are not perhaps so inimical to one another after all (cf. pp. 48–56).

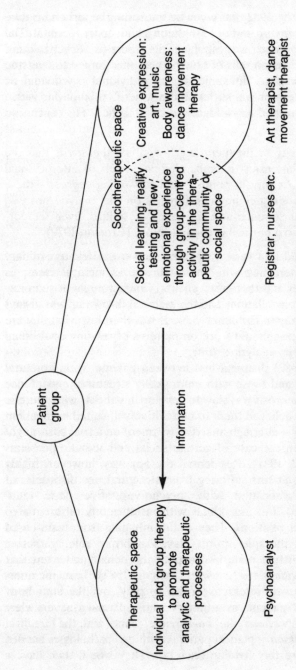

Figure 3 Basic design of bipolar models

Patient group

Therapeutic space
Individual and group therapy to promote analytic and therapeutic processes

Psychoanalyst

Sociotherapeutic space
Social learning, reality testing and new emotional experience through group-centred activity in the therapeutic community or social space

Registrar, nurses etc.

Creative expression: art, music
Body awareness: dance movement therapy

Art therapist, dance movement therapist

Information

Core assumptions: 1 Clear role allocation and therapeutic task assignment for each area
2 Interpretation of interaction and phantasies in the light of the realities of social coexistence

Ermann (1979, 1982) has given an interesting report on his time in the psychosomatic unit of Mannheim's University Hospital. The therapeutic approach was bipolar in its thrust (cf. Schepank and Studt 1976). Ermann tells of how he was once forced to overstep the usual discretion threshold during individual psychoanalytic therapy. The tension was such that the patient's relationship with a particular nurse had unavoidably to be broached. His conclusion was that:

> The specificity of inpatient psychoanalytic therapy is that the analytic relationship is embedded in a web of interpersonal structures. At certain points – and to varying degrees – these other relational ties impinge directly on the analytic process; conflict, transference and resistance crystallize, even temporarily, around a particular configuration. (Ermann 1979)

Patients figured in a variety of roles: as ward-mates, as ordinary individuals interacting with their fellows, as medical cases, as nurses' charges and therapists' clients. Conflict might arise in any one of these constellations and the material thrown up was always worth processing in Ermann's view. It was therefore vital that the analytic therapist should work on patterns of relating established outside the strict analytic setting.

Ermann (1982) distinguished between patients with structural ego disorders and those with neurotically structured egos. Since transference neurosis was slow to develop in patients with neurotic structures, he believed them to be relatively ill-suited to inpatient psychotherapy – although analytic treatment on a trial basis might be indicated in the case of certain social and somatic problems (Ermann *et al.* 1981). Residential therapy was, however, highly desirable for patients suffering from structural ego disorders, or disturbances associated with 'psycho-vegetative basic fault' (Ermann 1983), i.e. individuals with insufficiently differentiated self and object relations. They could only gain from team-based therapy. The therapist group played a proxy role, gathering together conflictual material on patients' behalf and exercising *integrating auxiliary ego functions* (Ermann 1982). Team members had their separate interactive roles to play, but the staff body functioned for patients as a unitary whole. Ermann nevertheless distinguished between the *interpretive* plane and the *creative*, *active* and *normative* planes; patients with ego pathologies needed to know where the dividing lines lay. They would then have a chance to observe integration in action: individual tasks performed jointly after proper coordination. In such an environent, the stage was set for the team to perform surrogate ego functions on the patients' behalf.

Such considerations led logically to the embracing of a more integrative approach to the whole treatment process. Ermann has subsequently written on his experience in a residential setting where patients with structural ego disorders were offered individual analytic therapy in a truly integrative environment (Ermann 1985). Unified models of this kind are increasingly common and seem to be doing well (cf. pp. 48–56). I too moved from a bipolar to an integrative stategy in the course of my work in the inpatient field (cf. Chapter 4).

COMBINED INPATIENT–OUTPATIENT MODELS

The models we have discussed so far were put into practice in residential settings. Attempts have however been made to combine the inpatient and the outpatient approach to psychotherapy. This is of course only feasible in big teaching hospitals, with fully-fledged outpatient departments, or in hospitals with a large regional catchment. The inpatient element has tended to remain bipolar, the main difference from the arrangements described above being an expectation that patients would commit themselves to a prolonged period of outpatient treatment after leaving the ward.

Heidelberg University's Department of Psychosomatic Medicine was the scene of several experiments in combined inpatient-outpatient group therapy. Work centred on alexithymic patients and the names generally associated with the project are Bräutigam (1974, 1978b) and von Rad and Rüppell (1975). The literature refers to a range of alexithymic traits found in psychosomatic patients (cf. Nemiah and Sifneos 1970; Freyberger 1977; von Rad 1983). They are usually lacking in phantasy and prone to concrete thinking. Their ability to understand themselves and others is deficient and they are alienated from their own feelings and emotions. Object relationships are rudimentary and unstable; in order to maintain rapport, they need to have the object present in front of them. Alexithymics also have a tendency for intellectual arrogance. The processes are complex and I cannot go into any further detail here. Suffice it to say that Bräutigam (1974) saw alexithymia as a defence strategy, dissenting in this from Nemiah and Sifneos (1970), for whom it was an ego defect. One undisputed fact is that the psychosomatic patient speaks through his body; inducing verbalization is therefore a priority in any kind of psychotherapy.

Since the majority of alexithymic patients come from less-educated backgrounds and have difficulty putting things into words and conceptualizing, Bräutigam and his Heidelberg team soon opted for a group-oriented approach. They found that the group format generated a higher emotional charge than individual therapy and offered broader scope for identification; even the silent participant was set to gain something. Entering into dialogue with a variety of other individuals was seen as a learning experience in itself, helping to diffuse patients' fear of their own aggressive impulses. Strong affects were more likely to find motor outlet in a group than in a dyadic setting; resulting physical manifestations could then be worked through interactively as part of the therapeutic process.

Intensive group therapy sessions were held daily throughout the patient's inpatient stay, which lasted for a maximum of two to three months and was followed by two to three years of groupwork in an outpatient setting. The inpatient component was designed to loosen patients' defences and enable them to stand back from their normal social world (Bräutigam 1974). The residential period was essentially seen as an initiation phase; there was never any question of an inpatient-only option. The inpatient setting offered multiple opportunities for breaking down defences: intensive groupwork; non-verbal therapies, e.g. art therapy, autogenic training (Bräutigam 1978a); plus the whole experience of life in a community. As with all bipolar models, the therapeutic/social space dichotomy was retained; everyday coexistence – the *therapeutic community* element – took place in *social space*. Accordingly, the Registrar took responsibility for administering drugs, carrying out physical examinations, assuring compliance with the house rules etc. Team meetings provided a forum for pre-empting splitting reactions in patients.

The initial belief that the wards were little more than a place for social learning and behavioural adjustment gradually came to be questioned. Reporting on their Heidelberg experience, Becker and Lüdeke (1978) highlighted the therapeutic significance of ward life. Patients found that they at last had 'leeway to be themselves';

the ward became a 'refuge' where they could ventilate inner conflict without anxiety. There was great potential for ward staff to do more than simply represent social realities and stimulate communication; they too could have an interpreting remit. In other words, the ward was beginning to be seen as a dimension of analytic or therapeutic space. Becker and Lüdeke recommended keeping formal structures to a minimum. Doctors and nurses should avoid appearing in stereotypical guise; patients needed maximum freedom to use them as objects, although nurses might inevitably find themselves cast in a maternal role. The authors noted that conflict re-enactment was most likely to take the form of acting out in the inpatient environment; this could usefully be backed by non-verbal therapies (Becker 1981). Ego-syntonic acting out of the kind encountered was viewed as true *action* – an integral component of human growth. The self was effectively 'putting itself on the stage'; *acting out* no longer carried negative overtones of resisting remembering (Freud 1914). If acting out is 'managed' properly, the response from the therapists can prove highly educational; the patient actually lives through a 'corrective' experience.

Practical experience convinced Becker and Lüdeke that the analytic process could fruitfully draw for its material on events in social space. Acting out was seen to constitute a dynamic form of self-disclosure. Complemented by social learning on the ward, this self-enactment opened the way for new experience and unlocked the workings of intrapsychic processes. The necessary corollary, we might add, is thorough interpretive clarification. Acting out or re-enactment of pathogenic conflict will not yield therapeutic results unless properly worked through. Old primary object relationships can then be distinguished from new therapeutic relationships, silencing the mechanisms of neurotic repetition.

Heidelberg's initial advocacy of 'group therapy only' eventually gave way to a more flexible approach; where indicated, individual therapy, or a mix of individual and group methods, were made available to patients (Jonasch 1978; Sellschopp and Vollrath 1979). Some anorexics, for example, simply did not respond in groups. Combination treatment was liable to induce transference splitting, but this was not necessarily a problem. As Jonasch pointed out: 'Patients with disorders of early onset, and those suffering from psychosomatic complaints, find at their disposal a whole team of people willing to apprehend their needs' (ibid.).

Splitting in the transference means that the patient has at least one 'good object' with which to relate, e.g. a nurse. Clinicians at Heidelberg devised three approaches to the treatment of long-standing disorders: group therapy alone; the combination approach (individual plus group); and individual treatment only. Autogenic training and art therapy were offered in all cases and patients experienced the effects of therapeutic community living. In order not to break the flow, patients kept the same therapists when moving on to subsequent outpatient therapy (cf. Kordy *et al.* 1983).

Hanover University's Department of Psychosomatic Medicine experimented for a while with similar methods (Freyberger 1977, 1978; Künsebeck *et al.* 1978; Drees *et al.* 1978), as did Rüger (1981) in the outpatient unit at the Berlin Psychiatric Hospital. During my time in the Neurological Department of Bonn's University Hospital, we too advocated a combined approach for the treatment of neurotic and psychosomatic patients (Quint 1969, 1972; Janssen and Quint 1977).

In their discussion of the Hanover unit, Drees *et al.* (1978) highlighted the inclusion of a cognitive component in the thera-peutic spread on offer. Two parallel inpatient groups were set up, both with input from nurses; one followed analytic, the other behavioural principles. The analytic group worked with psychoge-netic alexithymic pathologies; patients were offered 'training in the use of phantasy and the emotions' (Drees 1981). Behavioural methods were introduced to help individuals with disturbances stemming from current relational difficulties; here the emphasis was on enhancing perception and altering established patterns of behaviour. The analytic-behavioural model was eventually aban-doned in favour of a run-in phase of supportive psychotherapy, followed by inpatient group therapy or outpatient family therapy (cf. Lehrmann *et al.* 1987).

The account given by Rüger (1980, 1981, 1982) of a combined inpatient-outpatient experiment at the Berlin Psychiatric Hospital sheds further light on the influence of a residential milieu on therapeutic processes. He was primarily concerned with assessing the effectiveness of group therapy in an environment where a vast range of therapeutic methods was practised. Rüger started his patients off with a three-month period of inpatient treatment. Group therapy took place in a closed group of eight, although patients otherwise were distributed across four psychiatric wards.

They were expected to participate fully in ward activities and came face-to-face with the fact that there was more than one variety of therapeutic approach. Rüger was in no position to dictate the parameters of inpatient life, nor the way members of the clinical staff related to patients. He therefore had to structure his therapeutic strategy around group therapy sessions. This he saw as a potential advantage, since the mixed setting with its interweave of influences provided a foretaste of outpatient realities. Any conflicts arising – small group versus hospital, small group versus therapist, therapist versus ward – could then be worked through in the group.

A considerable degree of regression was observed as a result of pressure from the large group (Rüger 1980, 1981). Patients tended to stick tightly together in the small group, seeking security in membership of a close-knit community. The group gradually ꞁohered into a family, which people then found hard to leave. Regressive tendencies grew so pronounced that malign regression threatened. The fact that patients forged strong emotional ties with one another actually turned into a problem, given that they had to part after a mere three months. Rüger urgently recommended follow-up outpatient treatment, since he feared that patients would otherwise be unable to handle the realities of discharge. Instances of therapeutic failure and broken-off treatment were attributed to the potent mix of neurotic personality structure and clinical life.

We might however put a slightly different gloss on the events Rüger witnessed. Because of the top-down nature of inpatient psychiatric care, patients feel moved to congregate in a small group under the protective and dispensing wings of the therapist (Bion 1961). When therapy is over, loss anxiety and a sense of abandonment frequently follow. Three months is a long time, yet not long enough to work through the processes of separation. Neurotic structures need not therefore be the sole cause of severe regression during inpatient therapy; an equally powerful contributing factor is the organizational structure of the unit within which the small group functions. This is corroborated by virtually all reports of bipolar strategies, where life in the therapeutic community is split off from therapy proper. Until the entire clinical environment is encompassed, and all the players are harnessed in pursuit of a common goal, therapy will never be wholly successful – a conviction endorsed by Novotny (1973) in his study of the various strategies deployed in analytically oriented psychiatric hospitals in the United States.

INTEGRATIVE MODELS

Intimations of an integrative dynamics were in fact very much present in the original conception of a therapeutic community (see pp. 26–35), since the aim was for every member of the professional staff to function as an integral part of the community as a whole. Transposed into our clinical context, the psychoanalyst might expect to find unconscious traces of the passage of an entire therapy team in the deep recesses of his patient's psyche. The full spectrum of unconscious relational configurations therefore requires thorough therapeutic scrutiny.

The first tentative moves towards integration were made in small inpatient psychotherapy units (ten to fifteen beds). One of the earliest descriptions of an integrative model is the account given by Pohlen (1972, 1973) of the *Munich Cooperation Model* (cf. Pohlen and Bautz 1972, 1974, 1978). He and his team were interested in developing a format for brief group-analytic therapy which allowed for therapeutic use to be made of the whole social dimension of the hospital. Their stated purpose was to: 'design for the clinical setting an organizational model capable of taking in the sum of group interaction' (Pohlen 1973).

Pohlen (1973) built on the findings of research into the sociology of hospital structures. Societal patterns have a tendency to replicate themselves within institutions. 'Clinicogenic' phenomena arise, leading to distortions in the structures of communication and blocking the creation of a proper therapeutic milieu. In order to pre-empt this, Pohlen devised what he called a 'bifocal' organizational model, where the dynamics of group processes would foster 'equitable and reciprocal interchange between staff and patient groups'.

Analytic therapy was organized in groups comprising patients with a range of disorders and behavioural profiles. This non-homogeneity was intentional; a specimen group might include schizophrenics, depressives, obsessionals and hysterics (Pohlen 1972). Members of the ward staff (nurses, social workers) had a clear therapeutic remit. They held structured one-to-one meetings with patients and played an integral role in group-dynamics sessions attended by the entire ward group (staff plus patients). The purpose of one-to-one and group contact with the ward staff was to foster a critical awareness in patients of how their behaviour came across in varying relationship contexts. Whereas the group analyst was expected to focus on unconscious factors, the ward staff concentrated more on conscious behaviour. In nurse-patient relations, Pohlen called for primacy to be given to 'descriptive interpretation' over 'causal interpretation', along the lines: 'Let us see what you are doing', rather than: 'Let us see why you are doing it'.

Balint groups provided a forum for the full team to discuss staff-patient interaction in the various fields, with the focus on counter-transference and problems relating to the professional hierarchy. The idea was that the insight gained from this exercise would impact directly on group-analytic work and filter through to inter-relations in other therapeutic areas. Teamwork developed the capacity of the professional staff to think reflexively; the spin-off for patients was that their stereotyped image of doctors and nurses underwent modification (Pohlen and Bautz 1972). The immediate therapeutic goal was 'to train and strengthen the ego with a view to consolidation of the reality principle' (Pohlen 1972). Hope was held out of 'a quantum increase in practical ego capability', equipping patients to relate better to the world out there (Pohlen 1972; Pohlen and Bautz 1974).

As it grew in sophistication, the bifocal model took on a distinctly *bipolar* hue (Pohlen *et al*. 1979; Kauss 1981). Two clearly defined therapeutic areas were marked out: analytic and non-analytic. Each was acknowledged to influence the other and an attempt at integration of the two took place at team meetings. Group analysis, plus individual and family therapy, were located in analytic space; routine rounds by nursing and medical staff, individual discussions with nurses, ward meetings (for talking through day-to-day conflicts) and art therapy, belonged in non-analytic space. Pohlen and his team found that patients were liable to 'repeat' pathogenic infantile experiences in both these areas and acting out could be triggered in either when situations became acute. It was hoped that, by observing the attitude of therapists towards them, patients would learn new patterns of relating and, thanks to interpretation of their own conduct, acquire new insight.

In view of its integrative qualities, Pohlen's original treatment model (1972) exercised considerable influence on the theoretical development of inpatient psychotherapy in Germany. Arfsten and

Hoffmann (1978) have mentioned it in their writings. They organized their practice at Freiburg University's Department of Psychotherapy around the needs of patients with disorders of early onset, in particular those with borderline personality structures (Arfsten *et al.* 1975; Hoffmann *et al.* 1981). Such individuals required an inpatient arrangement which would 'bear them up' whilst remaining 'bearable'. Outpatient therapy was not an option, since they simply did not attend. Because of the many different relationship configurations on offer, ward life provided a *holding environment*. Inpatient therapy was felt to prepare patients for outpatient follow-up by 'raising their tolerance threshold'.

Individual therapy was contra-indicated in the authors' view; the object relationships their patients formed with therapists were too unstable. They therefore recommended groupwork only. Levels of disturbance were such that outbreaks on the ward could not be discounted. Arfsten and Hoffmann took their lead from Pohlen in conceiving of the ward as a *dynamic unit* within which patient and therapist groups 'were located in bifocal relation to one another' (Arfsten and Hoffmann 1978). Any link forged by a patient with a member of the permanent staff working on the ward could be used therapeutically.

The task of the therapist group was to stand united, receiving and handling transference splitting and any other type of multiple transference reaction. Via acting out and verbalization, patients effectively 'put on stage' their inner conflicts. The ward became a place where infantile conflict could be repeated and its affects revived. Equally, scope was given for 'putting order into disturbed inner worlds' and giving patients a new perspective. By processing the material it had jointly gathered, the therapist group knitted together what patients had torn asunder, reuniting split-off elements. Staff roles varied according to speciality: therapists homed in on conflict; nurses provided analytic confrontation and clarification (Arfsten and Hoffmann 1978).

Given the rigorous group orientation of this model, no provision was made for individual therapy; intensive group sessions were conducted by one male and one female analyst. There were however 'therapist surgeries', where individual clinicians made themselves available to patients for brief consultation. This promoted transference splitting, since patients could choose their contact person. The main purpose of these one-to-one talks was to discuss patients' progress and sort out administrative matters such as transfer, discharge etc. If a patient tried to turn one of these encounters into a therapy session, the therapist was not expected to give in, but instead to find out why the problem could not be talked through in the group.

Daily team discussions were of the essence if the ward was to remain a *dynamic unit*. The Clinical Director – who had no direct contact with patients – provided supervision. The team had to ensure that it fulfilled its task, one major element of which was to uphold the delicately constructed web of relationships on the ward. Where patients sought to destroy what had been created, the team was duty bound to resist and restore.

Artificial separation between social and therapeutic space was avoided and the dichotomy between therapeutic and non-therapeutic staff overcome. The model was still deficient in my opinion, none the less. Patients with disorders of early onset were effectively 'refused' the scope inherent in a dual system for strad-dling verbal and non-verbal lines of communication. Winnicott (1951) talked about the *intermediate area* between symbiotic object relationships and individuation. A space of this kind is of vital importance to those suffering from structural ego disorders. This may explain why Trimborn (1983), looking back over his own experience with the *dynamic unit* model, came to the con-clusion that inpatient admission interrupted the omnipotence phantasies of borderline patients at too early a stage. Their *basic fault* was that they had never experienced an intermediate area; their world so far had been bereft of *transitional objects* or *subjec-tive objects*. It was the purpose of the psychoanalytic setting to make up for this lack. Therapy allowed them for the first time to experience spatial and temporal continuity, since they could rely on the presence of the analyst etc. Trimborn rightly noticed that inpatient therapy promoted a high degree of splitting and re-gression, often accompanied by extreme forms of acting out. He deduced from this that ward life positively impeded the develop-ment of an intermediate area, something only outpatient psycho-analytic treatment could deliver. He saw a particular danger in the overlap of social and therapeutic space. Important community relationships were formed in social space, whereas therapeutic space was the arena of the imagination and phantasy. The realities of the inpatient setting forced patients into object relationships too sophisticated for their level of maturity. It cer-tainly behoves any psychoanalyst working in a clinical environment to heed this warning, yet Trimborn surely goes too far in concluding that borderline patients should never be offered inpatient therapy. As I shall be illustrating later, my experience has taught me otherwise (cf. also Janssen and Wienen 1985).

Another early experiment in inpatient psychotherapy took place in the Department of Psychosomatic Medicine at Gießen University (Fürstenau *et al.* 1970). Drawing on the principles of ego psychology, the protagonists sought to provide adequate levels of ego support and a basic climate of security. An element of confrontation was introduced as therapy progressed, designed to bring about gradual ego strengthening.

The therapeutic team (staff group) around the Registrar acted to create the requisite climate on the ward; confrontation was reserved for group therapy sessions. The approach was thus two-pronged, yet integrated. The staff group consisted of: the Registrar, the nurses and the art therapist. The Registrar made a daily ward round and coordinated the work of the team. The nurses saw to patients' comfort and well-being, seeking to induce a degree of 'preverbal attachment'. The nurses and the art therapist were also expected to encourage self-exploration.

The ward was envisaged as a holding environment, offering security and ego support. Group therapy sessions were for confrontation with the harder facts of life; patients faced things that oppressed or embarrassed them, working through worrying or shameful material. A proper balance between ego-support and confrontation was essential if this model was to function properly. The therapist group held together thanks to a free flow of ideas and information among all members of the professional staff.

Inspired by this model, Stephanos (1973) produced a design for treating individual patients in a ward setting, abandoning the notion of group therapy altogether. The staff team nevertheless continued to act as 'a single structured entity'. Instead of attending group sessions, patients were visited on the ward by the psychoanalyst, accompanied by the nurses and the art therapist. This configuration constituted the therapeutic setting. Stephanos baptized his new approach 'analytically oriented psychosomatic therapy', taking his conceptual lead from work on pathogenesis and psychosomatic disorders by the French school of object relations theorists (Stephanos 1978a, 1979).

Since the needs of psychosomatic patients were at the forefront of such work, two psychoanalytic criteria in particular had to be met. These individuals required what Winnicott (1960a) termed a *facilitating environment*, i.e. a therapeutic milieu resembling the original world of the infant. The setting also needed to exercise a *holding function* (ibid.) for the patient. Psychosomatic patients tend to be locked into symbiotic patterns of relating and this holding dimension gave them the security to take their distance from the therapeutic objects in front of them; in this way they could break out of the symbiotic bond. The therapist himself had to be prepared to face the patient's 'psychosomatic peculiarity', i.e. his lack of phantasy life, the absence of any real faculty to form contacts, the sense of divorce from his inner self and his inability to process psychic material.

Another key concept for Stephanos (1978a, 1979) was *taking care*. During therapy-induced regression, patients were entitled to a sense of fundamental security – the product of the attitude described by Winnicott (1951) as *primary maternal preoccupation*. The holding dimension of the therapeutic relationship was achieved thanks to carefully 'dosed' closeness on the part of the therapist. The patient needed to be at just the right distance: far enough away to move freely, yet within reach of narcissistic succour. In this way he discovered the power of his desire for symbiotic union with the therapeutic object and learnt to relate properly to the 'good object'.

Taking care and providing a *facilitating environment* were consecrated terms for the ward group, especially the nurses. These were the concepts on which ward activities centred, whereas the focus of psychoanalytic rounds (analyst plus nurses and art therapist) was on therapeutic confrontation and interpretation. According to Stephanos (1978b) patients experienced the visiting analytic constellation as a *family*; in their phantasies about the relationship between the analyst and the nurses, disturbed individuals were confronting the oedipal scene. Like Arfsten and Hoffmann, Stephanos saw the inpatient setting as a ready-made focus for transference. His implicit words to the patient were:

> Here you have a family, our ward team, which is keen to accept and care for you. You will find in the psychoanalyst a father figure. He is accompanied by his co-workers, the nurses and art therapist; they – in particular the ward sisters – are mother figures. Your fellow patients are your brothers and sisters. What you need to do is integrate the therapy team, i.e. your

family, into your inner world. You can then step back and
observe the way your life has changed. (Stephanos 1978b)

The art therapist and nurses were expressly acknowledged as
recipients of transference reactions. Stephanos (1979) believed
that psychosomatic patients were driven to overpower the maternal object (the nurses) by the dynamics of their relations with
their real mother. They soon discovered that the nurses belonged
to the psychoanalyst and this generated frustration and aggression.
In order to safeguard possession of the object, they found themselves obliged to introject it as 'an internal agency, a libidinous
internal object' (ibid.). This internalization of the good,
libidinously-cathected mother constituted the first decisive therapeutic step.

As therapy progressed through its stages, the nurses in their role
as transference objects acted both as early libidinous objects and as
oedipal-phase sexual objects. The painful process of disillusionment experienced by a patient – the nurse belonged to the analyst
– left him frustrated. Contrary to what happened in childhood,
however, he was able to tolerate this frustration thanks to support
from the *facilitating environment*. As time went by, the nurse
became little more than a mediating *transitional object*, for the
patient now believed he could gain possession of the 'good object'
(father-analyst) via the maternal object (nurse) owned by the
father. This jostling for influence with analyst and nurses helped to
structure the ego. In the best-case scenario patients overcame their
fear of the analyst and yielded to his influence. They were released
from the mother as omnipotent object and, as individuals, could
begin to operate on oedipal territory. Stephanos argued the need
for follow-up outpatient treatment if the process were to be sustained. This would be delivered mainly by the nurses and could be
expected to last between two and four years (Stephanos and Zens
1974). One to two years might elapse after termination of therapy
before any quantum improvement in ego structure could be
observed.

The Stephanos experiment was a consistent and determined
attempt to preserve the dyadic format of the analytic relationship
inside the multipersonal hospital milieu. The psychoanalyst
remained the final focus of transference reactions; nurses and the
art therapist functioned broadly speaking as mediating transitional
objects. The group dimension intrinsic to any inpatient treatment

setting was played down in favour of the one-to-one relationship between patient and analyst. Nurses admittedly had therapeutic significance in that they figured as maternal transference objects; yet they were nurturing and 'silent' mothers, with no allotted role as interpreters of psychic material.

Holding high the motto: 'Inpatient therapy is always group therapy', Möhlen and Heising (1980) subsequently reinstated group therapy at the Gießen psychotherapy unit. Group-analytic sessions were run by the Registrar, who confined discussion during his routine rounds to medical and administrative matters. The nurses were available to patients for private discussion, attending in particular to problems of an individual nature.

Like Arfsten and Hoffmann (1978), Möhlen and Heising (1980) favoured the integration of social and therapeutic space. This was necessary, they argued, in view of the frequency of *splitting transference* or *transference splitting* in the clinical setting. Ward life offered a 'multipersonal transference system', which re-activated primitive defence structures and object relationship patterns, as well as inducing splitting of the transference (Kernberg 1975a). The move towards integration of therapeutic intervention was a conceptual response to splitting. The integrative strategy comprised: 'osmosis' between social and therapeutic space; the involvement of all categories of professional staff in therapy; the granting of equal importance to the totality of relational constellations in which patients found themselves; regular team meetings for everyone concerned with the therapeutic process; and therapeutic working through of acting out by patients in both social and analytic space. The purpose of this integrative strategy was to overcome splitting and promote integrated self and object representations.

Each of the approaches I have described has in its way influenced my conception of integrative psychotherapy. Some particular concerns – such as the dynamics of institutional organization – have not received the attention I would have liked, yet the overall picture is positive. Changes have clearly taken place in attitudes towards analytically oriented psychotherapy for inpatients. Several of the ideas on therapeutic communities originally put forward by Tom Main (1946) have recently been dusted off and put to work in new ways. Nor is there any lack of fresh input. The experiments we have seen illustrate the impact of developments in psychoanalytic thinking (e.g. object relations theory) –

not to mention all the work done in Germany on group-analytic methods.

COMBINED PSYCHOMEDICAL APPROACHES

Combined medical and psychosomatic models are based on a broad, rather than a narrow, definition of psychosomatic illness. The contention is that any disease or complaint, regardless of etiology, has somatic, psychic and social aspects. Weiner (1977) in America and von Uexküll (1973, 1979, 1981a) in Germany have been among the foremost proponents of this approach. The somato-psycho-social position is that all disorders are ultimately psychosomatic, since their nature, course and prognosis are influenced by a combination of psychic, social, genetic, virological, immunological, physiological and biochemical factors. This comprehensive perception of disease offers an alternative to the purely organicist approach of so much modern-day medicine (von Weizsäcker 1948). The experiencing subject, social matrix and all, is brought in from the cold.

Committed psychosomatists have been endeavouring to introduce psychotherapeutic working methods into medical departments and general hospitals. Köhle and his team (Köhle *et al.* 1976, 1977; Köhle 1979; Köhle and Kubanek 1981) built on the theories of von Uexküll (1973) in devising their *Ulm Model*, which aimed to cater for a variety of situations. The majority of their cases involved organic disease (77.3 per cent); only 12 per cent of patients suffered from traditional psychosomatic complaints and 5.9 per cent from functional disorders (Köhle and Kubanek 1981).

Köhle and his team described their unit as a *medico-psychosomatic ward*. Figure 4 illustrates its organizational structure, highlighting the two main areas of psychotherapeutic interest: relationships between patients and nurses, and between patients and physicians/psychosomatists. The parameters of the doctor's round provided the psychotherapeutic setting for his work. His attitude was patient-centred and modelled on the guidelines laid down by Balint and Norell (1975) for psychotherapy in the surgery.

The nurses assessed patients' nursing needs and carried out ward rounds. Their function was not solely to act as mediators between doctors and patients; they were active and autonomous contributors to the overall therapeutic task. The common goal of

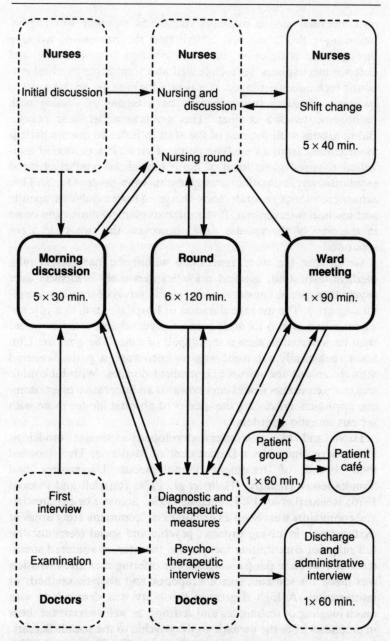

Figure 4 The organization of a psychomedical ward
Source: Köhle et al. 1977

all concerned was to establish viable and two-way working relationships; this 'reciprocity' facilitated the process of *working through* the realities of illness. Pathological conforming and defence mechanisms were discussed and supportive psychotherapeutic techniques deployed. It was rare for patients on this ward to be given intensive psychotherapy as a means of dealing with pathogenic psychic conflict. The psychosomatist held regular Balint groups with the rest of the staff in order to discuss patient management from an analytic point of view. If a particular individual required some form of more specialized conflict-oriented psychotherapy, outpatient arrangements were made. One and the same practitioner generally took charge of both psychotherapeutic and medical intervention. If the internal medical dimension came in the way of therapeutic work, however, the two tasks were separated.

Given that the ward functioned within the parameters of a medical institution, medical priorities inevitably held sway over psychotherapeutic considerations (e.g. in terms of length of hospital stay etc.). The average duration of hospitalization in a psychosomatic unit is two to three weeks; psychotherapy can no more than be initiated in such a short spell of time. The goal the Ulm team realistically set itself was to encourage a patient-centred attitude among the nurses and medical doctors. With luck more and more clinicians would edge towards an integrative psychosomatic approach, enhancing the quality of hospital life for those with serious somatic disorders.

Hahn and his co-workers developed a similar model at Heidelberg University's Department of Medicine. They labelled their brand of treatment 'Simultaneous Diagnostics and Simultaneous Therapy' (Hahn *et al.* 1974; Reindell and Petzold 1976; Reindell *et al.* 1977; Petzold 1979). Somatic or psychosomatic complaints were seen as examples of 'communicating areas of dysfunction', involving organic, psychic and social elements; the full range of contributing factors was therefore considered *simultaneously* when making a diagnosis or offering therapy. Provision was made for somatic, sociotherapeutic and analytic methods of intervention. A high degree of flexibility was demanded, with much juggling of techniques and settings, as well as constant shifts in emphasis from the somatic to the psychic to the social. Somatic interests inevitably took priority (Petzold 1979; Deter *et al.* 1979; Deter and Reindell 1981), with psychoanalytic imperatives (e.g.

attention to transference reactions) suffering the same fate as in the Ulm experiment.

The range of psychotherapeutic treatment available was impressive none the less. Individual therapy was provided on a case-by-case basis in line with needs (Deter *et al.* 1979). Groupwork focused on how the fact of being ill was processed internally, with attention to the compensatory strategies patients deployed in order to cope with the psychic and social repercussions of their condition (Deter and Reindell 1981). Groups were structured around specific issues and the group leader's role was more one of medical adviser than of group therapist. Patients with the same complaint (e.g. bronchial asthma) were sometimes treated in a homogeneous group (Deter and Allert 1983). The objective throughout was to bring people to a medically appropriate understanding of their illness; the conjunction of medical care and psychosocial learning would ideally predispose patients towards the idea of working therapeutically on emotional conflict. This strategy certainly succeeded in some cases, as Deter and Allert (ibid.) have demonstrated in their account of subsequent outpatient work with a number of bronchial asthma sufferers.

Wittich (1975) was doubtful that decent analytic or psychosomatic work could be done in somatic departments, even if the necessary methodological tools were made available. The ever-present danger was that psychotherapeutic criteria would be subordinated to the presuppositions of organic medicine. At the best, 'pseudo' accommodation would be reached between the two disciplines. My feelings are more positive. Bringing a psychotherapeutic dimension into a traditional hospital environment can hardly fail to improve the quality of hospital life for somatic patients – and there is always a chance that they will derive the motivation to pursue fully fledged psychotherapy at some later stage.

Departments of internal medicine have proved particularly keen to adopt patient-centred methods (cf. Filter *et al.* 1981). It is here that the traditional psychosomatic disorders are generally treated: ulcerative colitis, Crohn's disease, bronchial asthma; also anorexia, bulimia, migraine and other organic disorders with neurotic complications, e.g. diabetes mellitus, myocardial infarction etc. Approaches have tended to be pragmatic rather than theory-led. Feiereis (1982) produced an inventory of recommended procedures for use in the treatment of psychosomatic patients. He suggested that non-verbal and exercise-oriented techniques (such as relaxation, autogenic training, music therapy, physiotherapy, respiratory exercises, concentration therapy and occupational therapy) be combined with individual analytic therapy or theme-centred group therapy. After four to six weeks, around 80 per cent of patients with morphological or functionally defined organic conditions would be expected to show measurable levels of improvement in their condition.

Another interesting experiment in this area has been described by Bepperling (1974, 1981). His dream was to see psychiatry and psychosomatic medicine incorporated as a matter of course into mainstream medical practice in general hospitals. Twenty years of his working life were devoted to bringing about some kind of integration between psychosomatic and organic medicine. He launched out orienting his theories towards the requirements of somatic medicine, but soon conceded the futility of parachuting psychosomatic ideas and methods into an institution committed to the principles of natural science (Bepperling 1981). He therefore set up his own special psychosomatic unit, to which patients from medical departments were referred for complementary psychosomatic therapy. He described the new venture as a *psychosomatic workshop*.

The workshop had the capacity to treat thirty patients; each individual was offered the type of therapy best suited to his current pathology and 'pathogenic biography'. Bepperling placed analytically oriented therapy (individual and in groups) at the centre of his treatment strategy, which essentially involved coming to grips with psychosomatic problems through teamwork. Most patients started out in individual therapy, since the intimacy and protection of a one-to-one setting were felt to be necessary if the unconscious roots of neurotic behaviour were to be uncovered and the relevant psychosomatic connections established. Group-analytic therapy followed, with the same therapist in charge. An additional programme included: functional relaxation, autogenic training, dance movement therapy, hypnosis and music therapy. *Interactive therapy groups* were set up to analyse the group dynamics generated by the realities of clinical life. The large group – which broadly speaking came under the responsibility of the nurses – formed the locus for 'intramural social therapy': role playing, conflict rehearsal, dialogue games and biofeedback. The large group setting was designed to foster 'a spirit of therapeutic cooperation'.

Despite his catholic approach towards technique, Bepperling steered an analytic course. His premise was that non-processed traumatic experience should be retrieved into consciousness; re-actualization would reveal pathogenic patterns of object relating, which could then be worked on therapeutically in the clinical setting. The concept of a *psychosomatic workshop*, where various interactive levels are brought together, suggests the beginnings of an integrative strategy. Given that Bepperling followed a consistently psychoanalytic approach, hospitalization periods were generally longer than in the other psychosomatic models we have considered. It needs to be remembered, however, that he was operating with a relatively restrictive definition of psychosomatic illness and did not attempt to treat the whole range of internal medical disorders. The main lesson I have learnt from him (Bepperling 1981) and from Köhle and Kubanek (1981) is this: if a psychosomatic unit is to function successfully as an integrated entity, it must have independent status as an institution.

CLINICAL PSYCHOTHERAPY: THE PRAGMATIC APPROACH

The models described so far either gave methodological underpinning to the concept of inpatient psychotherapy as a remedy for severe neurotic disturbances or introduced psychosocial criteria into the organization of traditional hospital medicine. In this section I look at clinical institutions which have taken a more eclectic slant on psychotherapy, either because of a preference for the pragmatic approach, or for practical reasons (e.g. the public policy requirement that *Kurkliniks* be provided for pensioners).

Langen (1956, 1978) introduced the notion of *multidimensional clinical psychotherapy*, i.e. he chose eclectically from psychiatry and psychotherapy in order to offer an *active* form of psychology-driven therapy in the clinical setting. The model is of historical interest only, so I do not intend to dwell on details. Langen drew up a list of what he saw as the operational parameters of clinical psychotherapy: 'a sheltered climate for the psyche; a fixed time frame; a group environment; the possibility of drug therapy where indicated'. In 'active and synthesizing fashion', he handpicked a series of therapeutic methods which, to coin Kretschmer's term, 'had purchase'. Psychoanalysis, individual psychology, analytical psychology, hypnosis, phased active hypnosis were all drawn on and deployed in individual interviews, group discussion and multi-personal exercises (phased active hypnosis). The aim was to 'purge' the existing situation of its conflictual elements and anchor newly gained insights in the deeper layers of the psyche (the 'depth person'). A variant of educational therapy was used to this end. The therapist in Langen's model not only set an example and spurred the patient to action, but also performed an interpretive role. As for nurses, they were 'the doctor's assistants'; their function was to 'uphold authority', but not to carry out 'lateral analysis'. They took charge of patients on the ward, giving equal attention to everyone and making sure that order was maintained and punctuality respected.

The pragmatic approach is followed by necessity in the big *Kurkliniks* which have been set up in Germany to provide psychotherapy and treat psychosomatic disorders. Their flexibility is limited by the requirements of the hospital operators and by the short duration of treatment (usually six weeks). Patients referred to these institutions are often suffering from chronic problems (persistent neurotic symptoms, character disorders, psychosomatic complaints) which might entitle them to invalidity pensions, i.e. there is *secondary sickness gain* at work. In most cases, group therapy proves to be the most viable strategy. Ahlbrecht (1969) found that group discussion noticeably relaxed somatic fixation, while Mentzel (1976) gathered patients together in the hope of fostering an understanding of psychogenesis and modifying illness behaviour. Harrach *et al.* (1981) sought to achieve a similar end via a combination of group therapy and non-verbal techniques. Brief focal therapy (Mentzel 1969) has also made inroads in *Kurkliniks*. Ahlbrecht *et al.* (1972) highlighted the need for therapeutic work to combat institutionalization. They aimed to counter passivity through sport, games, gymnastics etc. Therapeutic community structures, with joint staff-patient management, were also believed to boost motivation for groupwork. The common purpose of all the therapeutic approaches used in *Kurkliniks* was to shake patients out of their *sick role* and instil into them an awareness of the psychic causes of illness (Mentzel 1981).

Given their restricted remit, such institutions are bound to opt for pragmatism and shun theoretical pathfinding. There is nevertheless a danger of their becoming too eclectic and disorganized, leaving the patients bemused in the face of such a vast array of possibilities. Mere concatenation of psychotherapeutic and other variegated techniques is not in itself therapeutic, however impressive the spread. Such motley combinations defy serious evaluation and render it impossible to assess the impact of transference and countertransference reactions.

THE LARGER PSYCHOSOMATIC CENTRES

The format devised by Wittich for the big psychosomatic centre he headed in Gengenbach offers an illustration of how the eclecticism we saw above can be avoided. The analytic approach to psychosomatic medicine was given absolute priority – and the institution as a whole managed accordingly. The function of the clinical environment was comparable to that of 'an alert, beneficent and unobtrusive therapist' in the psychoanalytic setting (Borens and Wittich 1976). The therapeutic goal – unimpeded development of patient capability – was mirrored by the workings of the institution. Analysis of relational disturbances in therapeutic space and within the therapy team enjoyed top priority, since phantasies and processes inside the staff group were all of central diagnostic significance when considering the difficulties of patients.

The theoretical position underpinning day-to-day functioning of the hospital owed much to the work of Alexander Mitscherlich (1969) on two-phase repression and to research by Cremerius (1977b) into the genesis of psychosomatic symptoms (Borens and Wittich 1976; Wittich and Buchmüller 1981). The thesis was that patients suffering from psychosomatic disorders were in fact alexithymic only in the early stages of illness. Alexithymia signalled a defective ego and was specific to individuals from lower social strata; poorly developed phantasy structures coexisted alongside a potent superego (Cremerius 1977b). Since capacity for verbal expression was so limited, there was either no perceptible transference response, or transference manifested itself solely in the shape of acting out, vegetative reactions or psychosomatic symptoms (i.e. the physiological alarm bell).

The function of the hospital environment was to facilitate repetition through action in the here-and-now (Wittich and Buchmüller 1981). Emotions and phantasies would then begin to surface. Inside the therapy group, and as members of the community of patients, individuals started to tread a path from symptom to conflict and from symptom to interpersonal communication. This corrective social and emotional experience broke through the alexithymia (Borens and Wittich 1976). Behavioural disturbances, labile states and regressive anxiety were part of the course and needed to be seen in a positive therapeutic light, even if the result was a degree of upset and destabilization within the team.

As for methodology, Wittich and his co-workers favoured a multidimensional approach to psychosomatic rehabilitation, drawing on the spectrum of recognized clinical somatic procedures and psychotherapeutic methods. Choice of strategy was none the less guided by analytic considerations. *Cardinal therapy* was the name given to the analytical therapy (group or individual) component (Wittich 1967, 1975, 1977; Wittich and Enke-Ferchland 1968). In addition the authors recommended the use of art therapy, dance movement therapy, baths, massage, autogenic training etc. Great conceptual flexibility was demanded if therapy was to be patient-centred and not method-driven; the phase-by-phase schedules drawn up for patients with ulcerative colitis and cardiac neurosis stand as eloquent monuments to therapeutic openmindedness (Enke and Wittich 1965).

The Gengenbach team did not believe that linear analysis of transference was feasible in the multipersonal environment of a large institution; too many ancillary social influences came to play (Enke *et al.* 1964). Group therapy was therefore the preferred locus of both social learning and corrective emotional experience. Three types of groupwork took place: analytic psychotherapy in the small group, reality-oriented work in a ward group and large group gatherings for the purpose of disseminating information (Wittich 1975). A *personal doctor* took overall responsibility for the individual patient's treatment and well-being. As Clinical Director, Wittich saw himself as exercising integrative functions and upholding the institution's therapeutic goals; he also had an advisory role vis-à-vis the patient's *personal doctor*. The Gengenbach model stood the test of time (Wittich and Buchmüller 1981) and is still in operation.

A psychoanalytic approach was also followed by Widok (1981, 1983) in his work at the Schömberg Hospital for Psychosomatic Medicine. Since transference 'knew no boundaries', he saw the whole clinical environment as a stage upon which patients played out pathogenic conflict. If this re-enacted material was to be worked through therapeutically, the big institution needed to be broken down into smaller, relatively autonomous entities. The optimum entity in a hospital was a therapy team acting as a 'unitary psychotherapeutic person'. The word 'unitary' did not imply that everyone thought and behaved alike, but rather that the purpose of team endeavour was to follow up all the various ramifications and splittings of transference therapeutically. Widok's goal in his big centre was identical to the one that I have always pursued in my smaller operations, namely undintingly to challenge working practices and team processes in the interest of the dynamics of patient therapy. Where he dissented somewhat from me methodologically was in advocating independent supervision by a practitioner from outside the institution.

As we have seen from these last two examples, psychoanalytic methods are not restricted to small units only. The work done in the bigger hospitals has injected much analytic and psychotherapeutic input into the debate on hospital organization. The experience and insights gained are of relevance to anyone involved with the institutional dynamics of hospital management.

Our survey has taken us through exciting territory; inpatient analytic psychotherapy is present on many fronts and in many forms. No single conceptual approach holds sway, however, which explains the difficulties experienced when trying to draw comparisons between institutions (cf. Göllner *et al.* 1981). The lack of a stable theoretical model underpins existing divides among the professionals over the theoretical import of transference, regression and therapeutic remit. The role of the nursing staff is a particular hot potato.

Many impressive methods have been devised and a vast spread of verbal and non-verbal techniques is available to practitioners, yet there has been a shortage of hardcore theoretical work, with practical testing of hypotheses. Further research into concepts and methods is certainly required. My journey through recent clinical history has none the less revealed a growing interest in integrative approaches to inpatient psychotherapy – which is very gratifying.

Chapter 4

A comparison of therapeutic results in a bipolar and an integrative setting

My own first venture into the realm of group-analytic inpatient psychotherapy was during my time at the Psychotherapy Department of Bonn University's Neurological Hospital. The approach we followed there was bipolar in its thrust, but hands-on experience soon convinced me of the need to come up with an integrative treatment model. This is what I did and the result was put into practice at the Centre for Psychotherapy and Psychosomatic Medicine in Essen, where I spent nine years.

From the very beginning, the intention was to back experimental work with hard results. The switch from a bipolar to an integrative strategy offered an ideal opportunity for comparative study. I therefore embarked on a comprehensive analysis of the two models (Janssen 1980), my working hypothesis being that the environment within which therapy takes place exercises a decisive influence on therapeutic processes and outcome.

Let me first of all say a little more about the theoretical underpinning of the two approaches, exploring how this determined choice of organizational structure. I shall then move on to an analysis of therapeutic processes and results. My aim is to keep as close to realities on the ground as possible, enabling those who are active in similar settings to draw their own comparisons.

GROUP-ANALYTIC THERAPY IN A BIPOLAR INPATIENT SETTING (MODEL 1)

When establishing his bipolar model, Quint (1972) worked on the assumption that four 'spheres' exert their influence on the development of the therapeutic process:

- the outside world the patient leaves behind him on admission;
- the new world he enters when he joins the ward and mixes with his fellow patients;
- group-analytic psychotherapy;
- non-verbal therapies, e.g. creative therapy, exercise therapy.

He concluded that the main thrust of the treatment effort should be on group-analytic therapy, which he envisaged as taking place in *therapeutic space*. Conceptually, *therapeutic space* was separate from *social space* – the 'real life' area where patients encountered the Registrar and nursing staff etc. Experiences in social space would be analysed in group therapy.

The bipolar approach was designed to ensure that patient-patient and patient-staff relationships were allowed to develop freely without being subjected to immediate analytical interpretation; the therapeutic process proper could then be contained within the area occupied by group-analytic work. Patients would experience their time on the ward as a real-life event, interacting with their fellows and learning to cope with the institutional constraints of the hospital. When agreeing to admission, individuals accepted temporary removal from their normal world. Neurotic or psychosomatic problems had in any case rendered life outside untenable. The challenges they met on the ward would be similar to those outside, except that there was a perceivable structure to events. Neurotic conflict could be unrestrainedly played out in both social and therapeutic space, although only in the group-analytic setting would any attempt at interpretive clarification be made.

Having been involved in the practical implementation of this model, I now propose to look in more detail at how Quint's theoretical assumptions materialized.

The duration of inpatient therapy was between three and a half and four months; patients were treated in closed groups of eight. Some of these continued to meet weekly for a one and a half hour outpatient session for up to a year after their members had left residential care; we firmly believed in working through the process of separation and social reintegration (cf. pp. 35–48).

The psychotherapy unit was not a physically discrete entity, but part of an open psychiatric ward. Our patients did however have their own dining room and recreation area. General ward rules applied across the board, i.e. mealtimes and bedtime were fixed, as were the periods during which the Registrar and nurses could be consulted on administrative matters. The timetable for group therapy, exercise therapy and creative therapy had to be arranged to fit in with the rest of the ward. Patients congregated socially in the recreation room. The nurses encouraged people to take on ordinary ward duties, e.g. making beds or serving meals, but there was no obligation. The Registrar had a multiple remit. He saw to it that the house rules were understood and obeyed; arranged visits home; made appointments for medical consultations and ensured that drugs (if prescribed) were properly dispensed and administered; and dealt with administrative matters. His contact with patients was either one-to-one or in *group-living meetings*.

These were held once a week under the leadership of the Registrar and lasted for a maximum of an hour. The meeting brought together the Ward Sister, other members of the nursing staff, the creative therapist, the exercise therapist, plus all patients on the ward. The purpose was to allow patients and therapy team alike to air their views on organizational matters. The group-living meeting equally provided a forum for tackling problems of social coexistence on the ward and talking through patients' family or professional problems.

The nursing staff, whose responsibilities spanned the psychiatric and psychotherapeutic sections of the ward, performed sociotherapeutic, supportive and organizational tasks. They worked with the Registrar to ensure that the institutional parameters were upheld and the house rules obeyed; they administered drugs and encouraged patients to undertake ward duties. In their individual dealings with nurses, patients had a chance to discuss relational difficulties, ask questions, put forward their views etc. The aim was for the nursing staff to act in ego-supportive fashion, steering clear of attitudes which might prove alienating. Patients would then take heart and venture to raise their personal difficulties in group therapy. The nurses were well placed to temper frustrations generated by the therapeutic process and stood by patients in cases of ego decompensation. The nursing remit extended to organizing extra-institutional activities, e.g. theatre visits, social events. Most importantly, nurses were there to interact and foster social contact within a protective environment.

Sixty-minute group-analytic sessions were held five times a week in a group room physically separated from the actual ward. The group was led by a psychotherapist in training analysis, who was familiar with group therapy. He exercised no other functions on the ward. A group observer (also in psychoanalytic training) looked on from outside the group; the session was talked through with him afterwards. Quint (1972) drew on the theories of Kemper (1958) in devising the format for group therapy. The therapist refrained from all active guidance or indirect influence. His brief was to interpret, pinpointing how the behaviour of one patient was often an unconscious expression of the mood of the group. Wherever possible, the group's relationship with the therapist was analysed in terms of a transference reaction, i.e. the group was conceived of as an *individual* (Argelander 1963/4, 1968, 1972). Tensions between the two poles (the group and its leader) were then examined and interpreted.

A supervision group met once a week for one and a half hours to discuss progress in group therapy. All analytically oriented psychotherapists working in the hospital took part in these sessions, including those in training – even if they were not directly involved in the treatment of patients on the ward (e.g. they saw them only as outpatients). Supervision was led by the Head of Department and gave practitioners the opportunity to bounce ideas off one another. In this way they gained a grasp of the dynamic processes at work within individual patients and the group as a whole.

Creative therapy sessions, which were held four times a week, gave patients the chance to make something for themselves. Working with clay, wood or paper enabled them to give non-verbal expression to feelings and ideas that had been reactualized in the course of psychotherapy. At the ward meeting (see below) we looked at these artefacts in the light of the overall therapeutic process and discussed how patients could be induced to take their representational efforts further. The therapist might invite one member of the group and one member of the therapy team to produce a symbolic rendering of themselves as individuals, or of the whole group; another potential exercise involved jointly portraying the group. Patients discussed what they had produced in the group-living meeting and in group therapy (cf. Janssen 1978). This dimension of creative therapy involved input and guidance from the therapy team. Time was equally set aside however for patients to explore their creativity without external guidance.

Exercise sessions were attended five times a week. The focus was on gymnastics and ball games, the aim being to involve patients in some kind of physical activity. We seldom incorporated exercise into the actual therapeutic process.

The purpose of ward meetings was to integrate the various areas of endeavour into a coherent whole. The Head of Department chaired proceedings, which took place once a week It was expected that everyone involved in therapeutic work would attend. News and views on the course of therapy were exchanged among members of the full treatment team (nursing staff plus therapy team). Areas of tension were pinpointed and, where appropriate, elaborated.

EXPERIENCE WITH THE BIPOLAR TREATMENT MODEL

We persevered with this approach for about six years, until the time came for thorough critical analysis of the interpersonal and group-dynamic processes involved. The shortcomings of the model could no longer be disguised (cf. Janssen and Quint 1977), but we did not throw up our hands. On the contrary, we pressed forward all the more resolutely in our search for a more promising answer to the challenges of inpatient psychotherapy.

In order for readers to appreciate what we were up against, let me briefly run through the deficiencies of our bipolar strategy. Patients began to regress quite severely immediately they were admitted to the unit. We attributed this to the fact that they had been abruptly removed from their familiar surroundings and plunged into a communal group situation. As regression deepened, neither the group therapist, nor the Registrar, nor the nursing staff felt able to sustain the separation between social space and therapeutic space.

The psychoanalytic rule of abstinence was only partially obeyed by the group therapist. When infantile conflictual patterns were re-enacted during group therapy, he inevitably allowed things he knew about patients' behaviour on the ward to filter through into his comments. He was unable in other words to rely solely on material thrown up by the specific group situation and began to look to the link between regressive processes and events on the ward. He found himself taking an interest in patients' phantasies – about the hospital, its nurses, its Registrar and Head of Department. Transference reactions engendered outside the group-analytic structure entered his field of vision. As group therapist, this placed him in a quandary. It was simply not possible for him to remain within the agreed parameters of the therapeutic setting. He had to adduce his knowledge of events outside group therapy in order to comprehend events taking place within it; yet the only way to remain true to the official format of the setting was to blot out everything occurring beyond the pre-set bounds.

The other side of the coin was that the Registrar and the nurses sometimes felt moved to abandon their purely *social*, real-life role and don a therapeutic hat. Acting out on the ward and clashes with the institutional setting were not unknown; non-therapeutic staff could hardly avoid venturing an interpretation of the libidinal or aggressive impulses they were witnessing. The problem was that there was no provision for this *lateral therapy* to be integrated into the overall therapeutic strategy.

Patients' private meetings with the Registrar, ostensibly to sort out administrative or medical problems, also tended to become the locus of lateral therapy. Transference to the doctor developed alongside transference to the group therapist, leading to lateral or splitting transference. The Registrar then allowed himself to be drawn into interpreting the reactions he observed and, in so doing, stepped out of his prescribed role.

He also tended to find himself in deep water during the group-living meeting, where patients would try to impose a group-therapist role upon him. Such gatherings consequently took on the guise of parallel group therapy sessions, occasionally developing a dynamics which ran counter to the thrust of official groupwork. Patients either idealized experience in the parallel group, or else devalued everything that happened there, with the result that *group-living* time was used to play out personal psychodynamics in the here-and-now. This was not a bad thing in itself, but the remit of the meeting was such that the material thrown up could not be put to proper therapeutic use.

As for the nurses, their restricted mandate left them ill-equipped to identify the nature of the behaviour they encountered on the ward. They were liable to perceive infantile neurotic conduct as a response to day-to-day events. This triggered a *social space* rejoinder and the result was a pool of unprocessed counter-transference reactions. Despite team efforts to clarify what was happening, relationships often remained locked in their pre-established grid. Guilt feelings led the staff members concerned to split themselves off from the therapeutic endeavour. Pseudo-therapeutic theories took shape, undermining patient treatment and team motivation.

Mutual exchange of information and ideas was supposed to be engaged in at ward meetings; yet the flow of news was usually in one direction, with nurses briefing therapists. The original conception was that the whole gamut of therapeutic relationships would be analysed, with particular emphasis on intra-group processes; achievement of an integrated treatment strategy required that level of interchange. In practice there was often so much to report that the allotted hour barely sufficed to set the stage, let alone grapple with the issues. The real reason for this lack of proper exchange lay deeper, however. Something was wrong with the structure of relations within the treatment team. Ultimately, nurses and creative therapists were in one camp, analytical therapists in the other. The analysts were apt to see the nurses as their 'assistants', which tilted the balance of narcissistic task-investment. Some therapeutic roles were clearly more equal than others; the nursing staff were but handmaidens to the psychotherapists. This amounted to a de facto ban on therapeutic input from non-analysts. People kept quiet about things, in particular their own conduct and feelings. Countertransference began to be acted out; a nurse might yield to a patient's desire for closer contact and invite him home for supper one evening. As the outcome was probably a friendlier and more relaxed patient, there was a temptation for that nurse to phantasize that hers was the better form of therapy.

Once we came to analyse incidents such as this, we saw that the nurses were reacting defensively to what they experienced as a professional snub: 'You are not therapists, so you had better stick to your nursing role.'

On top of this, the nurses faced a conflict of loyalties, since they had simultaneously to service the standard psychiatric section of the ward. They were caught between the psychotherapists and psychiatrists, unable to play on either side, yet part of the game. The best solution was to go it alone; if the other parties could not get their act together, then the nurses would.

These issues of personal esteem were thrashed out in the supervision group. Even within the body of psychotherapists, we discovered, degrees of task-identification varied. Therapists working only with outpatients found it hard to relate to the inpatient model. They clashed with the inpatient team over professional worth, seeking to profile themselves as offering greater 'value and efficiency'. Focus in the supervision group was consequently more on the dynamics of inter-professional rivalry than on the processes at work within the patient group.

We had to concede that the various fields of therapeutic interaction (group-analytic therapy, Registrar-patient contact, nurse-patient contact etc.) had not been sufficiently integrated into a mutually enriching whole. It was clear that certain preconditions would have to be fulfilled before we reached our goal. This entailed:

1 Securing acceptance among the entire therapeutic staff of the need for each professional grouping to identify with the psychoanalytic approach, i.e. commitment to a common task.
2 Obtaining a staff complement dedicated exclusively to inpatient group-analytic therapy; we could not afford to have people simultaneously championing psychiatric principles.
3 Making sure that the nursing staff and non-psychoanalytic therapists (e.g. art and music therapists) were able to exercise a therapeutic role commensurate with their personal and professional identity. Analysts had to be prepared to share their knowledge and leave space for others to play a confident and productive part in the inpatient enterprise. Liaison with the outpatient sector was also necessary to ensure that everyone understood the purpose of the different levels of therapeutic intervention.
4 Saying goodbye to the notion of therapy-free 'social space'. The everyday scene in a hospital setting constituted a therapeutically potent source of insight. Any irruption into life on the ward of re-actualized infantile conflict needed to be seen in a constructive light – the apparent distortion of clinical realities in fact exposed material deserving of interpretation.
5 Convening frequent meetings of the treatment team to discuss interaction with patients, in this way promoting interdisciplinary cooperation and generating a true dynamics of debate. So as to ensure an integrating analytic presence, it was important to place a psychoanalyst in charge of proceedings.
6 Allowing patients the opportunity to see a therapist on a one-to-one basis. Individual contact fostered identification with the treatment process – although the facility was not to be used as a

backdoor means of re-introducing an individual-therapy-only strategy for inpatient analytic work. Practitioners disavowed the group dimension of hospital life at their peril. This was not to deny that an overemphasis on the group dimension – on the wards or in psychotherapy – had in the past led to disorientation and severe regression.

So much for our conclusions. It was in 1977 that a blueprint for a new, integrative treatment model actually took shape. I was by then operating in a different hospital, with different staff structures. For theoretical and practical guidance, I and my team looked in particular to Fürstenau *et al.* (1970) and to Arfsten and Hoffmann (1978). Psychoanalysis was beginning to address the treatment of structural ego disorders (cf. pp. 11–20) and the emergent techniques seemed readily transposable to an inpatient setting. Whereas our strategy under the original bipolar model had been to work on resistance and transference in the context of group therapy, the presence of patients with structural ego disorders shifted our perspective. Armed with a new integrative model and winged by fresh ideas on transference, we set out into unexplored terrain.

AN INTEGRATIVE MODEL FOR INPATIENT PSYCHOANALYTIC THERAPY (MODEL 2)

Some institutional and staffing prerequisites

We carried out our experiment in an autonomous department, attached to the Rhine District Hospital and Medical School. Departments of General Psychiatry and Child and Adolescent Psychiatry were accommodated within the same complex. Our unit comprised two wards of fifteen beds each. We also had an Outpatient Clinic, where patients referred to us underwent preliminary examination. Direct admission without prior assessment was not possible.

The treatment process began with what was known as a *diagnostic meeting*, attended by all departmental therapists. This was the forum for deciding whether, in a particular case, outpatient or inpatient therapy was indicated. Ten medical and psychological specialists were employed in the Department (three psychologists, seven medical practitioners). In line with integrative principles, each had tasks to perform in the Outpatient Clinic (preliminary screening) and on the wards. I do not intend to dwell on the finer points of psychoanalytic diagnosis and treatment formulation here; this is an area I shall be dealing with more exhaustively later. With the exception of acute psychoses, or alcohol and narcotic substance dependence requiring withdrawal treatment, our coverage extended to: neuroses with incapacitating symptoms, e.g. severe forms of hysteria, obsessional neurosis, anxiety neurosis, cardiac neurosis, suicidal depression and pharmacological substance dependence; personality disorders, e.g. borderline personality disorder; psychosomatic disorders, e.g. severe functional organic disturbances, anorexia, bulimia, ulcerative colitis, Crohn's disease, hypertension, severe migraine and some cases of bronchial asthma.

The Head of Department and the two Consultants exercised mainly advisory functions. All medical and psychological practitioners were either trained psychoanalysts/psychotherapists, or were in training at the time. Twelve nurses and one Senior Nursing Officer operated in the Department. Our aim was for members of the nursing staff to be versed in the general tenets of psychoanalysis. We therefore held special in-house seminars on subjects such as: the theory of neurosis; psychosomatic medicine; psychoanalytic concepts of illness; the basic principles of analytic psychotherapy and group-analytic therapy; and the dynamics of large organizations.

Several nurses took up our suggestion that they enter group-analytic training. All attended regular *Balint groups*, where they worked on recognizing the dynamics of interpersonal relations and coping with interactive situations. This programme of continuing training ensured that we had a group of nurses who felt comfortable with the analytic climate. We could also rely on them to tutor any new nurses who joined the Department. The Senior Nursing Officer, who had completed the requisite level of analytic training, carried out supervision for the rest of the nurses.

Our art and music therapists had also been through an analytically oriented training programme. They generally saw patients one-to-one, although some work was done in groups. Once the Department had become established, we took on a dance movement therapist as well. Weekly supervision sessions were organized for each area. Since creative therapists operated in the *extra-*

verbal field,[1] it was important to keep their analytic sensitivities alive.

Together these professionals (medical and psychological practitioners, nurses, art and music therapists etc.) formed the *treatment team*. The integrative model was put into practice from the very outset in the Essen Department, although minor amendments (e.g. the addition of dance movement therapy) were made subsequently. My intention is not to go into the mechanics of launching a new project, nor to dwell on the small changes that were sometimes necessary. What interests me is how theory affected the patients we treated over a given period. Committed as we were to ongoing assessment of methods, a major exercise in evaluation was carried out, spanning the period from the end of 1977 until the middle of 1979 (cf. pp. 91–3). This means that I am in a position to take the reader through the phases of practical implementation of a conceptual idea – a story which culminates in Chapter 5 with an account of the model in its final state.

The point of departure

We set out to create a setting that would do justice to the lessons of the bipolar model (see pp. 70–4). *Integration* was the key. Within the multipersonal matrix of the inpatient environment, patients were to be given the opportunity to re-enact inner conflict in the here-and-now, opening access to the object relationships of their infantile world. With the support of the therapy team, individuals would gain the courage to venture into new and therapeutic forms of interrelating, acquiring the experience and insight to modify existing psychic patterns. The whole range of interaction and object choice in the multipersonal arena had to be analysed in order to ascertain whether, in any particular instance, infantile configurations were being replayed. A dual focus was therefore required. We needed to observe the impact on the working alliance of events in the real-time social setting; yet it behoved us equally to be alert to signs of the unconscious resurfacing of infantile behavioural patterns, i.e. transference reactions.

The operational code we adopted was as follows:

– The thirty patients in the department were divided into four

[1] For elucidation of this term, see pp. 135ff.

treatment groups. Each of the two wards had one group of eight to ten and one group of five and six.[2]

- Organizational parameters grew out of everyday institutional imperatives: admission and discharge procedures; timetabling requirements (group therapy, individual therapy, nurses' rounds, music and art therapy); mealtimes; recreational activities; weekend leave. The sum total of all these equalled the setting. In other words, our model turned what had traditionally been described as 'social space' into the actual framework within which the therapeutic process was to take place.
- All members of the professional staff were integrated into a single therapy team, each individual taking charge of a specific field of therapeutic interaction.
- Jointly and severally, the team and its members were responsible for upholding the institutional framework and safeguarding the therapeutic process. This meant maintaining the boundary-setting and holding functions of the Department and ensuring that the dynamics of transference was allowed to develop freely.

Nobody was in a position to predict how – and according to what timescale – object relating would materialize in individual cases. We accordingly made no attempt to place a deadline on the duration of treatment. On admission patients effectively entered into a contract with us. We explained that they should probably reckon with a minimum stay of four months, assuring them that the question of discharge would be properly talked through well in advance of the final decision. The corollary from the therapists' point of view was that they had to keep a clear picture in their own minds of the individual progress of patients. Keeping track in this way simultaneously equipped them to answer eventual queries from the hospital operators.

The different therapeutic fields and analytic tasks

A cursory glance at the Department's operational code might suggest that everyone finished up doing everything – which was not in fact the case. We were very careful to distinguish one therapeutic task from another. Figure 5 correlates the different aspects of

[2] It was agreed from the start that the smaller groups would be homogeneous, i.e. dedicated to therapy conceived for one specific disorder (ulcerative colitis, anorexia, obsessional neurosis).

Common task: upholding the therapeutic framework (holding and boundary-setting function)	
Setting	*Methods*
1 Group-analytic therapy: four sessions a week: one hour (group therapist plus nurse as co-therapist).	Interpretation and confrontation in relation to multidimensional transference generated during interactional replay. Focus on large-group process. Impact of: ward dynamics; here-and-now group events; processes operating within individuals.
2 Individual analytic therapy: two or three pre-admission interviews; optional sessions during inpatient stay; ± five post-discharge sessions.	Safeguarding the working alliance. Auxiliary ego functions in cases of regression. Interpretation and confrontation. Focalization and coordination of therapeutic process. Admission and discharge procedures. Drawing up of reports.
3 Nursing activities: individual contact two times a day: scheduled ward rounds; informal contact.	Caring and diatrophic relationships. Encouraging patients to voice difficulties, complaints etc. – requisite action commensurate with setting and institutional framework. Clarification: highlighting of aspects of manifest behaviour; also interpretation of relational patterns.
4 Registrar: surgery.	Dealing with somatic problems. Organic treatment where necessary. Contact with other medical departments and institutions in the case of referrals for second opinion.
5 Music therapy.	Production-oriented music therapy: self-portrayal and affective actualization. Communication-oriented music therapy: interaction at different psychodynamic levels (from symbiotic to oedipal) with the other (music therapist) as responding object.
6 Art therapy.	Objectification: plastic representation of inner images and moods. Product of artistic creation as mirror of self (ego-supporting function).
7 Dance movement therapy.	Promoting communication among members of group. Relaxation exercises to heighten body awareness.

Figure 5 Therapy fields: setting and methods

the setting with the therapeutic methods used in each interactional field. Dance movement therapy is included under *setting*, although it had not yet been introduced at the time the survey in question was carried out. I will be coming back to this diagram in Chapter 5, when I look in more depth at the theoretical underpinning of the integrative model.

Group-analytic therapy

Inpatient group-analytic therapy took place in closed-open groups of eight to ten or five to six patients. Newcomers were admitted only if another patient left the group; once in, people stayed until their residential treatment was over. Groups met four times a week for one hour. The two larger groups were led by an analytically oriented group therapist, with a nurse who had been through group-analytic training acting as co-therapist. The two smaller groups were conducted by a group therapist only. Since people's theoretical backgrounds in group therapy varied, weekly supervision sessions were organized to coordinate views and approaches. The respective group's remaining treatment team watched proceedings in group therapy from behind a one-way mirror; discussion then followed. My vision of the role of the group analyst in a hospital setting owes much to Foulkes (1964, 1975) and his multidimensional model. It behoves anyone working in a residential environment never to lose sight of the three levels of psychodynamic functioning in the small group: the reflexive-interactional; the oedipal; and the pre-oedipal (cf. Heigl-Evers and Heigl 1973b; Kutter 1978; Sandner 1978).

What we learnt in the bipolar setting led us to modify our attitude towards the group dynamic as such. Previously we had modelled inpatient group therapy on what happened in the small-group outpatient constellation. Now we began to broaden our vista, looking not only at small-group processes (e.g. transference on to the group therapist/therapist duo), but also at relational interplay in the large group constituted by the hospital community. Accordingly, transference to other therapists now needed to be encompassed. Group therapists were expected to work on and interpret large-group events, processing transference material in the here-and-now. No human manifestations were out of therapeutic bounds: patients' feelings about the setting; their attitudes towards each other; their ideas, sentiments and phantasies – all were worthy of interpretive clarification.

As co-therapists, nurses represented the wards, introducing the events of ward life into group therapy and commenting on actions by patients. They were closely bound up with the dynamics of ward interaction and therefore well placed to join in analysis of transference reactions – be it to themselves or to their colleagues. The nurse plus group therapist configuration proved to be a true *transference trigger*, propelling patients – who were often trapped inside pre-oedipal, symbiotic configurations with mother representatives (e.g. nurses or their individual therapist) – along the road of oedipalization.

Individual analytic therapy

Individual analytic therapy was designed to allow the one-to-one relationship established with a particular therapist during the first outpatient interview to continue during residential treatment. Compared with their group counterparts, individual therapists concentrated more on fostering self and ego development; they also ensured that the working alliance was sustained. If a patient needed special back-up, his individual therapist was there to take on auxiliary ego functions; he might even act as a surrogate for an ego disintegrating through severe regression. Where appropriate, transference reactions were interpreted in the here-and-now. Lack of therapeutic focus could also be remedied on an individual basis.

Following discharge, patients were invited to attend a fixed number (usually about five) of one-to-one sessions. This provided space for working through the process of separation from the hospital and helped them to re-adjust to the outside world. Where further psychotherapy was indicated, arrangements were made.

Nursing activities

The nurses' therapeutic field was the ward, where they entered into both formal and informal contact with patients. Twice a day they spent fifteen minutes or so with each individual as part of their scheduled rounds. In addition, people came to them for medication etc., or simply because they wanted to chat. Nurses also took charge of newcomers, introducing them to the parameters of inpatient life. The nursing remit could ultimately be described as looking after patients' needs, both day-to-day and therapeutic, throughout their hospital stay. A point was made of having a rota system for ward rounds so as to ensure that every nurse met every patient at regular intervals.

The prime perception of the nurses was therefore of a caring, nurturing and diatrophic group, ready to assist in making sense of the complex web of social interaction on the ward. They were not there to boss everyone around, but rather to lend support and to listen, encouraging the articulation of thoughts and feelings. We did nevertheless urge them to be frank in their feedback, using their personal insights to illuminate interactional processes and manifest behaviour. They clarified, *concretized* and occasionally interpreted. One of their main areas of intervention was invariably to talk patients through their frequent clashes with the actual setting itself. Input from the nurses helped to put a perspective on actions.

Registrar

Close liaison took place between the nursing staff and the Registrar who, as physician with responsibility for the ward, took charge of patients' somatic needs. He held a regular surgery to which people came with organic complaints. Where necessary, referrals were made to other departments or institutions for medical treatment. He also prescribed drugs etc. The Registrar never acted as individual therapist for a patient on his ward. He did however exercise a helping remit vis-à-vis the team on whether a patient really had an organic problem, or simply craved more and more medical tests as a means of evading psychical difficulties. If patients somatized to the extent that they caused disruption (e.g. anorexics), he stepped in as an auxiliary ego. From the point of view of individual patients, he was their *hospital GP*.

Music therapy

Practical emphasis in analytically oriented music therapy nowadays is on active production and communication, backed by a fledgling reception-theory component (cf. Willms 1975; Schmölz 1976; Strobel and Huppmann 1978). We worked with Orff instruments plus piano. Sessions were generally held in a dyadic setting so as to lead patients step-by-step through the various stages. We found pentatonic music suitable for therapeutic purposes, since results were not dependent on the rote learning of musical engrams; individuals felt free to produce the sounds that sprang spontaneously from within.

At the first session the music therapist explored the patient's musical sensibilities, asking what kind of music he liked etc. Sometimes as a warm-up the two of them would listen to a recorded piece together. Then the patient was usually invited to play something himself. If the very idea of this threw him, hearing the therapist go through some rudimentary sound-phrases often helped. Active therapy began with single note sequences by the patient; the therapist responded in kind where this seemed appropriate. The next step was to combine notes and produce real compositions, matching mood and sound. This led naturally into improvisation. The patient was by now equipped to join in music-making with others. An equally important part of active therapy was to talk through what had occurred. At the end of each phase, the patient was asked to comment on the feelings that had been aroused in him. The therapist too gave a perspective on inter-action. Something intimate had been portrayed in musical form; it remained to clothe it in language.

Art therapy

Art therapy took place both one-to-one and in the group. Patients were asked by the therapist to convey the essence of their inner-most selves through a process of *objectification*. The aim was that coloured images should be produced straight from the emotional core. The therapist all the while offered advice on how to give concrete form to abstract ideas and feelings. Anything touching on the life of the emotions was a fit subject for pictorial exploration: fear of visual representation itself; affects such as anger or a sense of abandonment; dreams; fairy tales; family scenes; relationships with primary objects, partners, therapists etc. Where the ideas portrayed failed to hang together, verbal clarification was required before the patient could properly come to grips with the material he was spontaneously producing. This often proved to be the case where events on the ward were getting people down. Pictorial representation, however confused, always came first. This was a sacrosanct principle. Reflection and talking through were for afterwards.

Our point of departure was that therapeutic processes are indivisible. It was not a matter of isolated things happening in discrete therapy fields; what counted was the overall dynamics between treatment group and patient group (cf. Figure 7, p. 109). Therapeutically significant events took place in the space generated by the interplay of forces. As I shall be illustrating below, patients occupy different areas within that spatial configuration depending on their specific infantile patterns.

Team meetings

Given the indivisibility of the therapeutic task, we saw no reason to privilege any one particular relationship constellation (e.g. therapist–individual patient, therapist–group). While different practitioners had different things to offer, the essence of the integrative approach was that everyone worked together in pursuit of a common goal. The team's *basic rule* was that members should always be open about their interaction with patients.

The forum for this honest exchange was the *team meeting*, which had several guises (see below). I have always believed that a group cannot perform its task satisfactorily unless it has access to some kind of integrating agency. For this purpose we introduced the figure of *psychoanalytic adviser*. As fully fledged analysts, the Head of Department and the two Consultants held ultimate responsibility for the therapeutic process and were therefore well placed to fulfil this role. This precluded them of course from direct contact with patients.

I shall be discussing the role of psychoanalytic adviser again in Chapter 5, when we come to look in more depth at the integrative arrangement. For the time being I propose to concentrate on the organizational aspects of team meetings. Agreement was reached in advance on who should attend, how long proceedings should last (usually one hour), number of participants etc. All gatherings – apart from the diagnosis meeting – were multidisciplinary. In most cases the psychoanalytic adviser kept a record, which he circulated to the therapists concerned.

The diagnosis meeting (four a week)

The patient's initial contact clinician – and subsequent individual therapist – introduced the case. The therapist group then produced a psychodynamic formulation (cf. Figure 6, p. 89) and decided whether or not inpatient therapy was indicated. Lastly, an individual treatment plan was drawn up and entered in the case file.

The ward meeting

Each of the four therapy teams met once a week to discuss an agenda of their choice – although the assumption was that they would give priority to topical issues. Certain patients might be causing concern; medical problems needed addressing (e g. desirability of medication) and so on. Conflict within the team was another matter frequently arising. The one fixed requirement was that a patients's *admission scene* be analysed. This was our jargon for events surrounding the arrival of a new patient in the Department; initial response to all fields of therapy was examined. Questions of admission and discharge were also discussed. Separate ward meetings were held for each treatment team; there was no mix.

The progress meeting

Every two to three months the relevant treatment team met to assess each patient's progress. Patterns of relating in the various therapy fields were examined and an attempt made to establish a conceptual picture (*progress Gestalt*) of the re-enactment of infantile behavioural configurations. Plans were then drawn up for future therapeutic action. These meetings were attended by all therapists directly involved with the patient's treatment.

The group-process meeting

Members of each treatment team watched proceedings in their patients' one–hour group therapy session from behind a one-way mirror. They spent the following hour analysing the group process and how it had evolved. Comparisons were drawn with what was happening in other therapy fields.

The full-team meeting

This took place once a week, usually on a Friday. The whole team, i.e. all four treatment groupings, attended. The prime focus as the weekend approached was on *problem patients*, who were perhaps unhappy about leave arrangements. Conflict within both patient and therapist groups was talked through and time was set aside to deal with organizational matters of concern to the whole team.

The post-discharge meeting

Four to six months after inpatient treatment had ended, the patient's individual therapist reported on progress in outpatient therapy during the immediate post-discharge phase. The *discharge scene* was discussed and it was possible to look back with some detachment over the whole course of inpatient treatment. A decision was then taken on whether further therapy was required.

Outside the frame of these regular meetings, *ad hoc* liaison took place between doctors and psychologists (to arrange admission dates and preliminary interviews etc.); meetings were convened with the hospital management to discuss administrative and therapeutic matters; briefing sessions were arranged with art, music and dance movement therapists. The full staff team also met at intervals for thorough-going debate on therapeutic methods and the structure of the setting.

COMPARATIVE ASSESSMENT OF MODELS

Methods for evaluating results in psychotherapy

Inpatient psychotherapy, like anything else, relies for its further development on research into the success of methods already in place. I therefore undertook a random-sample survey, comparing and contrasting results achieved under each of the two models with which I had been involved (see Janssen 1981a for a detailed account).

The methodological challenges facing anyone seeking to monitor the results of analytic psychotherapy have been taken up at length in the literature (Dührssen 1962; Dührssen and Jorswieck 1965; Cremerius 1962, 1968; Bergin 1971; Malan 1973; Graupe 1975; Göllner and Deter 1979; Kächele 1981). Inpatient work offers no fewer hurdles. It is beyond the scope of this book to explore the minutiae of hypothesis-testing theory and process research; I simply refer the reader to the work done by Kächele (1981).

The assumption underpinning the survey was that psychoanalysis is an empirical science. Brenner (1968) in fact called it primarily descriptive, i.e. the corpus of knowledge grows out of observation and interpretation. The psychoanalytic process is in some sense an exercise in *therapeutic research*. Material thrown up by the analytic situation is worked on systematically; hypotheses are formed; observations are recorded, evaluated and finally interpreted.

The nature of the clinical environment in which we were operating dictated certain practical considerations. The instruments of evaluation could not be too cumbersome; we had to respect the institutional framework; methods needed to be replicable if we were serious in our intention to monitor therapeutic practice on a routine basis. Homing in on each separate therapy field was hardly a realistic option; nor was it desirable. What interested us was the integral effects of inpatient therapy.

Before I move on to my own eventual choice of assessment method, let me first consider some of the approaches used by other researchers. The Menninger Clinic (cf. Kernberg *et al.* 1972), like Malan (1963), opted for a naturalistic-style survey (cf. Remplein 1977). A project team was formed at the Menninger to collate the data routinely recorded by therapists on their clinical charts. Clinical case histories were then drawn up. Some predictive and quantitative research was also done. When the time came to assess the results of therapy, clinical judgements were underpinned by a commitment to psychoanalytical conceptions of the cure process. When Malan (1963) was considering the results of brief analytic psychotherapy (focal therapy), he drew up 'Assessment and Therapy Forms' for individual therapy fields, on which he entered details of treatment. In line with analytic principles, he then *worked through* the material he had obtained *retrospectively*. Throughout this exercise he looked to the therapist group concerned – the *Workshop* as he called it – for supervision.

Like other psychoanalysts before me, I felt that the methods used by Malan (1963, 1976) might be usefully transposed to the inpatient setting. Meyer (1978) had already applied Malan's technique to the evaluation of brief analytic psychotherapy for psychosomatic patients. The Heidelberg team (Bräutigam *et al.* 1980; Engel *et al.* 1979a, b) too looked beyond standard rating scales and psychological tests. In cooperation with the therapists concerned and independent assessors, clinical data were reviewed in the light of analytic criteria (ego strength, superego pathology, drive integration and object relations).

Malan (1976) proposed the following sequence for investigating the effectiveness of analytic psychotherapy:

- drafting an inventory of all known disorders and symptoms;
- establishing psychodynamic hypotheses to explain symptom formation from a psychoanalytical perspective;
- drawing up for each patient a list of *appropriate reactions*, in advance of outcome interviews;
- holding outcome interviews with these patients and comparing results against above lists;
- formulating an assessment scale.

The concept of 'appropriate reactions' clearly presupposed an established set of values. Malan's psychic yardstick was derived from the psychoanalytic tradition which placed stress on heterosexual satisfaction and the achievement of harmonious relations with others. Therapeutic goals were absolute, tinged with notions of the ideal; any loss of symptom predicated on the patient's social or career demotion was suspect and should not be classed as therapeutic success. Malan (1963) devoted considerable attention to what he termed the 'false solutions', often accepted as hard currency. The problem lay in misguided apprehensions of recovery. I certainly agree with him that the way to avoid these perceptual pitfalls is to make systematic use of the psychoanalytic interview as a control instrument (cf. Cremerius 1962; Beck and Lambelet 1972; Danckwardt 1976; Meyer 1978; Schwarz 1979; Bräutigam *et al*. 1980; Rüger 1981).

The chosen method of assessment

Transposing Malan's methods to the inpatient setting called for certain adjustments, which I shall now outline.

There were various stages to the production of a *psychodynamic hypothesis*. We started by compiling an exhaustive list of symptoms, basing ourselves on the results of pre-admission psychiatric and medical examinations. An introductory psychoanalytic interview was held, a personal history (anamnesis) taken and a therapy team meeting convened. We were now ready to establish a psychodynamic diagnosis and formulate a treatment plan. Unlike Malan (1963), we did not assume an ideal or absolute therapeutic goal; our focus was more on the specific needs of the individual in front of us.

When operating in the bipolar setting (Model 1), I assessed therapeutic progress by consulting records of group therapy and reports on the work of the supervision group. A final statement on outcome was drawn up around two months after termination of inpatient (or post-discharge outpatient) treatment. This was a collaborative exercise, involving the group therapist (me) and the group observer, with occasional help from the supervision group.

This bipolar experience was useful when it came to devising a method of evaluation which would cater for the integrative model. We now required a more horizontal approach to the monitoring and recording of the therapeutic process; yet the exercise had to be practicable in the clinical setting. My solution was to set a time-table for recording the ideas and material pertaining to the various stages of therapy. The steps given below became standard practice in the integrative setting (cf. pp. 74–85).

1 Working on the basis of the report drawn up by the therapist in charge of the patient's first interview, the therapist group drafted a *psychodynamic hypothesis*. Drawing on the work of G. and R. Blanck (1974, 1979), we endeavoured in our formulation to do justice to the aspects of psychodynamic diagnosis shown in Figure 6 (Janssen 1980). Individual treatment goals were derived from the psychodynamic picture obtained.

2 One week into residential treatment, the *admission scene* was analysed. We looked at developing relations in all therapy fields and set our observations against the initial hypothesis. Under the guidance of one of the team analysts, we then devised a treatment strategy.

3 Throughout a patient's hospital stay, meetings were convened (*ward meetings, progress meetings*) at one- to two-monthly intervals so as to examine and register progress in the various spheres (life on the ward; interaction with nurses; relations with therapists: group, individual, art, music, dance movement). The therapy team now had the material it needed to reconstruct the infantile scene. Where necessary, the original psychodynamic hypothesis was revised.

4 Four to six months after discharge, the *post discharge meeting*

took place. The staff team explored progress in the light of the initial hypothesis and evaluated developments in object relations. At this point a prognostic assessment was made of the likelihood of future disturbances.

---

1 Symptoms: type; variety; evolution.
2 Drive development level: fixation at the oral, anal, phallic stage.
3 Ego development;
   a) Ego strength: anxiety and frustration tolerance; instinctual outbursts;
   b) Self/object differentiation: identity diffusion, desire for merging, versus self and object constancy;
   c) Ego functions: thought; language; judgement; reality testing; synthesizing faculty;
   d) Anxiety level: anxiety about annihilation, object loss, loss of love, punishment;
   e) Defence level: e.g. projection; splitting; turning on self; isolation; repression.
4 Internalized patterns of object relating: reliving of early object relationships; parental imagos; real trauma e.g. experience of institutional placement.
5 Superego constellation: e.g. self-punishment; guilt feelings; rigid standards.
6 Self images: real self; ego ideal; grandiose self.
7 Current pattern of interpersonal relations: family; partner; profession.
8 Transference – countertransference.
9 Motivation for therapy: psychic pain; need gratification; inner hurt; conflict awareness.

Figure 6 Aspects and organization of psychodynamic diagnosis

When the time came for my retrospective research, I used the findings recorded in the reports of these meetings to assess the treatment process and its outcome, classifying results according to the grid established by Malan (1963):

1 *Resolution of conflict*
2 *Partial resolution*
   – substantial improvement in the human relations without improvement in, but without exacerbation of, the symptom;
   – limited improvement in both the human relations and the symptom.

3 *Clear-cut false solution*
  – Loss of symptom, with solution of the problem of human relations by withdrawing from it.
4 Loss of symptom, with minimal changes in the problem of human relations.

In line with Malan's model, I then allotted points:

– *Score 3*: Evidence for substantial resolution in the main problem.
– *Score 2*: Evidence for limited resolution in the main problem, e.g. partial resolution.
– *Score 1*: Substantial symptomatic improvement without appreciable changes in the problems of human relations; also *valuable false solutions*.
– *Score 0*: No change or deterioration.

Fully-fledged *outcome studies* were carried out in order to reach a judgement on the sustainability of change. When patients left the hospital, they returned to the influences of their previous social environment; it was always possible that they would be enticed back into pathological modes of object relating. Under the bipolar model (*Model 1*) outcome studies continued for up to three years after termination of inpatient treatment (see Appendix, Table 1). The research was carried out by me, in my capacity as group therapist, in liaison with the group observer, who had not been directly involved in therapy. We compared results and evaluated the level of change using the points scale given above.

  The key component of outcome research was a semi-structured psychoanalytic interview of one to one and a half hours. We covered a range of issues: the patient's current situation; any symptoms he was experiencing; interpersonal relations; his professional and family situation; relationships with friends; his handling of general social situations. Conflictual behaviour in social and personal relations was interpreted analytically. Standard questions were asked to ascertain whether there had been any further hospitalization or need for psychiatric/psychotherapeutic help since discharge; whether medication was being taken; how the patient was coping with work; whether he had had to change his job. Finally, we enquired how he felt in general about his inpatient stay with us. Looking back, did he feel satisfied with the range of therapies on offer?

Under the integrative model (*Model 2*), outcome studies were the responsibility of a therapist who had not been involved with the patient's treatment (Schwennbeck 1992). He began by going through the results of the customary assessment procedures: psychological tests; responses to the Gießen Questionnaire;[3] answers to a set of standardized questions relating to Malan's scale. Therapeutic outturn was then set alongside the initial psychodynamic hypothesis. The next step was to analyse reports from the various therapy fields (the assessor did not have access to post-discharge results) and draw up personalized lists of questions for the final assessment of each case. The highpoint of the outcome process was a semi-structured psychoanalytic interview, designed to ascertain how patients were progressing. Questions were asked about symptoms and the quality of current object relationships – a particularly sensitive outcome indicator. On the basis of this information, the assessor produced an up-to-date psychodynamic diagnosis and compared actual results with the therapeutic goal initially posited.

This method of assessment appeared to be the least disruptive of the therapeutic process. The information was readily available; we avoided bringing in an independent research team; yet we obtained the paving data for further, more sophisticated studies.

Models 1 and 2: results

Outcome studies were completed on eighty-seven patients. *Model 1* provided us with thirty-nine cases, treated in four closed groups over the period 1972 to 1976. There were seventeen women and fourteen men between the ages of 19 and 42; the average age was 26.2 years. Fifty-six patients were followed up under *Model 2*; they were resident in the unit between the end of 1977 and the middle of 1979. This group comprised thirty-four women and twenty-two men from 19 to 49; the average age was 30.

Table 1 (see Appendix) gives comprehensive details of all eighty-seven patients: age; sex; marital status; occupation; symptoms and their duration; diagnosis; duration of therapy; results of follow-up two to six months after termination of therapy; results of outcome studies over the months following discharge. Patients 1–31 were treated under *Model 1*; patients 32–87 under *Model 2*.

---

[3] *Gießener Beschwerdefragebogen* – a complaints questionnaire.

In the case of two groups (patients 17–31) assessment encompassed the one–year course of post-discharge outpatient group therapy; research began as soon as this ended.

Data on the social background of patients can be found in Table 2 (see Appendix). The majority of those admitted for inpatient therapy were women. This tallies with the generally observed trend that women are more likely to enter psychotherapy than men. Another striking feature is the over-representation of people in some kind of training (e.g. the students in *Model 1*). Otherwise the main clients were lower grade employees and public servants; the self-employed do not figure at all in the list and there were few people with a university education. Non-skilled workers were totally absent from *Model 1* and under-represented in *Model 2*. There were however more skilled workers and housewives in *Model 2* than *Model 1*. The statistics we have available are none the less too limited for valid conclusions to be drawn as to the correlation between social status and motivation for inpatient therapy.

If we consider the two to six month follow-up results for all eighty-seven cases (see Appendix, Table 3), the recovery pattern emerging is as follows: 20.7 per cent – no improvement; 33.3 per cent – fair progress as a result of therapy; 46 per cent good or satisfactory outcome (graded *3* or *2*). The picture differs somewhat if *Model 1* and *Model 2* results are considered separately. While the *no improvement* figures are practically the same (22.6 per cent and 19.6 per cent), noticeably more *Model 1* patients were graded *1* on outcome (fair). Moving on to the *good* and *satisfactory* categories (*Scores 3* and *2*), 51.8 per cent came under these headings in *Model 2* as against 35.5 per cent in *Model 1*. The differential here is pronounced ($p > 0.01$);[4] successful outcome proved considerably higher in *Model 2*.

Under *Model 1* we undertook *outcome studies* on twenty-nine out of the thirty-one patients (93.5 per cent). One woman had committed suicide (No. 4); one man (No. 22) had broken off treatment. At the time of the outcome survey, he was undergoing therapy for drug dependence and did not wish to take part. The individual timetable for outcome assessment is given in Table 1 (see Appendix). Studies continued for up to three years after termination of therapy.

[4] Chi-square relative frequency test.

As for *Model 2*, thirty-seven out of fifty-six patients (66 per cent) were followed up for outcome (see Table 1). Even after several years, the tendency was for *good* and *satisfactory* results to be sustained. There were seven *Score 3* patients (19 per cent); fourteen *Score 2* (38 per cent); seven *Score 1* (19 per cent); nine *Score 0* (24 per cent), i.e. 57 per cent achieved *good* or *satisfactory* results. The one caveat is that we only managed to reach 66 per cent of the original assessment group.

Taking *Models 1* and *2* together (see Appendix, Table 3), 51 per cent of the sixty-six patients studied for outcome achieved *good* or *satisfactory* results (*Scores 3* or *2*). Once progress had been achieved during therapy, patients seemed to maintain the momentum. Comparisons did however reveal that more patients in *Model 2* scored *3* or *2* (57 per cent) than in *Model 1* (45 per cent). We should perhaps sound a note of caution here all the same. When undertaking long-term outcome studies, clinicians must pay due heed to the influence of the patient's overall social environment. Where life circumstances were favourable (secure job; continuing financial support, in the case of a student; opportunity to pursue outpatient treatment; helpful relatives), we found that patients tended to move up a level (*1* to *2*; *2* to *3*) as time went by. Falling scores were often attributable, in part at least, to pathological family constellations or sudden redundancy.

Analysis of results

In Chapter 3 we looked at various units specializing in inpatient psychoanalytic therapy. Table 1a (see Appendix) offers an overview of the methods used to evaluate the success of the respective treatment approach. I do not intend to enter a critical debate on the validity of individual assessment techniques – which range from the simple questionnaire to sophisticated research designs (Göllner *et al.* 1978; Kordy *et al.* 1983). Suffice it to say that expectations have risen as time has gone by.

Where recovery rates were actually recorded in the Table 1a surveys, favourable outcome varied between 50 and 80 per cent. The longer the outcome investigation – and the more precise the instruments deployed – the lower the recovery ratio. I have so far been unable to ascertain to what extent differences in results were attributable to different theoretical assumptions or non-comparable patient pools.

Coming back to my research, 46 per cent of our patient sample achieved *good* or *satisfactory* outcome, i.e. less than the two-thirds mean generally quoted for psychotherapy. If however our results are compared with those of other departments carrying out fully-fledged outcome studies, we are broadly speaking on a par. Göllner *et al.* (1978) and Kordy *et al.* (1983) reported recovery rates of around 50 per cent. Were we to include our *fair* category in the count (loss of symptom or symptomatic improvement, but no appreciable change in the problems of human relations; valuable false solutions) the figure would rise to 79.3 per cent. This result would be in line with conclusions reached by other researchers. Systematic comparisons are not easy to make, since so many different criteria are brought to bear when evaluating success. The fact that the integrative model significantly outperformed the bipolar one in the *good* and *satisfactory* bracket does at least suggest that we are entitled to answer 'yes' to the question: do theoretical positions and organizational structures affect the nature of therapy? I have certainly found confirmation of the integrative hypothesis I ventured when working in a bipolar setting. Conceiving of the entire inpatient environment as part and parcel of therapy certainly does appear to enhance the quality of treatment – particularly for patients with structural ego disorders.

The influence of variables on any particular treatment scenario is a subject I have dealt with in some detail elsewhere (Janssen 1980). It behoves anyone passing judgement on therapy to keep in mind:

- Patient variables: duration of symptoms; lead symptom; age; motivation to seek therapy; pathogenic psychodynamics.
- Psychosocial variables: family situation and relational patterns; relationship with partner; other social factors.
- Treatment variables: theoretical model used; pattern of transference and countertransference; duration of therapy.

It was quite clear from my survey that symptom duration was a powerful determinant of *good* or *satisfactory* outcome. Where a patient had been suffering from the same symptom for a prolonged period, results were likely to be in the *fair* or *no improvement* brackets. I established that patients in this category had been living with their problem for an average of 8.5 years. A *good* or *satisfactory* score was most likely in patients with average symptom histories of 5.8 years. These findings are in line with the prognostic criteria for neurotic illness proposed by authorities such as Heigl (1972).

Little noteworthy influence on outcome was exercised by a patient's cardinal symptom (psychic, functional, organ-destructive), age or motivation. Younger people appeared to stand a slightly better chance of recovery, but results were by no means conclusive. Outpatient practitioners frequently cite *motivation for therapy* as a reliable pointer when deciding whether or not psychotherapy is indicated; a patient is motivated if he seems willing to explore and discuss aspects of his inner life. The inpatient equivalent must surely be an individual's willingness to become hospitalized. As far as openness is concerned, I have seen patients who started out in therapy veritably cowed by the pain their symptoms were causing them. To all intents and purposes they were passive, withdrawn and unresponsive. They needed to experience the support of the hospital setting for some considerable time before they were ready to peer beyond their somatic horizons. Only then could we truly speak of motivation for *therapy*.

Another aspect I assessed was the severity of *pathogenic psychodynamics*. This I did by checking the results achieved in therapy against a list detailing the patient's individual psychodynamic characteristics (cf. Appendix, Table 4). Both structural and developmental aspects were considered. The first structural step was to distinguish between *neurotic* ego disorders and *structural* ego disorders. Neurotic disturbances of the ego are functional; thought processes and reality testing are bound up with drive-defence conflict. In the case of structural impairment, certain ego functions are simply not operative because of a deficit in ego development (cf. Fürstenau 1977a). The developmental distinction I made was between oedipal and pre-oedipal disorders. This enabled me to ascertain the level of drive fixation – which sets the pattern for object relating. I also studied levels of anxiety and defence, since knowledge of these allowed for differentiation between psychogenetic disorders of early and late onset.

In *Model 1*, the distribution of oedipal and pre-oedipal object relating was fairly even, but oedipal patients tended to derive greater benefit from therapy than their pre-oedipal counterparts. This *un*evenness in outcome proved still more pronounced when I came to consider levels of ego disturbance. Most patients (24 = 77.4 per cent) were suffering from neurotic ego disorders; the seven who had varying degrees of structural impairment all achieved considerably poorer results. A similar trend could be observed in the case of anxiety and defence levels. Patients whose anxiety was located at the bottom end of the development line (anxiety about object loss and loss of love) were less accessible to therapy than those with problems of a higher developmental order (superego-induced anxiety, castration anxiety). Borderline patients with defence-related anxieties or fear of annihilation (which ranked low on the developmental scale) proved totally unreachable. The predominant defence schema was obsessional-phobic. In other words, the overall picture emerging from the bipolar model was of an inpatient setting suited to neurotic patients with intact egos and oedipal conflict behaviour. The likelihood of successful outcome decreased the earlier along the development line the disorder had taken hold.

When I moved on to my evaluation of *Model 2*, a mere glance at the cardinal symptoms and their duration left me in no doubt as to the severity and chronic nature of the psychic disorders treated. I again drew up a list of patient-by-patient characteristics and recorded the results (see Appendix, Table 4). Out of the fifty-six *Model 2* patients surveyed, thirty-eight (67.9 per cent) displayed pre-oedipal object relationship patterns – a marked increase over *Model 1*. Thirteen of the eighteen patients with oedipal problems (72.2 per cent), and sixteen of the thirty-eight in the pre-oedipal group (42 per cent), progressed towards *good* or *satisfactory* outcome, i.e. both oedipal and pre-oedipal success rates were higher than in *Model 1* (13.3 per cent: two out of fifteen).[5]

On the ego front, neurotic ego disorders predominated in *Model 2* also (thirty-seven out of fifty-six = 66 per cent). Similarly, these patients achieved better results than those with structural ego disorders or extreme ego weakness. Although more *defective ego* cases were handled in the integrative setting (34 per cent compared with 22.6 per cent), the impact of the ego-defect factor on outcome was roughly equal in both models.

I had however sensed greater pre-oedipal potential in *Model 2*. Corroboration came when I looked more closely at defence and anxiety levels. Borderline defence was manifest in seventeen out of fifty-seven patients (30.4 per cent), whereas the percentage was just 6 per cent (two out of thirty-one) in *Model 1*. More cases of depressive defence were also treated in *Model 2* (sixteen out of

[5] Several years have now elapsed and this trend has intensified. These days *only* patients with severe psychic disorders are admitted for inpatient psychotherapy.

fifty-six = 28.6 per cent); in the bipolar model, obsessional-phobic constellations predominated. Patients with borderline defence patterns were less likely to progress beyond the *fair* category than those with depressive or obsessional-phobic tendencies. Nevertheless, *Model 2* was more successful with borderline cases than *Model 1*. A similar picture emerged with anxiety levels. Thirty-two out of fifty-seven *Model 2* patients (57 per cent) suffered from anxiety about object loss or loss of love; yet therapeutic outcome in 53.1 per cent of cases (seventeen out of twenty-two) was rated *good* or *satisfactory*, against 31.2 per cent (five out of sixteen) in *Model 1*.

The main conclusion I drew from this comparative study of therapeutic outcome was that, despite the predominance of pre-oedipal cases in *Model 2*, results were generally more favourable than in *Model 1*. The integrative approach therefore seemed better suited to the treatment of structural ego disorders than the bipolar arrangement.

Let us not leap to conclusions, however. The fact that the integrative model outperformed its bipolar counterpart does not prove incontrovertibly that integrative inpatient therapy is the treatment *par excellence* for patients with structural ego disorders (cf. Arfsten and Hoffmann 1978; Möhlen and Heising 1980). Those of us working in the field have certainly found evidence that the integrative model meets the 'ideal' psychotherapeutic criteria we have set ourselves better than any previous approach (cf. Beese 1971b, 1978; Heigl 1972; Bräutigam 1974; Janssen 1981b). I none the less feel that patients are not always as well as they might be when we discharge them. This sentiment has been echoed by the team at the Cassel Hospital (Denford *et al.* 1983). Their conclusion was that borderline patients were being discharged on the grounds that they seemed well enough adjusted for the outside world, when in reality they were simply going through a depressive phase. Therapists should not allow themselves to be taken in by appearances. The Cassel team's view was that this type of patient needed further inpatient treatment if satisfactory results were to be achieved. My experience – and that of my immediate colleagues – has been that treatment duration, unlike other variables, is not a major influencing factor.

Psychosocial variables are a different matter. We did not need systematic studies to convince us of this; clinical evidence spoke for itself. Interpersonal relations, and the way conflict was handled

in the home environment, unequivocally played their part in therapeutic outcome. Formal research into the backgrounds of our
eighty-seven cases duly confirmed that neurotic constellations in
family and partner relationships (Mentzos 1976) not only exerted a
counter-pull on patients while they were in therapy, but actually
had a negative influence on outcome. A special pathogenic psychodynamics appeared to be at work. When we looked closer at
individuals in the *fair* and *no improvement* categories, we discovered that they mostly came from environments where personal
relationships centred on defence formations or instinctual gratification. Patients who broke off therapy mid-way frequently fitted
this mould – a finding endorsed by Dehe *et al.* (1979) in the
outpatient analytic context. Conversely, those who were rated
good or *satisfactory* managed during the treatment process to
change outside relational patterns for the better. They demonstrated higher degrees of individuation and learned to structure
their lives more autonomously; relationships with partners grew
warmer and more alive.

These results tally with the notion that patients need to be
removed from pathogenic environments if a true therapeutic process is to be engaged (cf. *inter alia* Heigl 1972; Kind 1972;
Bräutigam 1974; Schepank and Studt 1976). Taking a patient out
of a neurotic interpersonal constellation calls into question his own
defence structures and those of significant others. This may be
painful, but the results are fruitful therapeutically. The inpatient
therapist must of course be aware of the possible external repercussions of all this. Established interpersonal configurations not
only enable the patient to stabilize his defences and satisfy his
unconscious needs; they equally keep a complex system – perhaps
the entire family – on some kind of tack. Attention must therefore
be paid to the effect of the patient's treatment and transformations
inside the therapeutic setting on his social world outside. While
family or couple therapy may not be primarily indicated, it is
generally necessary in such cases to bring families and/or partners
into the treatment process.

At this point I should like to touch upon the problem of patients
who break off therapy in mid-term. *Therapy drop-outs* expose the
limits of any psychotherapeutic enterprise, inpatient or outpatient;
yet analysts in general have had little to say about patient desertion (cf. Graupe 1975).

When carrying out my evaluation, I drew a distinction between patients who decided very early on that inpatient therapy was not for them and those who went along with the process for a time, only to pull back later. Some lasted barely a week (over a period of seven years, we had roughly 3 per cent in this category). We simply failed to get through to them; a working alliance was impossible to forge. Being separated from their pathogenic object relationships generated levels of anxiety too intense to be broken down by therapeutic outreach.

The second category was different. Some of these patients did enter a working alliance and engage with others in the various therapeutic fields. Pathogenic psychodynamic workings began to unfold. Then, all of a sudden, they interrupted the therapeutic process, usually by not returning to the hospital after a break. With the exception of one female patient, most individuals in this category eventually resumed contact on an outpatient basis with their own particular therapist, often with a view to re-admission. Occasionally a patient would veritably plead to be discharged – against the wishes and advice of the therapy team. Outpatient contact was usually maintained under such circumstances. In other words, such patients did not give up on therapy irredeemably; they eventually re-contacted us or applied for outpatient treatment.

The reasons why people broke off therapy had to do with the dynamics of their own psyche. They could not cope with the vast interactional field in which they were obliged to co-exist with the therapists and their fellow patients. Some individuals were afraid of the closeness involved in sustaining a therapeutic relationship; others seemed unable to tolerate frustration and were excessively prone to acting out destructive impulses. One man fled the unit because he felt overwhelmed by the friendly attentions of his fellows (they gave him a birthday present). A woman patient preferred to break off treatment rather than 'give in' to the nursing staff, who wanted her to swap rooms with someone. Her room was her castle; if she could not keep it she would rather go away altogether. This dramatization with the nurses amounted to a replay of her pathological relationship with her mother. Patients who broke off hospital treatment clearly found the 'attraction' of pathogenic interpersonal arrangements in the outside world too powerful to resist.

Dehe *et al.* (1979) found that one of the causes of desertion lay in therapists' failure to recognize what was going on when patients entered the clinical environment. The natural priority for a newcomer is to reinstate familiar patterns of human relations; Mentzos has spoken in this regard of 'psychosocial defence' (1976). Established grooves suit neurotic defence structures, as well as providing surrogate gratification for warded-off infantile needs. Dehe's team saw evidence here of the power of the symbiotic, sado-masochistic and phallic-aggressive currents which often run beneath the surface in couple relationships. A patient coming to therapy with this variety of psychosocial baggage inevitably tried to superimpose his chosen format on relations with therapists. If the latter proved too slow in recognizing the stakes, they finished up playing the role in which they had unwittingly been cast: punishing partner, symbiotic superego or sundry infantile object. By the time realization dawned, it was often too late; interpretation of the transference reaction involved simply led the patient to break off therapy. Such individuals deeply resented being deprived of the gratification they drew from the pursuit of infantile dramatizations.

Some of our patients broke off treatment following the unmasking of unconscious interpersonal configurations; yet such instances were rare. People were more likely to depart as a consequence of unconscious acting out by therapists in the countertransference. Confronted with patients who were themselves acting out in an aggressive manner, therapists were liable to enter rejection mode. The advantage of the hospital setting was that other therapists could step in to cope with countertransference behaviour in their team colleagues. At least one therapeutic relationship was therefore likely to remain intact; countertransference acting out by one or more therapists did not in other words lead inexorably to the breaking off of therapy. This element of the multipersonal inpatient environment made it ideal for the treatment of structural ego cases, since these patients had a particular tendency to trigger countertransference behaviour in therapists. Individual strands might strain to breaking point, but the fabric held and the therapeutic alliance was maintained.

Thorough analysis of treatment variables was not easy under either model; inpatient psychotherapy involves imponderable amounts of therapeutic interaction and interrelating. An exhaustive assessment would have needed to pinpoint the precise field in which any particular treatment effect was achieved. In this regard evaluators of inpatient settings face still greater challenges than their outpatient colleagues (cf. Kächele 1981). We eventually decided to juxtapose the treatment parameters of the two models and attempt a comparison in terms of the correlation between therapy duration and growth of a true relational/transference Gestalt. This we hoped would take us forward.

It transpired that the duration of therapy had barely any influence at all on outcome. We might have expected to find greater evidence of therapeutic change in longer-stay patients (e.g. those who, in *Model 1*, had pursued group therapy as outpatients or, in *Model 2*, spent more time as inpatients); yet our results failed to corroborate this. No discernible improvement in outcome was produced either by the continuation of group therapy as an outpatient, or by above-average lengths of inpatient stay (i.e. more than 5.7 months).

My gloss on this superficially surprising result is as follows. A patient presents for treatment. The therapists already have an idea of the severity of his psychopathology. One fundamental variable is how well they succeed in grasping and recording the specific psychodynamics of that patient from the moment he enters the hospital and begins therapy. His initial object choices in the new multipersonal environment are indispensable pointers to inner workings. The team's first task is therefore to form as comprehensive a picture as possible of fledgling interaction in all therapy fields. Proper understanding of the dramatizations triggered by pathogenic psychodynamics paves the way for decisions on the nature, intensity and duration of therapy.

This brings us logically to the next treatment variable I quoted, namely the team's management of developing relationship constellations and its response to manifestations of transference and countertransference. My material was drawn from the records of interaction in the different therapy fields. Analysis of the comments entered for the thirty-one patients treated under *Model 1* confirmed our theories about the effect of a bipolar arrangement on the development of transference (cf. pp. 70–4). The distinction between therapeutic and social space led therapists to concentrate uniquely on events in group therapy; interrelating in the social arena was not considered important. Processes of transference or countertransference involving the Registrar, the nurses or other patients were never uncovered; acting out went unnoticed. The team often remained in the dark about certain things until outcome interviews were held. The repercussions of this missing matter have already been discussed.

Analysis of relational configurations in the integrative model pointed me in the direction of a special transference Gestalt, which I came to refer to as *multidimensional transference*. What took place in an integrative setting was enactment on the interpersonal stage of the many faces of pathogenic psychodynamics. Multidimensional transference permitted patients to rediscover internalized, libidinally or aggressively cathected (family) object relationships (with mothers, fathers, brothers, sisters etc.). Each patient's *group ego* (Ohlmeier 1976, 1979) was now *externalized* in the matrix of the multipersonal setting. Multidimensional transference might be described as the regressive re-enactment, in live interchange with therapists and fellow patients, of family constellations – those internalized relational patterns which 'set' psychic structure. The various aspects of the intrapsychic template find discrete, yet simultaneous expression in transference to the different therapists (cf. *Vignette 1*, pp. 157–9).

The concept of multidimensional transference can usefully be compared with that of *multilateral* transference in the outpatient group-analytic field (cf. Foulkes 1964, 1975). Similar processes also occur in one-to-one analysis, but are referred to there as *lateral transference*.

Another transference Gestalt that figured large in the inpatient setting was *transference splitting* (Kernberg 1975a; Volkan 1976). Non-integrated *good* and *bad* object representations became *split off* and projected on to different therapists. From the team's perspective, multidimensional transference was occurring. The patient however experienced a one-to-one or unidimensional thrust, since good and bad components coexisted in an unintegrated state alongside one another. Splitting transference reactions signalled borderline personality (cf. *Vignette 3*, pp. 161–6).

Unidimensional transference was particularly prevalent in certain patients during regressive phases. One relational field alone became cathected, e.g. that occupied by the individual therapist as over-idealized maternal object. One-dimensional transference equally occurred where the sole focus was on the hospital or therapy team as diffuse, yet unitary objects, e.g. in cases of transference to the object as oral-dispensing mother (cf. Van Eck 1972). I observed this especially in psychosomatic patients and learnt to gauge their therapeutic progress in terms of movement towards a multidimensional pattern.

Looking at the treatment histories of patients with *good* and *satisfactory* outcomes, I discovered that extreme regression did not necessarily trigger malign deviation of the therapeutic process. Favourable results were achieved by patients with potent symbiotic, idealizing, splitting or negative transference reactions. Multiple object choice allowed for the unfolding of specific transference Gestalts. Despite reactivation of negative and destructive reactions, patients were capable of sustaining a positive therapeutic relationship at a subliminal level; this acted as a guarantor of the working alliance. Even where they sought in their acting out to destroy the maternally holding setting (in cases of conflict re-enactment), or where the therapy team countered negative transference with acting out of its own, a positive dynamic could still endure. Lateral transference to other patients was also potentially useful as a catalyst for change, provided it was properly incorporated into the therapeutic process.

Summing up, the ratings edge enjoyed by the integrative over the bipolar model came into particular relief with the treatment of structural ego disorders. Its superior performance in my view sprang from the leeway it offered: for the unfolding of multidimensional processes; for transference splitting; for the re-enactment in the here-and-now of pathological patterns of object relating. There was real free flow, which could be observed by the therapy team and worked upon in a joint effort.

The integrative approach would therefore seem to offer the best way forward for those who see inpatient psychotherapy as a means of bringing about structural change in their patients. That was certainly the conclusion we reached and, on the basis of the results of our outcome studies, we set about fine tuning both our theory and our practice. In my final chapter I hope to communicate the essence of our new thinking.

Chapter 5

Integrative psychoanalytic treatment in the hospital setting
Towards a theory of practice

Fürstenau (1977b) proposed the term 'praxeology' to describe the effort to give theoretical underpinning to clinical practice. I now wish to venture a praxeology of inpatient analytic psychotherapy, hoping in the process to answer the question I raised in the introduction, namely: how can psychoanalytic methods be put to work in a hospital, with its complex interweave of staffing and organizational arrangements? The purpose of the analytic approach is to reactivate in transference patterns of relating which are an unconscious replay of infantile conflict. Analytic work then sheds light on the meaning of experience and behaviour, enabling the patient to gain insight into his internal object world. Discoveries made within the parameters of the analytic situation open the door to new experience (cf. Chapter 2).

This goal can be achieved in a hospital setting provided the many lines of interaction between professional staff and the patient can be harnessed in a common, psychoanalytically oriented endeavour. There are certain essential psychoanalytic requirements, which must be fulfilled:

- the provision of clearly defined and unchanging parameters, necessary to establish boundaries and provide a holding environment;
- constant availability of therapeutic partnerships;
- profound understanding of how therapeutic relationships fit into the pattern of transference and countertransference;
- a willingness to 'confront' patients in the analytic sense and interpret material arising from the interactive process;
- the provision of space for opening up new areas of object-experience in the context of therapeutic relationships.

As we have seen, inpatient conditions are not those of the outpatient clinic; the institutional framework is different, as are the therapeutic relationships on offer. Hospitals have their own organizational requirements: things must be run in an economic way; there are administrative structures to be respected; research needs to be done etc. The individual alone has little influence on such parameters. If inpatient analytic psychotherapy is to be more than mere *therapizing*, the requirements of therapy and hospital alike must be integrated into a concept that can be shared by all (cf. Novotny 1973). Some analysts dispute that their discipline can ever prosper within the frame of an institution governed by economic and other non-therapeutic criteria; these miscellaneous factors simply put a brake on the unfolding of transference and countertransference. My contention remains that psychoanalysis is an empirical science which can, under the right circumstances, thrive very well in a hospital setting.

Hospital analysts are of course called upon to demonstrate large measures of conceptual creativity and flexibility. They have to work alongside all sorts of other professional groupings; positively cathected relations are a must. The enterprise stands and falls on whether these other professionals are able to identify with the analytic goal, yet feel they have space for their own particular input. My personal experience suggests that such a climate is attainable.

THERAPEUTIC SPACE: UNDERLYING ORGANIZATIONAL STRUCTURES

A further comparison with outpatient psychoanalytic therapy may help to clarify the influence of institutional and staff-related factors on analytic treatment within the hospital. In the outpatient setting, it is the one-to-one relationship which is paramount (Fürstenau 1974); transference to the therapist naturally comes to the fore, since the patient directs all information and affects towards the one analyst, who in turn concentrates his attentiveness on the patient alone. An inpatient setting, however, with its web of multipersonal relations, offers many different lines of therapeutic interaction. Isolated consideration of transference in the two-person context thus takes in only one aspect of the total interactive process (Enke 1968; Wittich 1975, 1977; Danckwardt 1976; Ermann 1979). The analyst is not visible to the patient in classical outpatient psychoanalysis; a face-to-face situation involving the therapist as a real physical presence only arises if modifications are made to the standard procedure, e.g. in types of analytically oriented psychotherapy where the patient is seated, or in group therapy (Nerenz 1977). With inpatient psychotherapy, however, face-to-face is the most commmon mode. Patients are aware of the therapist's position and role within the institution, i.e. there is a social context to therapeutic interaction. In private practice the therapist may appear to patients to exist solely in the solitary splendour of the consulting room, whereas in the institutional setting he comes to be perceived within a relational field – factors not to be ignored.

Integrated inpatient psychoanalytic therapy can perhaps best be described as *psychoanalytic treatment through teamwork*. A human being in distress is incorporated into a group of patients and cared for by a group of therapists functioning in relationship to one another. Institutional parameters (degrees of flexibility inevitably vary) provide the setting in which treatment takes place.

Chapter 3 explored various types of inpatient therapy, showing how organizational principles and basic analytic/therapeutic suppositions colour the way therapeutic space is structured. Integrated approaches are taking time to penetrate. In the early days theoretical discussion focused solely on dyadic relationships, by analogy with the model of outpatient psychoanalysis; the hospital environment at the most provided a structure and afforded patients protection against acting out. Another trend was to view initial hospital treatment, e.g. in the shape of group therapy, as a crash-course for outpatient therapy in the same group. The models to which a theory of inpatient psychotherapeutic practice may usefully look are the bipolar and integrative ones, since they work with a concept of setting which explicitly incorporates the total institutional context. Let us briefly recapitulate the arguments (cf. Janssen 1985, 1986).

The main characteristic of bipolar models is that a line is drawn between the space proper to analytic therapy and that belonging to sociotherapy (cf. Figure 3, p. 41). Individual therapy and/or group therapy take place in analytic space, whereas 'real-life' or social space offers various settings – theoretically underpinned by the findings of social psychology – for social learning and emotional growth. A further dimension to social space is furnished by art and dance movement therapies, whose methods tally with sociothera-

peutic principles. Even in analytically oriented therapeutic communities, a bipolar approach is favoured. Management of the
social milieu is delegated to nursing staff, leaving analytic therapists with a clearly demarcated therapeutic area within which to
carry out interpretation. Intercommunication between fields is
bounded by the rule that analytic psychotherapists exercise discretion vis-à-vis the sociotherapeutic team.

The purpose of bipolar strategies is to concentrate transference
processes within therapeutic space and to preserve social space as
a testbed for more reality-oriented behaviour in cases where the
ego's strength is undermined by regression, or where transference
splitting occurs. My own bipolar experience, supported by the
results of team-process analysis and outcome studies (cf. Chapter
4), suggests that transference does not occur in therapeutic space
alone; transference reactions equally extend to individuals active
within social space. This might explain certain cases of therapeutic
failure – particularly if we consider the primitive transference
patterns associated with structural ego disorders. When a portion
of a patient's total transference becomes split-off on to staff operating in social space, transference-countertransference *binds* develop; yet under the bipolar model this phenomenon cannot
usually be worked through therapeutically.

Splitting of the transference is consistently observed and must
manifestly be seen as part and parcel of inpatient treatment (Main
1957; Plojé 1977; Danckwardt 1976; Janssen and Quint 1977;
Becker and Lüdeke 1978; Ermann 1979, 1982; Heising and
Möhlen 1980; James 1984). When a patient is admitted to hospital,
influence is exerted both by fellow patients in the group and by the
various therapists working on the ward. That patient's *significant
objects* will be chosen on the basis of past relational patterns and
he will view the relationship with his individual or group therapist
as no more than a privileged example of general interrelating
within the group. The complete transference picture can only be
rendered visible and open to therapeutic elaboration if the *entire*
interweave of multipersonal relations in the hospital is considered
as the matrix for the re-enactment of infantile relational patterns.

Integrative approaches address these concerns (to greater or
lesser degrees, cf. pp. 48–56) in that they see inpatient psychoanalytic treatment as the joint responsibility of the professional
staff as a whole. A key feature of rigorously implemented integrative models is that members of the staff team have a therapeutic

task to perform wherever and whenever they interact with patients; polarization between *social space* and *therapeutic space* representatives never comes about. An integrative inpatient treatment setting is one where the therapeutic and non-therapeutic interventions of each and every professional are conceived of as integral parts of a shared project; an environment where each protagonist, in his particular relational context, can foster an independent and analytically oriented therapeutic relationship with the patient. This of course means being open to the analysis of transference and countertransference processes.

In Chapter 4 (pp. 74–85) I looked at the assumptions underpinning my own integrative model, explaining the structure of both setting and therapeutic team. One of the challenges is to fit in with the institutional environment of the hospital whilst upholding the principles of psychodynamic therapy. Figure 7 shows how the patient group as a whole is embedded in a matrix of interrelations; the different fields correspond to the areas of expertise of therapists. Patient and therapist groups alike have to meet the challenges of social space and cope with transference and countertransference reactions; each individual patient experiences a therapeutic process involving reciprocal interaction between one group and another.

In our model, the large group of thirty patients was divided into four small groups; each of these was then allotted to a therapeutic team. This meant that the full therapist group, i.e. all hospital co-workers who had therapeutic contact with patients, was equally split into four. The therapeutic and non-therapeutic parameters of hospital treatment furnished the overall organizational framework for patient and therapist groups: admission and discharge procedures, house rules, mealtimes, leisure periods, bedtime, weekend leave, therapists' working hours (therapists and nurses worked day shifts, nurses also had night duties; doctors were expected to be on call), plus other statutory provisions. Therapeutic activity was scheduled within this institutional frame: e.g. group therapy, individual therapy, nurses' rounds, Registrar's surgery. Duration of treatment was agreed on a case-by-case basis according to how the therapeutic process was progressing (although sometimes length of stay had to be negotiated trilaterally, bringing in the hospital operators as well as patient and therapists).

No attempt was made to demarcate a purely therapeutic area

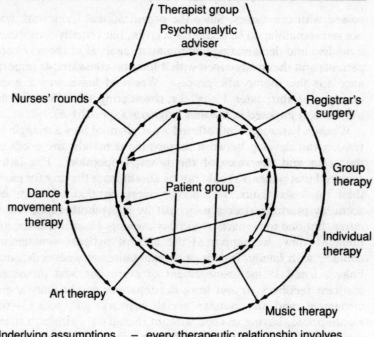

Underlying assumptions – every therapeutic relationship involves
coping with the institutional setting
– multipersonal relations offer scope for
multiple transference
– the therapeutic process entails interaction
between patient group and therapist group

Figure 7 Basic design of the integrative model

within the overall organizational framework, which was characterized by all sorts of social, non-therapeutic elements. On the contrary, the institutional context *was* the setting for the large-group
process. Discussion of how therapists and patients were managing
with the institutional parameters took place regularly within the
separate therapist teams and among the staff group as a whole
(full-team meeting). An integral part of all fields of therapeutic
contact (group therapy, individual therapy and especially nurses'
rounds) was that patients were asked about their interaction with
the institution itself. Discharge procedures and questions raised by
the hospital operators tended to be dealt with in the individual
therapy setting, whereas punctuality for meals, staying out too late
(free period = 6–10 p.m.), weekend visits etc. were usually dis-

cussed with the nurses. Since the organizational framework was not just something to be accepted as given, but actually constituted a holding and demarcating environment, analysis of the way both patients and therapists coped with it took on considerable importance for the therapeutic process. Weekend leave was a good example of this; later I shall be considering the effects of an alcohol ban imposed in the unit (*Vignette 3*, pp. 161–6).

Weekend arrangements offered a paradigm of how a triangle of tension can develop between therapeutic demands, the needs of the team and the rules of the hospital operators. The latter required that patients should not be absent from the unit for more than thirty-six hours, i.e. people were entitled to leave on Saturday morning after a joint visit by a psychotherapist and a nurse, but had to be back by Sunday evening. From a therapeutic point of view, we supported the idea of patients maintaining contacts with family, friends or acquaintances at weekends; such links assisted in the management of regression and promoted constant feedback to and from the inpatient psychoanalytic environment and the outside social network (cf. pp. 154–6). Furthermore, having to cope without therapists – although there was always someone who could be reached by phone via the hospital – was helpful in fostering ego stability (Green 1975). Separation challenged patients who were symbiotically bound to the hospital or their therapist to develop more autonomy. The very idea that they might be expected to survive for a weekend without therapeutic assistance was sometimes perceived as an imposition; anger ensued at the absence of the longed-for and all-satisfying maternal object. Such feelings were subsequently talked through, promoting more self-understanding in the patient concerned, who, as the therapeutic process advanced, gradually came to identify with the therapists when they said 'no' and developed greater inner autonomy (Blanck and Blanck 1974, 1979).

As the week went by, a patient began to manifest more pronounced regressive tendencies. She skipped group therapy and withdrew to bed, yet the Registrar could not ascertain any physical illness. The patient called the nurses to her bedside for a chat; she also requested a hot water bottle, which was provided. When the nurses discussed her need for this extra care they could find no reason for her altered behaviour. Just as the weekend was approaching, she suddenly asked to be allowed to stay in the hospital, saying she would only curl up in bed if she went home. The matter was raised by the nurses at the team meeting. The patient's individual therapist reported that the possibility of curtailment of inpatient treatment had been raised with her, following a question from the hospital operators. The patient was angry and disappointed, accusing the therapist of not having fought hard enough for her. The team could now see her desire to be mothered over the weekend in terms of regressive containment of her fear of separation. This was talked through with her. She subsequently allowed herself to feel anger towards the therapists for seeking to leave her on her own. Without any assistance from us she eventually solved the problem by arranging a weekend outing with a female acquaintance.

The fact that the team adopted a therapeutic attitude towards the weekend issue was tantamount to saying to the patient: 'We understand your desire for mothering and your fear of being alone. We think, though, that you will make out. We can confidently part from you without any worry or fear as to what will happen to you over the weekend.' Patients have varying motives for wishing to remain in hospital at weekends. The pattern just described is one of the most frequent, although some individuals might want to stay on because they think they need protection from threatening objects in the outside world. Therapeutic progress will only occur if individual motivation can be uncovered and analysed – regardless of whether, in any particular instance, patients spend the weekend in the hospital or not. Team members, especially nurses (doctors are often on call), are bound to want their weekends free wherever possible; team motives may therefore need to be analysed too.

Some patients deny their desire for symbiosis, or they somatize their anger and disappointment. We see this in psychosomatic and anorexic patients; also in depressive individuals with suicidal ideation. They simply cannot accept being in receipt of the care, nurture and outreach of the therapists. This may be a consequence of pseudo-autonomous postures or it can stem from feelings of guilt. We found that, if the team suggested to such patients that they might remain in the unit, their defensive strategy of standing alone and denying needs was often dropped. There will nevertheless always be those patients who require the protective milieu of the hospital at weekends to shield them from ego disintegration – which might take the form of acting out in cases of addiction and perversion.

Conflict also arose when patients overshot the bounds of weekend leave, either going off on a Friday, or failing to return until Monday. Such behaviour is motivated by a variety of factors. Patients may be fleeing objects within the hospital which they perceive as dangerous; or they may be getting at therapists who have not met their demands. Frequently this type of conduct also signals resistance towards the working through of neurotic patterns operating at an unconscious level in family or couple relationships.

> One young woman was admitted for inpatient treatment in a wheelchair, with both legs paralysed. She was oedipally embroiled at an unconscious level with her father, who suffered from cancer and was unable to work. Her parents had been reluctant to agree to inpatient treatment and, right from the outset, sought to exert control not only over her and her treatment, but also over the therapeutic team. The father would insist on collecting her on Friday, yet all attempts to discuss this with him or the patient ended in failure. Because the young woman related satisfactorily in other areas of therapy, the team hesitated for what proved to be too long in clarifying the situation. The father-daughter relationship, as reflected in the weekend scene, remained – for the duration of inpatient therapy at least – unelucidated. Looking back, it was clear that lack of resolve in handling the weekend rule had played a decisive part in impeding proper working through of the family conflicts underlying the patient's paralysis.

We see from these events surrounding a particular hospital parameter (in this case the weekend leave rule) that any dimension of setting can be utilized within the therapeutic process. Where a boundary is contested, opportunities arise for crystallizing therapeutic insight.

THE STRUCTURE OF THE PSYCHOANALYTIC TEAM AND HOW IT OPERATES

At the heart of this style of treatment is the relationship between patient group and therapist group, with the latter working as a team to perform joint therapeutic tasks. The decision to bring together all the professional players into one team, within which each exercises a specific function, was arrived at in the light of experience with the bipolar model (see above). We felt that the whole point of the inpatient setting was that it should provide the patient with a *facilitating environment* (Winnicott 1965), a good and reliable holding atmosphere (Balint 1968; Loch 1974; Fürstenau 1977b), which would enable infantile scenes to be re-enacted within the frame of the various therapeutic relationships. In order to create this climate, the team as a whole must form a relational matrix in which individuals are able to maintain their personal and professional identities. This helps to prevent narcissistic conflicts and identity crises of the kind arising where practitioners come to doubt the value of their own actions.

Little purpose is served by relying solely on the 'goodwill' of all involved. The manner in which the team is structured and led must generate a feeling that the identity of each individual and professional grouping will be preserved. Theories of identity, both psychoanalytic (Erikson 1956; Levita 1971) and sociological (Goffman 1967; Krappmann 1969), have greatly inspired me in my forging of ideas for team structure and leadership. The sociological school focuses in particular on action and identity in social situations (Janssen 1979). I later discovered that Main (1946) had put forward similar views when elaborating his concept of the *therapeutic community*, probably better described as a *psychotherapeutic community* (Wilson 1984).

Helped by these theories, I came to see the therapeutic actions of individuals within the team as examples of 'ego-identity balancing acts' (Krappmann 1969). The hospital is a social environment and all members of the therapy team must be conceded the right to safeguard their own personal and professional identities. Whenever a therapist relates therapeutically to patients or interacts with the team, personal *and* professional identity are expressed. In teamwork, the therapeutic interrelating of the psychoanalysts (medical doctors and psychologists) and the actions of other professionals (nurses, music therapists, art and dance movement therapists) all bear the imprint of professional and personal identity, empathy and countertransference, theoretical grasp and level of training (Thomä 1977). Every move made by a member of a treatment team is thus an identity-sustaining act.

Each individual consequently needs to be able to maintain his personal and professional stamp. In our context, this entailed ensuring that everyone in the therapist group was allowed to articulate whatever he perceived – within his personal and professional parameters – as being relevant to the interactive situation; no more status should be accorded to statements, insights and interpretations from 'experts' (individual or group-analytic psychotherapists) than to similar input from non-experts (e.g. nurses) – and vice versa in non-analytic matters. It had to be gradually instilled into people that their remit was not to 'interpret' other co-workers, but rather to speak for one segment of the relational whole. Experience with task-oriented teamwork has taught me that interaction which respects *identity* enables individuals to *identify* with the therapeutic purpose.

A team which is capable of working through personal and subjective material drawn from the interactive process is positioned within a group-dynamic continuum, impelled by both patient-induced and team-specific events: transference, admission episodes, separation from patients, actions by patients, reactivated individual conflicts manifested in countertransference, group conflicts etc. It is only possible to exploit this group-dynamic potential to the full therapeutic benefit of individual patients if proper organizational provision is made for someone to act as consultant or adviser to the team, i.e. a psychoanalyst who can stand back from the web of therapeutic interrelations and ensure that the team upholds its *primary task* (Rice 1965): facilitating therapeutic processes within the patient.

In the course of my endeavours to come to grips with the dynamics of team processes, I devised a format for the various team meetings (cf. pp. 74–85). Of considerable guidance here was Rice's concept of how organizations work, for which he drew on ego psychology and open-system theory (Rice 1965, 1969; de Board 1978). Kernberg (1976b) has also highlighted the relevance of such an approach (cf. pp. 26–35). By way of brief recapitulation, each individual, group or organization has a *primary task*, which involves coping with concrete assignments and reconciling performance of these with internal needs. In the case of individuals, it is the ego which (according to the structural model of psychoanalysis) functions as a mediating agency (Wälder 1930). Where individuals prove unable to cope with primary tasks, therapeutic intervention becomes necessary; in a therapeutic institution

or a group, responsibility for this lies with the group leader/
conductor.

The psychoanalytic adviser in our setting was effectively called
upon to perform the task of the ego by providing guidance and
reality-orientation (mediation) for the organization as a whole and
particular teams within it. Simultaneously, he functioned for team
and individuals alike as a comprehending transference object,
capable of displaying tolerance and defusing anxiety (Whiteley
1978). Such a role demands a constant double focus: on the
primary task of the institution and team and on the prevailing
group dynamics within the therapist group.

Group-dynamic processes within a team are many-sided. Some
intimation of this was given when I discussed the weekend rule and
more examples will follow. I now propose to describe and comment on a few brief scenes which illustrate the reciprocal interaction between patient group and therapist group; the adviser's
role in handling patient-induced or team-specific processes will be
highlighted as we go along.

One particular patient group always seemed to be saying 'no'; it
was silent and defiant, helpless and unable to do anything. In its
phantasies it seemed to be at the mercy of the therapists, who
'arbitrarily' changed appointments, went off on holiday and
failed to take the group and its members seriously. Yet the
group was incapable of articulating its anger and disappointment vis-à-vis these people who failed to meet its needs and
appeared to have nothing better to do than set restrictions and
bring about separation. What Bion (1961) termed 'fight-flight'
(phase of counter-dependence) began to develop, a phenomenon equally present in the therapist group. The therapists'
behaviour was retentive; they appeared helpless and useless,
apparently forever waiting for something to happen and barely
able to say anything about their interaction with the patients.
Sometimes they would openly attack the psychoanalytic adviser, even seeking to wrest leadership of the group from him;
at other times they preferred to explore their sense of being
dependent on him. He related their reaction towards him to the
dependent attitude of the patients – with their phantasized
vision of therapist power – towards them. With the therapists
behaving in retentive and helpless fashion, an interpretation
from the adviser to the effect that they were awaiting 'redemp-

tion' from him was doomed. By picking up too soon on the small amount of material imparted, he would have put the therapist group under additional pressure; his intervention would simply have smacked of norms and authority, thereby making the team feel more dependent and helpless. In any such scenario, patients try to please the therapists, whilst the latter seek to mollify the psychoanalytic adviser. If he sticks to his interpreting prerogatives, the therapist group becomes para-lysed and begins to undervalue its own interpretations; or else a power struggle develops over 'correct' understanding of the processes at issue.

Induced phenomena such as these can be made positive use of in the further course of patient therapy, provided the psycho-analytic adviser abstains from interpretation and instead reports on his or her impressions and observations, encouraging others to do likewise and actively eliciting a response if the therapist group seems to be holding back. The material needs to be unravelled and explored at some length before every individual can fully participate. Only if it can recover a sense of its own therapeutic competence will the therapist group be able to begin to interpret cogently the processes occurring within its own ranks and in the patient group (e.g. swings from depen-dence to fight-flight and back again).

This type of retentive group-dynamics does not necessarily mirror processes in the patient group; such patterns can equally spring from conflicts internal to the therapist team. Where personal rivalry occurs and is not openly discussed, the team as a whole may lose its ability to function. The arrival of new team members sometimes causes problems, as does the absence from the group of a familiar figure. Some members will decide to hold fringe meet-ings (subgrouping) in defiance of the established group meeting. Particular individuals may be afraid that other team members or the group adviser are impinging upon their space; rivalrous self-demarcation will follow – and so on. The task of the psycho-analytic adviser is not so much to home in on perceived conflict from the vantage point of group dynamics, but rather to facilitate free discussion of what pyschoanalytic teamwork means. Once specific examples of behaviour can be isolated and talked through – e.g. desire for demarcation; 'I know better' attitudes; blurring of task boundaries; unilateral steps to 'improve' patient contact –

consensus and cohesion within the group is restored.

The team's integrative capacities are particularly called upon where control over the impulsive and aggressive tendencies of either patient or therapist group threatens to slip away – or is actually lost. This is illustrated by the following example of a group process extending over many weeks.

The entire patient group was prey to aggressive tension. Several patients began firing 'machine gun'-like invective at the therapists, projecting on to them everything they perceived as 'bad'. The aggressive conduct of a patient suffering from obsessive-compulsive neurosis threatened to destroy the group. The hospital was truly under fire. In the phantasies of one therapist, a 'villain' was threatening him with a pistol. Other team members tried to put up defences against aggressive-impulsive patients by raising the possibility of discharge. Inside the therapist group, a nurse and the group therapist took up the aggressive tension and unloaded it in attacks on the psychoanalytic adviser and Ward Sister. The dance movement therapist no longer felt able to control the impulsive games being played out by the patients. Tension here was eventually released in actual motor form. One day, while playing ball in somewhat frantic fashion with a young man, a female patient broke her thigh. The patients began to panic. The young woman herself desperately needed to find someone to take charge and make her leg better again. Other patients denied the seriousness of her injury and tried to get her back on her feet. The dance movement therapist managed to find a doctor. The patients, however, reproached the therapists with not having tried hard enough; they could have prevented the accident. These accusations gave rise to feelings of guilt within the therapist team. What hadn't they seen? Why hadn't they exercised more supervision and kept a tighter rein? Things go off course without a firm hand. At this point, my job as psychoanalytic adviser was to ease the team back into a frame of mind where it could do some discriminating, analytical thinking; I was not there to do what, at the level of transference, they all wanted me to do, i.e. come in as Mr Administration and put things right.

We began by accumulating as many observations as possible relating to the 'accident'. It emerged clearly that the patient concerned was in fact 'repeating' private conflicts (or her pathological resolution of them) within the context of the group. Her answer to the problem involved demonstrating through her own actions how impulsiveness can lead to injury, damage or even murder. The background was as follows. Some time ago, she had gone camping with her then boyfriend. One night two men burst into the tent at night, raped and shot her. She was left with a comminuted fracture to her thigh and had to undergo lengthy hospital treatment. She also developed Crohn's disease. Her psychical response to this traumatic event was autistic withdrawal. She could not tolerate closeness of any kind. As therapy progressed, she began to open up little by little and became more impulsive, spurred on by the group dynamic outlined above. At the instigation of the group therapist she spoke for the first time of her 'accident' (as she and her husband labelled the tent incident), violating the agreement the couple had reached never to speak about it again. Traces of her anger against men had just begun to surface when the 'accident', i.e. the repetition of the traumatic situation, occurred. The therapist group now saw how, given the impulsiveness of the patient group and the patient's history, this latest 'accident' fell into place. The therapist team's feelings of guilt and its countering manoeuvres to establish more rules and control took on a new complexion when we came to reconstruct the total scene. In wishing to build in more safeguards, we had been seeking to contain patients' impulsiveness and prevent the repetition, in our setting, of traumatizing events. Ultimately, we were afraid of impulsive behaviour in the patients and in ourselves.

This hands-on experience of team processes, and the theoretical insights it afforded, led me to develop certain conceptual guidelines, which I have set out schematically in Figure 8. The basic rule for teamwork could perhaps be summed up as commitment to an ongoing, open exchange of observations and feelings within a matrix of interaction with patients. Regular team meetings and frank talking through are vital prerequisites if developing relational patterns within the various therapeutic fields are to be recognized and integrated into the whole-team dynamic.

The psychoanalytic adviser

In all fields of therapy, individual members of the team take on *primary tasks* vis-à-vis patients. During meetings of co-workers, where the therapeutic process itself is discussed, responsibility for

1 The psychoanalytic adviser: functions:	Constant provision of patient-oriented advice, plus assistance in structuring therapy; preserving institutional frame and creating discussion space; maintenance of therapeutic setting and team motivation; conflict-focusing; interpretation of scenes played out by patients; forging of links between therapeutic fields.
2 Team meetings: the need for continuity:	Regular team discussions, with compulsory attendance by everyone involved in the therapeutic process; no observer status.
3 Team members: the primacy of honest portrayal of situations:	Open discussion of observations, actions, experiences, expectations, ideas, dreams, and feelings expressed by both patients and therapists; discretion applies only vis-à-vis the outside world.
4 Countertransference: patient-related interpretations:	Maintenance of boundaries between patient group and therapist group; upholding the therapeutic identity of each team member.
5 Each professional grouping within the team: preserving therapeutic identity:	All areas where interaction takes place are equal; maintaining therapeutic space for each component field.

Figure 8 Conceptual guidelines for managing the primary tasks of the team

primary task performance lies with the psychoanalytic adviser, who has no contact with the patients. As an analyst, he exercises reality-matching ego functions, providing assistance with interpretation and offering empathy and understanding. He is also conversant with the organizational and administrative framework of the institution. As regards supervision, the psychoanalytic adviser's task involves using his capacity for empathy, understanding and interpretation to help team members to elaborate the scenes played out by patients, as well as their verbal utterances. Subsequently, all the interrelating strands from different fields can be pulled together. With the assistance of the psychoanalytic adviser, the team comes to understand the *transference Gestalt* of individual patients, linking up previously un-linked material and devising means of therapeutic interaction and interpretation.

With regard to reality-testing, the psychoanalytic adviser ensures that the institutional frame is respected (e.g. liaison with hospital management and the hospital operators). He also verifies that there is proper provision for talking through (e.g. meeting times must be arranged and therapists convened). Where conflict arises or regressive tendencies begin to hold sway, the adviser is there to maintain the team's work space. Analysis of conflict within the therapist group furthers understanding of processes within the patient group. Once therapists come to identify with the psychoanalytic adviser's approach, his example is passed on in their therapeutic interaction with patients.

Several examples have already been given, and more will follow, of the psychoanalytic adviser's functions as an interpreter of material. I propose now to concentrate for a moment on his institutional role; he must after all uphold the clinical setting, make provision for team discussion and generally foster a working climate.

> Given that there is no fixed term to treatment – duration is generally around six months – we are constantly being asked by the hospital operators and health insurers to justify continuing inpatient therapy. It is up to a patient's individual therapist to respond to any such questions. Transference-countertransference patterns may develop in the course of consultation, with both patient and therapist perceiving this intervention from a third party as an 'intrusion' into their relationship. A patient's symbiotic attachment to his therapist is

justifiably seen in some cases as an important phase in the therapeutic process; if the powers-that-be come along and suggest placing a limit on the duration of treatment, therapists are entitled to feel vexed. They do not always give adequate thought to the relational ramifications, however. There is a tendency to blame everything on the health authority or insurance company representative, who is seen as an outsider with no understanding of the situation. Therapist indignation leads to a dismissive attitude towards third-party medical opinions and the individual representing the relevant authority or company understandably becomes irritated. I have always insisted that such matters are dealt with at team meetings, or in full liaison with those concerned. Several benefits derive from this: the intruding party is brought into the fold and no longer features as a threatening object from outside; the structure of the relationship between patient and individual therapist can be analysed and we are all forced to think thoroughly about the patient's progress. The third party medical expert is duly given a full report and the patient informed of any curtailment in treatment. Helping the team not to fall victim to patients' phantasies of heaven on earth is one of the foremost tasks of the psychoanalytic adviser. Once a therapist is reconciled to a time limitation being placed on a particular course of treatment, he can set about preparing the patient for the moment when the bond with the hospital will have to be loosened.

The role of team psychoanalytic adviser emerges with particular clarity when it comes to dealing with addictive acting out and cases of somatic decompensation. One borderline patient, having started out idealizing the whole therapeutic process – and especially his individual therapist – responded to mooted termination of therapy by stepping up his alcohol consumption. He drank excessively for all to see, appeared in a drunken state before the nurses and, in a supreme gesture of provocation, brought alcohol on to the ward. This patently ran counter to his contract with us. Several reminders to the effect that he was contravening the rules remained unheeded. The matter therefore came before the team meeting. The broad sentiment in the therapist group was that the psychoanalytic adviser now needed to intervene. He should declare the patient unfit for treatment, preferably recommending that he be transferred to somewhere else. I began by discussing with the team the possible causes for the patient's acting out in this addictive way. We uncovered that initial idealization of his individual therapist had given way to deep disillusionment with her. I was not satisfied that this exhausted the issue of whether the patient should, or should not, continue in therapy. We therefore decided to offer the man a kind of contract: therapy could continue, provided he undertook not to leave the unit; otherwise he would be sabotaging his own treatment. This was an offer he felt able to accept. The new arrangement brought with it a degree of structuring; exceptions to the rule were made at weekends only. For quite a while he managed to stick to the contract, although in a state of growing anxiety. His individual therapist was there when he needed to talk to someone and she proved able to handle his wilder phantasizing. He dreamt that snakes were gnawing at him and choking him. He felt he was in a dungeon and there were two people in his head fighting with one another. He imagined he saw a small child in the lap of a 'big black mama' in the jungle. These images showed how hard he was having to battle with the negative affects springing from his relationship to his mother. He longed to be free of all this and cherished the idea of becoming a travelling salesman. Manifestations of alienation and depersonalization came to the fore. He grew hypersensitive to noise and, one weekend, nearly resorted to actual violence in the course of an argument with his mother. Then, on Father's Day, he failed to return to the hospital and got himself very drunk. He did not show up again until two days later and realized full well that he had effectively discharged himself. We still kept in touch with him and discussed alternative treatment possibilities. Any moves we made were nevertheless consistent with the therapeutic thrust of psychoanalysis – an important qualifier if the team is to come to identify with the process.

Maintaining a proper analytic attitude can also be difficult in the presence of certain psychosomatic patients. Watching weight-loss in anorexics is liable to induce fear of death and morbid phantasies in the observer. The Registrar may panic and have premature recourse to force-feeding. The patient's individual therapist, who knows more about the underlying causes, meanwhile sees no cause for alarm. Calls for medical intervention – including transfer to a Department of Medicine – often turn out to have more to do with the team's death-fears than the patient's bodily condition. Sometimes the process operates in reverse. We once had an anorexia patient with impending ileus from faecal impaction. The nurses worked themselves into such a state of anxiety over the required medical action (administration by them of an enema) that I had to step in and work through the episode with them.

The psychoanalytic adviser can also become a transference object for the therapist group as a whole, or for individuals within it. He may function as the third party in a triad along with the therapist and the patient. At times his role is close to that of the pre-oedipal father (Rotmann 1978), who 'intrudes' into the mother-child dyad. He is equally an object through which the child (patient) and the mother (therapist) can ease themselves out of the symbiotic relationship they have developed. The two parties to the dyad finish up better able to tolerate absence and its emotional consequences, i.e. the psychoanalytic adviser functions here as a growth-facilitating object.

Team meetings

Further ideas on the role of the psychoanalytic adviser and the nature of teamwork grew naturally out of the very design of inpatient analytic therapy. *Continuity* turned out to be of the essence. We realized that therapist teams had to meet regularly; the *team meeting* was born. It was not generally found helpful to allow members of other teams to attend, even as observers. Only at full-team meetings did all staff groups congregate together. In a hospital environment, regular meetings mean that ongoing consideration is given to the therapeutic progress of individual patients. If any particular therapist appears to be losing interest in a patient, this can be interpreted as a problem of countertransference.

Team members

Equally important is the creation of a climate which bolsters therapists' willingness to be honest with themselves and others. A process of stable therapeutic advance is not possible unless people are ready to enter into a frank exchange of observations with one another. Interaction with patients – pleasant or otherwise – must be discussed in all its dimensions. It is essential to know about therapists' ideas, expectations and interrogations. They need to report back on dreams that they or their patients have had, acknowledging positive and negative countertransference and explaining where and why they have been moved to intervene. Within the therapist team, therefore, the discretion rule cannot apply. Everyone must be abreast of the therapeutic process. This explains why we instituted the practice of allowing members of the team to watch from behind a one-way mirror while their colleagues were engaged in therapeutic contact. Whenever this happens, patients must obviously be informed.

Countertransference

A further principle grows logically out of what has just been said. Transference and countertransference – in the shape of feelings or actions – must always receive patient-oriented interpretation. It is up to the psychoanalytic adviser to see to this. Team meetings should not become training groups for therapists. Provided this rule is obeyed, the boundary between patient group and therapist group can be maintained, safeguarding the therapeutic identity of each individual team member. In my experience, this is a vital precondition if people are to feel free to discuss their positive and negative countertransference reactions. This after all might entail relating dreams they have had about patients or reporting on emotional entanglements. Management of countertransference – especially in its aggressive forms, which tend to be taboo – is of paramount significance for therapeutic work. If corroboration is required, the following scenes provide it.

A patient presented for inpatient treatment with severe depression and in a cachectic state as a consequence of Crohn's disease. For weeks she failed to emerge from her shell. Eventually one of the nurses managed to tempt her into partaking of some semi-solid food, prepared especially for her. This proved a positive experience and she began to cultivate an intensive relationship with the nurse in question, constantly seeking contact. The hours earmarked for nurses' rounds were clearly not enough; she truly clung to this nurse, even suggesting they might stay in touch once inpatient treatment was over. The nurse felt 'totally swallowed up' by the patient and started to fear for her own autonomy. She dreamt of being encom-

passed by a jelly fish. It became obvious that she was experiencing the reawakening of aspects of her own unresolved mother-
daughter relationship; she was manifestly afraid of becoming
inextricably embroiled in the new situation. Only if she counter-
reacted by putting on a display of distance, and even aggressive-
ness, was she able to keep her relations with this patient within
reasonable bounds. At the team meeting she recounted her
dream and spoke of the fear that was driving her to ward the
patient off. What she had to say clearly affected other group
members and left them at a loss for words. As an analyst, I
viewed the symbiotic dimension of the patient's object choice –
which I conceived of in terms of Kohut's notion of self-object
(Kohut 1957) – as an important element in her cure. I could
nevertheless understand the nurse's fear in the face of such an
intensive attachment and appreciated her need, for reasons of
self-preservation, to fight back and establish boundaries.
Working on the transference-countertransference dimension of
the nurse-patient constellation would, I suspected, be of little
avail. What was required was a willingness on the part of the
rest of the team to support her through this difficult relationship. I therefore directly addressed the fear aroused in her by
the patient's intense relational bond and made it clear that I
understood her need for protection. The team was much
relieved, having anticipated that I was going to pass judgement.
It could now get down to coming to grips with the configuration
in hand and individuals were able to discuss their own reactions
when confronted with similar relationship structures. What is
more, as therapists, they were likely in future to have more
understanding for any disappointment shown by the patient – a
necessary condition for proper working through.

There were other occasions when I felt that team members might
open up more to discussion of their own contribution to situations.
Take the following example:

A nurse who was new to the ward, and still somewhat unsure of
herself on psychotherapeutic ground, behaved in a rather laid-
back and jocular fashion towards her charges. Meanwhile, a
woman patient was feeling lost and abandoned over the departure of another nurse. The new recruit was the perfect object;
the patient proceeded to lambast her for her off-hand and
seemingly uncaring attitude. This put the nurse on the defensive

and led to a row between her and the patient. An older nurse appeared on the scene as part of her routine round and chided the patient for behaving aggressively; the new nurse might leave if she did not meet with a more friendly reception. The patient – rightly – took this as a rebuke and went with her problem to the group therapist. He was in a quandary, unsure what to make of the nurses' conduct. My role as psychoanalytic adviser was to elucidate the processes involved. I pointed out that in all our interaction with patients, whether we like it or not, personal input plays a part. Patients are entitled to hold the mirror up to us. Our professed wish, after all, is that they should use the therapeutic relationship to ventilate their affects, regardless of how agreeable or disagreeable the result might be to us. This proposition met with a highly charged response from the nurses, who had expected me to lend them more support. None the less, attitudes towards the patient changed as a result of my intervention – to the positive benefit of the therapeutic process.

Being honest with oneself and others is not only good for the patient; the therapeutic identity of all concerned is strengthened. Individuals are free to structure things in their particular field as they see fit. Since all relational fields are deemed equal at team meetings, people are likely to speak more openly about the personal dimension of their interaction with patients. The ever-recurring tendency to impose pet conceptions or therapeutic approaches upon others stands in the way of frank discussion of transference and countertransference processes. Prescriptive rules (e.g. nurses shall only discuss such and such; the dance movement therapist must always encourage this or that response) do little to foster therapeutic identity at individual or at team level.

Ongoing debate ensures that, whilst there is broad scope for individual therapeutic diversity, core agreement on the overall objective is preserved. Theoretical assumptions and institutional parameters are debated; the nature of the working alliance is held up for scrutiny; processes are thrashed out. The safeguarding of therapeutic identity means that the patient is guaranteed a supportive atmosphere. Destructive action against this holding environment exposes the roots of longstanding mental disturbance. Rigorous analysis of manifest behaviour gives access to the underlying causes of aggression.

There are however occasions where individual therapist teams fail signally to come to grips with severe forms of acting out by patients. The deadlock can never be broken by those immediately involved, yet the full-team meeting usually manages to lay bare the hidden problem. Valuable feedback comes from members of other therapist teams, priming the group dynamic. The psychoanalytic adviser is therefore not alone in exercising integrating, reality-testing ego functions on behalf of the team; the large group itself can step in – at least as a back-up.

Working through re-enactments of infantile object relations is needless to say not an end in itself; the acid test is whether patient therapy is enhanced. Our experience has been that exercises in intra- and inter-team elaboration do have an impact on subsequent interaction with patients. Structured meetings provide individual players with insight into the totality of the therapeutic process; they can then target their own efforts accordingly. Let us consider the following example:

A power struggle developed between a male patient and the music therapist. He felt she was ordering him around and refused to do what she proposed. She tried to encourage him by playing something herself. He began tentatively to respond, even venturing to play along with her. Afterwards he wanted to be patted on the back and told how marvellous he had been. He sought to prolong the session, but the music therapist felt pressurized and said: 'Let's leave it there for today.' The patient was hurt and reacted with a fit of anger, refusing to attend music therapy again. The music therapist came to the group with this material. The problem initially seemed to be specific to her one-to-one relationship with the patient; yet input from the group soon shed fresh light on the situation. The man was driven by a compulsive striving to achieve autonomy; hence his defensive and contrary behaviour. One particular contribution from a nurse was illuminating here. Her relations with the patient were also characterized by a jostling for power; he was afraid she would dominate him. She once broached the question of his relationship with his mother, at which point he began to cry, saying how much he would have liked it to be a happy one. The nurse was struck by this abrupt change of affect. The team now began to see what he was so afraid of, namely that music therapy would rekindle his enormous need for warmth and oneness and bring back all the childhood pain. This explained his obsessional striving for autonomy and his resistance to any upsurge of desire.

Talking these things through helped the music therapist to understand the patient's ambiguity, i.e. how he could be so anxious and at once so willing to let himself go (manifested in his desire to overstay his appointment). Because of her countertransference – she had become irritated by his battle for autonomy – such insight had eluded her in her one-to-one interaction with the patient. I did not raise the question of countertransference with her directly; she actually discovered it for herself through what other therapists had to say. Next time she and the patient met, her attitude was different. She no longer let herself be drawn into the power struggle, but instead encouraged the patient openly to use the music as a means of getting close to her. She also accepted that he found it hard to see sessions end.

This example involved two individuals, but similar constellations occur on the multipersonal front. In the wake of an observation session behind the one-way mirror, discussion in the therapist group concerned focused on whether or not two particular patients were benefiting properly from therapy. The men in question were constantly vying with one another, seeing to it that quiet never reigned and stopping any manifestation of emotion from surfacing. Two women in the group mildly played along with this strategy, while two others simply sat silently by in overtly depressive mood. Anger pushed the group therapist to intervene and suggest that the men simply did not wish to cooperate in the process of therapy; their rowdiness and bickering was an obvious stratagem to avoid having to be part of the group. This thesis seemed to enjoy favour with the other therapists in the team; the nurses however kept out of the discussion, unable to contribute in that they did not share the group therapist's annoyance. As psychoanalytic adviser, I insisted at this point that we address the general climate on the ward. It turned out that one of the men had been acting in a helpless, regressive manner. On returning to the unit after the weekend he told the duty nurse that he felt unwell and actually vomited. She gave him a cup of tea and he went to bed. The next morning he did not bother with group therapy; all he cared about was the nurses. He seemed distant and only came properly to when one of them enjoined him to go along to the group. Now that they had this additional information about events on the ward, the other therapists began to get a new perspective on things. These two men had doubtless been vying and bickering with one another in the group as a means of fending off the emptiness and depression they felt inside. The vomiting episode signalled a degree of somatization. Once the group therapist had grasped the processes at work on the ward and in the group, she was able to change her attitude towards the pair. She came to see their behaviour as an attempt to 'delegate' their depression to the two silent women.

Provided the team can work through the dynamics of the inter-active process, new momentum is given to therapeutic action in all fields. The psychoanalytic adviser is not there simply to investigate transference and countertransference within the various areas; his remit equally involves stimulating the whole therapist team to come forward with comments and information. To this extent he differs somewhat from the supervisor in outpatient analysis.

The advantage of this approach is that therapists learn both directly and indirectly about transference and countertransference reactions; this helps them to bring new insight to bear in their relations with patients. A circular process is engaged: working through in the therapist group; feedback to the patient via new patterns of therapeutic conduct; more thinking and working through in the therapist group – and so on.

TASK-SHARING WITHIN THE TEAM

The team's role in promoting the therapeutic process can be summarized as follows:

– Shaping and maintaining clinical parameters: a boundary-setting and holding function.
– Fostering the working alliance and securing the link back to the 'real world'.
– Exercising a maternal holding and facilitating function where regression leads to the reactivation of primitive transference patterns and ego decompensation; plus the provision of physical care and treatment in the case of somatic illness.
– Interpreting and working through re-enacted conflicts.

There is no fixed allocation of roles in integrative therapy (e.g. these people do the nursing, those see to interpretation). Each instance of therapeutic interaction with the patient is dealt with in its own right, taking account of how past conflict is replayed in the particular clinical setting. Therapeutic priorities crystallize as hands-on experience intersects with theoretical reflection. Figure 5 (p. 78) suggests a possible way of breaking down therapeutic tasks. The fact that therapy takes many forms (group, individual, art, dance movement, contact with the ward staff) does not detract from its analytic thrust.

The idea behind the integrative model is for conflict to be re-enacted within the matrix generated by interaction between patient and therapist groups; this involves one-to-one and multiple relations. Authors such as Bräutigam (1974), von Rad and Rüppell (1975) or Arfsten and Hoffmann (1978) advocate group therapy alone in the hospital setting. We have found problems with this, particularly when faced with narcissistic or borderline cases. A combined approach (cf. Kordy et al. 1983) appears better suited to the pathology of patients with structural ego impairment. Nor is it enough to look just at interaction between patient group and therapist group; patient-patient relations and the whole culture and climate of the peer group are equally deserving of therapeutic illumination.

There are three basic planes within the integrative model, corresponding to:

- confrontation and interpretation (group therapy and individual therapy);
- extra-verbal creative activities (art, music, dance movement therapies);
- holding, supporting and nursing/medical care (nurses, Registrar).

Differing degrees of emphasis are placed on each of these, depending on the problems and psychodynamics of the individual patient or patient group.

Group-analytic psychotherapy and individual therapy

Our overall approach involved a mix of one-to-one and group interaction, but the group remained the prime setting for confrontation and interpretation. Experiments with psychoanalytic methods in small groups have shown that, in taking on roles and engaging with one another, patients replay internalized patterns of parent-child interaction (Foulkes 1964; Heigl-Evers and Heigl 1973b). Heising *et al.* (1982) see this potential for 'the repetition of early childhood object relations through interaction' as something peculiar to the structure of groups.

The hospital unit comprising patients and therapist team was viewed for our purposes as a structured large group. Research into large groups operating on psychoanalytic lines, e.g. therapeutic communities (Kreeger 1975), has uncovered that the processes at work differ from those generated in small groups or in a dyadic relationship. Pre-oedipal (or pre-individuation) conflicts, e.g. at borderline level, are more likely to become reactivated in the large group setting than in a small group or one-to-one therapy. The dynamics of large groups promotes more pronounced regression to early developmental phases, with a blurring of self and ego boundaries and an exchange of self-aspects among members of the group (Bion 1961; Pines 1975; Kernberg 1976b). The large group setting in a hospital unit fosters interactive replay of primitive object-relations patterns.

The four weekly sessions in the small group provided an opportunity to work through in the here-and-now the various object relations patterns and defensive strategies created by multipersonal interaction. Group therapy allowed for the processing of conflict generated around – and not simply within – the small group. In a hospital setting, group therapists and nurses cannot afford to direct their sole attention to the current situation inside the group; they must look beyond, embracing the whole spectrum of inter-action, even outside the unit. Relations with other therapists are paramount. The full-team meetings are where all dimensions can be highlighted and explored; insights acquired are subsequently put to use in the small group context.

A further illustration of the interplay between group processes and life on the ward is seen in the following example:

> During group therapy the patients had grappled with the question of strict, withholding mothers. On St Nicholas' Day[1] patients put out their shoes in the confident expectation that the nurses would fill them with sweetmeats. This placed the nurses in a quandary. Their initial reaction was to do as the patients wanted and their eventual decision not to do so made them feel

[1] *Translator's note.* In some European countries St Nicholas (commonly identified with Santa Claus) brings gifts on 6 December.

like bad mothers, bent on frustrating their children's wishes. During group therapy patients homed in on these bad nurses who denied them what they wanted; interaction with the nurses had reactivated infantile conflicts patients had experienced with their real mothers. They were now in search of a nurturing mother who would satisfy their needs and turned their sights on the group therapist. He had gone up to the nurses on the ward with a bulging shopping bag in his hand. The patients admitted to having believed in their phantasies that the bag was full of goodies for them. Disappointment ensued when they discovered that he was no more willing than the nurses to take on the role of nurturing mother.

Relations between patients as they live out their lives on the ward provide particularly valuable material for analysis in the small group, although the therapist must remember that reactivated patterns of infantile behaviour – varying in nature and intensity – will play their part too. Living together in the unit means negotiating agreements and developing social skills, which in turn helps people come to grips with the real world. Patients may decide to call a meeting to discuss when the television can be on, or hold a ballot if someone has to swap rooms etc. The therapist team's sole remit is to ensure that the basic parameters are respected; therapists should not interfere in the decision-taking.

Sometimes patients form alliances against therapists (cf. *Vignette 3*, pp. 161–6) or enter into mock sibling rivalry. Competing subgroups are set up, with members recruited from different wards; 'pairing' occurs. Mutual support is equally a feature of life in a hospital; patients often help one another in cases of decompensation. All of which demonstrates that the processes at work within the patient group are variegated. Particular therapeutic insight can be gained from studying those instances of patient-patient interaction where infantile object relating is replayed; therapists can usefully envisage what is happening in terms of positive or negative *pairing* (see also pp. 153–4). The following example involves a mother-daughter configuration, one of the possible forms of pairing.

A new patient (47 years old) came on to the ward. In her career as a nurse she had devoted herself body and soul to her patients, but had recently begun to sink deeper and deeper into depression. This left her feeling helpless and debilitated. She was separated from her husband, but claimed to enjoy a warm and sincere relationship with her grown-up daughter. Her daughter found her so weakened and unable to cope that she no longer recognized her. Feebleness was not her uppermost trait in the unit, however. The strong mother soon returned to the fore, demanding and dominating, yet concerned for the well-being of her fellow patients. We came to understand her inner difficulties in terms of a reactivated loss syndrome. When the patient was 4 years old, her mother died from a serious illness. The child was placed in the charge of very strict foster parents. In order to win the affection of her new mother and father she refrained from demanding anything for herself. Yet the need for oral gratification was still there, meeting with partial compensation when she became a nurse and started to care for other people. From the very outset we sensed the power of her oral-narcissistic needs (e.g. when she demanded the attention of the nurses or battled for her fair share at mealtimes). She was allocated space in a room occupied by a young anorexic/bulimic woman, who very much wanted the whole room to herself. The newcomer was perceived as domineering by this possessive patient, whose life was effectively one long struggle with the bad, withholding mother who set limits on her desires. Her bad maternal introjects could now be projected on to the new patient, whom she accused of coercing her and seeking to appropriate her room. The older woman in turn took on the role of all-denying mother vis-à-vis the girl. The battleground was the disputed room and the object of strife a particular shelf, half of which was for one, half for the other. The argument flared up every time there was a perceived incursion and the subject was frequently ventilated during the nurses' rounds. These discussions were supplemented by thorough talking through in the group and both patients benefited from having light shed on the constellation into which they had become locked.

Individual psychoanalytic therapy is a necessary complement to group dynamics in our experience; the one-to-one relationship helps to maintain the therapeutic alliance and foster positive identification with the therapeutic task. Right from the start of treatment – which begins effectively with the first pre-admission interview – the degree of empathy between individual therapist and patient constitutes a decisive motivating factor. Keeping up this dyadic relationship throughout inpatient therapy ensures constancy in the working alliance. Individual therapy sessions are voluntary in that patients and their individual therapists can arrange a meeting whenever the dynamics of the therapeutic process so require. In the hospital setting, things usually fall into place with a regular weekly session. This allows a specific transference pattern to take shape (cf. vignettes, pp. 157–74). Where patients systematically avoid individual therapy, or else press for it all the time, the psychic schema involved can be discussed at the full-team meeting.

Dyadic relationships are particularly important for therapeutic continuity in cases of regressive breakdown, gross acting out and somatic decompensation. A patient's individual therapist is the person best placed to take on the role of auxiliary ego and act as a surrogate for certain ego functions. He becomes a positively cathected object, providing coordination and support throughout the therapeutic process, maintaining motivation and providing structure and insight.

Let us consider the case of a 35-year-old borderline patient. This man suffered from numerous neurotic and psychosomatic disorders, with brief psychotic episodes. He projected the potent and aggressive tension inside himself on to external objects, which he consequently perceived as all-powerful and violent, bent on evil and out to destroy him. In its extreme manifestations this led to paranoid misrepresentation of reality and transference psychosis. Projective identification as defence was particularly visible in group therapy, or when he came in touch with the nurses. Difficulties also arose at a later stage with music therapy (cf. the example on p. 140). He claimed that the nurses were persecuting him with their constant demands that he keep to appointed therapy and mealtimes. The nurses viewed him as a shrieking, angry child, forever making capricious demands. Whenever they said 'no' or told him he was going too far he would rant and rave and threaten to wring their necks. In group therapy he terrorized patients and therapist alike, rushing out at will and breaking into a rage if anyone made to address him. He would have been beyond the reach of therapy were it not for the positive, binding transference he had built up towards his individual therapist (on splitting of the transference, see pp. 156–74). He idealized her. In her presence he was the model good little boy. He would have liked to have her all for himself. This relationship was strong enough to ride out stress, e.g. if the therapist was away. She became for him a reparative object or *self-object*, offering sanctuary when things reached crisis point in other areas. (This case is taken up again on p. 177.)

Another of the individual therapist's fundamental tasks in our model was to help patients work through the process of separation from the hospital. The duration of treatment was not prescribed in advance and, at some point, varying from patient to patient, the process of parting had to be set in motion. This might happen at the initiative of the therapist, in the wake of a query from the hospital operators or health insurers, or at the request of the patient. Therapeutic advance in such a situation can be measured by the way in which patients wean themselves from the hospital, e.g. to the accompaniment of separation or loss anxiety, by playing down the therapeutic relationships established or, more maturely, by engaging in mourning (Trimborn *et al.* 1981; Denford *et al.* 1983). Depending on the particular case, this process can take up to two months after inpatient treatment has ceased. We deemed therapeutic headway to have been made if, by the end of their hospital stay – or in the course of their five follow-up interviews – patients proved able to internalize the object relations they were leaving/had left behind, anchoring inside themselves the positively cathected holding object (Stephanos 1978a). This momentum can continue long after the entire treatment sequence is over, as our outcome studies have confirmed. Every time a patient comes back to a unit for further treatment – or simply drops in to say hello – his action speaks for itself. Specific affects invariably accompany parting; there can even be disavowal of the time-limit placed on hospital treatment. It is essential for the dynamics of inpatient therapy that the team work through these things with the patients.

Art therapy and music therapy

Art therapy and music therapy are located in an *intermediate* field in terms of psychoanalytic theory (Winnicott 1971); they allow patients to have recourse to 'extra-verbal' forms of expression when re-enacting conflict within the clinical setting.

Psychoanalytical research into creativity provided me and my colleagues with the impetus to transform these traditionally practical forms of therapy into analytically oriented tools (Janssen 1982; Janssen and Hekele 1986). Patients often enter a labile state as a result of clinically promoted regression, in which case music and art therapy come into their own. The development of creative ego activities is fostered via a process of 'symbolic concretization' (Müller-Braunschweig 1974, 1977) or 'symbolic communication' (Naumburg 1966; Kramer 1971). The 'product' created gives symbolic representation to conflicts within the personality (Müller-Braunschweig 1974, 1977). A shift takes place from a system of language-based symbols to musical and visual symbolization. Music and art differ from ordinary language in that they belong to the realm of presentative (able to be known or perceived immediately) symbols, whereas language is discursive (Langer 1965). Discursive systems are characterized by syntagmatic sequences of symbols (words), whilst presentative systems are paradigmatic and therefore able to represent differing and even contrary things at one and the same time. Examples of presentative systems are musical works (Klausmeier 1976) and paintings (Kramer 1971). This is why I chose to use the term 'extra-verbal' (rather then non-, a- or pre-verbal) to describe that which lies outside the direct scope of language. The epithet 'extra-verbal' points to the change that musical and visual symbols undergo when described in words. Language is only able to subsume them discursively; it cannot communicate their presentative qualities.

What has just been said touches upon one of the special features of the *intermediate* area occupied by art and music therapies. From a psychogenetic perspective, creativity in these areas bears the mark of the child's experience over the period of separation from the mother. This is the phase when the infant relates to 'transitional objects' (Winnicott 1951). Playing with a transitional object (e.g. a piece of rag, a doll) helps the child to part from its mother; inner reality and outer reality, subjective experience and objective experience come together. In this sense, the products of musical and artistic creation are both *transitional objects* and 'subjective objects' (Winnicott 1971). They are not truly 'third-party objects' or 'surrogate objects' as Müller-Braunschweig (1974, 1977) would have it; they can better be likened to the transitional objects of early childhood, for they stand in close relation to the person producing them and, as 'subjective objects', figure as 'partners' in a process of intensive emotional exchange.

'Subjective objectification' using images and sound enables patients with psychosomatic disorders or structural ego impairment to overcome their emotional inability to express themselves through the spoken language (Bräutigam 1978a). A quotient of anxiety is removed and they emerge better able to explore their inner selves and reclaim the world of their imagination.

Music therapy and art therapy act on different areas of experience. The former is more likely to provide release from anxiety and tension (Kohut 1957; Kohut and Levarie 1950; Willms 1975). According to Kohut, it is the regressive experiencing of primitive narcissistic equilibrium in musical expression which releases tension, whereas production of a painting or drawing involves coordinated activation of unconscious ego-components and impulsive id-tendencies. These formations take on new contours as they pass through the filter of the unconscious and coalesce in the final product. 'Concretization' in the shape of a picture allows intrapsychical processes to be communicated in symbolic form (Müller-Braunschweig 1974). The picture provides a locus for the trial transposition of impulses perceived as dangerous. 'The orderedness within the picture, together with the reflection back provided by the finished product' help the ego to gain mastery over, and reintegrate, these dangerous stirrings (Müller-Braunschweig and Möhlen 1980). Pictorial representation is in this sense 'ego-friendly' and can play a structuring, organizing and ego-supportive role in therapy.

A 19-year-old patient was admitted to the unit with the following profile: obsessive controlling tendencies, panic-like anxiety attacks, outbreaks of crying and screaming, a history of suicide attempts and a compulsion to indulge in self-mutilation. For a long time she kept her distance during art therapy sessions, painting self-deprecating pictures. One day change was heralded in art therapy. She had recently begun to act obsessionally and complained of stomach pains and constipation. The art therapist sensed some considerable disturbance. Possibly the girl wanted to communicate something, but could not get it across. The therapist urged her to paint what was going on inside, but she only cried. Then she paused and reflected for a moment. Without a word she set resolutely about painting a square with arrows pointing outwards from it. Big, watching eyes were positioned around the edges. Contemplating the finished product, she experienced afresh the anxiety and unease that had overcome her when told by others that a fellow patient had masturbated. She now managed to describe the nature of this reactivated anxiety. It was as if she was being asked to run naked through the town; all eyes would be on her naked body; her father would find her too plump and womanly; a creature might crawl up under her skirt. The eyes in her picture turned into stern onlookers, ready to punish and pass judgement. In psychodynamic terms the picture allowed the patient to acknowledge her id-anxieties and guilt feelings and to put them into words – something she had not so far been able to do. The presentative symbolism of the picture granted her direct sight of an inner process, triggering the recall mechanism and making verbalization possible. A reciprocal process was set in train: verbalization in group therapy; visual representation in art therapy. Disturbing sexual desires were represented by consuming rings of fire.

Pictures like this make way for what might be described as a form of creative self-actualization which is appropriate to the needs of the ego. Raw material varies and may originate in transference scenes or affective states: anger, despair, the emptiness of depression, loneliness etc. Object-images and self-images are generated. Contemplation of the finished product sparks off ideas as to what is going on in the picture, in turn promoting verbalization (cf. Naumburg 1966; Jakab 1968). Little by little the patient begins to uncover the significance of inner processes. The role of the art therapist is not to interpret or point the way, but rather to promote self-discovery. Patients need to see for themselves that presentative symbols are a means of communicating with the therapist; they must believe that spontaneous creative expression will help them to learn about themselves. Only then will the joy and pleasure of creative activity be sustained. They will come to see their efforts as reflecting their inner selves and providing a mirror for self-confrontation. The therapist's main function is to provide clarification and ego support. By encouraging patients to exercise their creative faculties and explore their innermost selves, he effectively acts as a narcissistic back-up object. Whether or not the art therapist has become integrated into the patient's overall transference schema emerges from the creative output produced.

In our model, production and communication were the central pillars of music therapy. Productive music therapy focuses on communication with the self; working with sound facilitates self-portrayal, self-actualization and self-discovery. Communicative music therapy involves encounter with an object (the music therapist) who will reply in musical form. Therapy cannot become communicative until there is rapprochement between patient and therapist and between patient and transitional object (sound or sound creation).

Productive music therapy involves giving musical form to experiences, happenings, moods, here-and-now predicaments etc. Scenes from other therapeutic configurations are worked through in musical mode; once something has taken shape, the implications in terms of experiences and affects can be discussed in words.

Communicative music therapy means encounter with the other, in this case the musical object. In analytic terms, music itself can be conceived of as a transitional object, as we have seen already. The real object is the music therapist, whose first task is to inspire and set an example, encouraging patients to make use of the transitional object. As therapy advances the focus will be more on listening, before the process culminates with the therapist as musically responding object. Throughout the progression from single notes to more complex tunes, the musical response from the therapist serves to extend the perceptual range of patients; their initial interest is in the subjective object 'music', gradually shifting to the objective object 'music therapist'. Productive music therapy (i.e. engaging with the transitional object 'sound' or 'sound creation') is nevertheless only one dimension of the therapeutic process; there is equally a need to promote individuation. To this end, individuals must be encouraged to recognize and acknowledge the objective object 'music therapist' as musically autonomous.

Many patients find it difficult to cope with an object perceived as musically 'other'. Sound, rhythm and volume are wielded in an effort to stand up to what is apprehended as an opposing force. Faced with the dilemma of the other, some regressed patients seek merger through homophony when faced with an object with a different mode of expression. Borderline patients often use music to manipulate or destroy the other object, whose very separateness is perceived as a threat. Obsessive-compulsive patients seek to impose their orderliness in a bid to keep the alien object under control. In a similar way to transference in psychoanalytic therapy, these forms of musical relating set the tone for the future progression of object relations throughout music therapy. This object-oriented dimension is well illustrated by the following example:

> The patient – who has already been briefly mentioned above (see p. 134) – presented with low-level borderline pathology and was in a severely regressed state on admission. During music therapy he sought homophonic union with the therapist and seemed uncannily able to second guess every note, every musical statement she was about to produce. He was particularly fond of the mellifluous and rippling sound of the xylophone, the instrument he favoured when acting out his desire for merger. The therapist felt like a mere pawn in his colonizing game. This patient simply refused to stand back and reflect upon what he was doing. In his comportment he oscillated between two ego-states, coming across either as threatening and aggressive, or as sweet and friendly. At any moment he was capable of switching from one mode to the other. His quest for merger with the music therapist intensified as time went by. He seemed to take possession of her as object, pressurizing her to meet his wishes, e.g. to have coffee or go swimming with him. Whenever she tried to take her distance he would erupt into fits of anger, which was then projected on to both therapist and music. From then on he could no longer bear music, finding it oppressive and threatening. He felt persecuted by sound and was no longer able take part in music therapy sessions.
>
> His insistent desire for merger, coupled with the music therapist's efforts at demarcation, had clearly induced a build-up of destructive rage. As frequently happens with transference psychoses in borderline patients, he employed projective identification as his defence against such anger; he either had to destroy the threatening object pursuing him, or flee from it.

The importance of musical object relating emerges clearly from this example. Working with sound bears on the emotions and promotes self-encounter and self-actualization. With a little explanatory back-up from the therapist, self-realization may well ensue – thanks to the expressive qualities of the presentative musical symbols. This is one dimension. The therapist also functions as an *objective object* by being present and responding in musical mode. Here we have interaction through music; patients can pursue themes in line with the rhythm of their unconscious relational needs. The dynamics underlying these patterns of musical relating can be readily observed and described, e.g. in terms of a compulsion to control the object. A patient's striving for homophonic union may signal symbiotic longing; it behoves the music therapist to go along with this. Having someone to accept this desire for symbiosis is a positive experience. As therapy takes its course, the patient can begin to abandon the search for musical merger and learn to see the other musical object as a true objective object. In this way music therapy furthers the process of individuation, enabling patients to differentiate between self and object (Mahler *et al*. 1975).

Once they are able to accept the other as a separate musical object, patients' further musical communication with the music therapist – now a true partner – is marked by a more mature level of symbolic integration. They are ready to engage in spontaneous play, using the music to move close, then stand back; to turn towards the other, then away; to experiment with near and far. Since they are no longer dogged by anxiety and desire for merger, the way is free for true engagement with their musical partner. They are capable of falling into step and of taking the lead; they can yield to other rhythms without fear of being unable to re-establish their own. Musical interaction of this kind stabilizes the process of individuation and constitutes a living exercise in self-assertion; such qualities are especially valuable for those with disorders of early onset.

The numerous patterns operating at an unconscious level mean that there is a broad range for the deployment of musical strategies. Music therapy at its most sophisticated involves individuals in an interchange of musical symbols; participation is mutual, with the self retaining its coherence, yet able to perceive and acknowledge similarities and difference in the other. The symbolic mode and emotional charge of musical expression mark it out from verbal communication.

The following example demonstrates once again how musical interaction can boost the process of individuation and at the same time illuminates certain deviations from standard analytic practice.

The patient was admitted to the unit complaining of anxiety attacks, a fear of suffocation and difficulties in swallowing. All she could eat was baby food and chocolates. Her initial response in music therapy was to strive compulsively for perfection, although she could not maintain her high standards for long. Her manner of playing revealed a desire for attachment. She became sad and dejected, turning to soothing, rocking rhythms. She readily understood that these lullabies and nursery tunes were an expression of her desire for closeness and, in her improvisation with the music therapist, her attachment longings became particularly manifest.

Her style of musical interaction was constantly changing. She could be provokingly self-assured, determined to have her own way; she would then reject any approach by the therapist and insist on leading the show. There was no question of her entering into the spirit of improvisation in these moods; she would simply look cross and refuse to be drawn in. At the other extreme she could be very clinging, eager for close musical union with the therapist. When asked to reflect upon her musical experiences, she voiced her fear of being unable to find the common ground with others that she none the less sought. Her musical behaviour made her aware of the dichotomy within her; she wanted to be independent and her own person, yet needed someone to lean on. In musical interaction she acknowledged and explored her dependency, only to break out and assert her separateness from the therapist.

This constant seesawing from contrariness and self-demarcation to extreme attachment behaviour proved persistent. A family therapy-style approach was therefore adopted; the matter was talked through and saying 'no' was actually 'prescribed' to her as a positive means of making headway. It was suggested that she make a point of playing against the tune struck up by the music therapist; simultaneously she was encouraged to see her desire for attachment as useful and facilitating. Her fear of her own desires began to evaporate and she came to see the things she sought as perfectly permissible. It was now quite feasible for the music therapist to say: 'Let's relax and play the same tune together.'

This therapeutic strategy turned the patient's hitherto self-contradicting tendencies into the proper stuff of musical creation. She learned to allow that side of herself which sought incorporation to play its part in the musical process; 'oral greed' was no longer accompanied by guilt. She constantly craved new forms of gratification from the music therapist, taking whatever

she could get. Her longing knew no bounds and time lost its
meaning; she could not let go. She desperately wanted the
therapist all to herself, which meant that she kept trying to
arrange extra appointments. The therapist herself felt able to go
along with all this, even though the process took its toll and
seemed to rob her of her own musical autonomy. Sometimes
the two of them would spend a whole hour at the piano. The
experience of having her incorporating tendencies tolerated in
this way helped the patient to accept that the other musical
object existed in its own right. She was ready to venture a new
beginning, in both musical and verbal interaction. Her playing
during improvisation became freer and more imaginative; she
was no longer tied to the format set by others, yet her newly
found independence was quite without anal defiance.

By way of summary, we can fairly say that playing music
loosened the patient's initial defences as reflected in her compulsive need for perfection; regression to oral-aggressive
instinctual aims ceased. The music therapist became a positively
cathected object – a 'musically other' object. She played an
enabling role in allowing the patient to emerge from regression
and pursue the relationship in a more equal and less dependent
fashion.

Dance movement therapy

Dance movement therapy was introduced into our integrative
model at a relatively late stage; our experience here was therefore
less extensive than in the art and music spheres. Other hospitals
have had longer and deeper involvement, producing a corpus of
theoretical work (cf. Becker 1981). Concentrative dance movement therapy has been described as *pre-verbal, phase-specific
psychotherapy*. Psychosomatic patients in particular enter 'body
and soul' into forms of action which open up access to their
physical selves. They begin to think and feel at the level of primary
process; symptom fixation and ego-syntonic defence mechanisms
can then be abandoned. Exercise-oriented therapy in no sense
reinforces the ego's capacity for symbolization; on the contrary, it
positively promotes regression.

In our unit we focused on the group dimension of dance movement therapy (cf. Becker 1981), offering individual therapy in
special cases and for particular purposes. Each patient attended a

group session two or three times a week; optional groups were devoted to techniques such as concentration and relaxation, the aim of which was to induce in patients a state of physical and psychical abstraction through concentrated attention on individual bodily functions (muscle activity, breathing, heart beat). At a general level, dance movement therapy in a group setting enhances patients' awareness of their own body and its motor potential; exercises are designed to improve carriage, balance, motor skills, agility, strength and endurance.

Nowadays, communication is being brought more and more to the fore in dance movement therapy. In motor interaction, we sometimes glimpse a direct reflection of the group-dynamic processes at work in analytic group therapy or in certain one-to-one relationships. There is scope for leading and being led; some individuals toe the group line; others prefer to carve out a space for themselves, or maybe invite someone else from the group to join them; ball games are played etc. Let us return briefly to our integrative model.

> We had several severely regressed groups who spontaneously decided to create a 'womb' for themselves by covering things over and shutting out the light. Other patients acted out a desire for merger by taking one another's hands and seeking rapprochement – which we found caused great anxiety for the anorexics among them. We learnt that one patient was perceived by his fellows as a danger; during a ball game they set about trying to drive him away and destroy him by hurling the ball in his direction.

Full-blown acting out was usually avoided, since the whole point of dance movement therapy is that it places a structure on things. Insights gained during sessions could therefore be worked through in analytic group therapy. Far from being counterproductive, we found that it made therapeutic sense to operate the two techniques in tandem.

We probably came closest to the core of the therapeutic process when we had occasion to tailor dance movement therapy to meet the needs of a specific treatment plan. The potential for understanding individual patient dynamics proved astounding.

> Three years previously a 40-year-old patient had developed dyskinesia of the head and neck jerking, which sometimes left

her head bent abnormally to the left. Lack of motor control was particularly acute at night. She also complained of tension in the neck and chest muscles. Eleven years before, she had suffered briefly from spasmodic torticollis, followed by depression. We interpreted the diffuse nature of the motor disturbance as an expression of unresolved conflict surrounding separation and individuation in her first year of life. Her hyperkinetic symptoms told the story of her endeavour to demarcate herself from an overstimulating mother. Anger and aggression were diverted into uncoordinated movements. A sequence of muscle relaxation and muscle tightening exercises was devised for dance movement therapy. During relaxation the patient was encouraged to go all floppy, at which point the dyskinesia vanished and she let herself be lulled by the voice of the therapist. The tautening exercises were designed to bring her out of relaxation in controlled fashion, so that her muscles would learn to respond to upsurges of aggressive tension with a degree of coordination. With back-up from analytic therapy and normal dance movement sessions, the patient reached a point where the hyperkinetic motor disturbance had virtually ceased.

The realm of the nurses and Registrar

Caring and support are the key contributions of nurses and the Registrar to the inpatient analytic enterprise. I have already echoed Winnicott (1965) in talking about the *facilitating environment* provided by the hospital. Yet the environment will only be holding, facilitating and supportive if the whole team is involved in making it so. Maintaining the hospital as a viable setting is the responsibility of the entire therapist team. A particular role falls none the less to the nurses working on the wards. We have seen what can happen in the course of therapy to borderline patients and those suffering from structural ego disorders; regressive reactivation of early mother-child constellations leads to potent negative transference. The brunt of this is borne by the mainstays of the inpatient setting, the nurses. They are frequently viewed by patients with suspicion; destructive and aggressive acts are then specifically targeted on them. They are also in the frontline whenever somatic and psychosomatic crises occur.

The nurses are bound to be most directly affected whenever conflict is deflected on to the hospital parameters (patients failing to turn up for meals, infringement of the no alcohol rule, leaving the unit before schedule at the weekend and so on). The first task the nurses perform in these circumstances is to encourage those concerned to think through their attitude towards the setting. Therapists and patients alike have problems with the supportive frame around them; they oscillate between an almost obsessional need for order and predictability, and an equally strong pull towards negative acting out in all its arbitrary, addictive and aggressive guises. What is significant therapeutically is not so much what is going on at the day-to-day level, but the unconscious motivation underlying any particular act against the setting. Where therapists compulsively require that all the rules be obeyed at all times they have clearly sided with the institution. If, as in the bipolar model (e.g. Heigl and Nerenz 1975), a strict line is drawn between nurses, who are responsible for order and discipline, and therapists, whose job is to interpret, the former inevitably become associated with the issuing of decrees and meting out of punishment. The latter meanwhile interpret in the background. Such a division of labour stands in the way of good therapeutic practice, especially in cases of ego impairment where everything is split into good and bad objects anyway. Under an integrative concept the nurses exercise auxiliary ego functions on behalf of patients. This is possible thanks to their attention to, and identification with, the inpatient setting; they actually represent this setting vis-à-vis the patients. If patients can be induced to think through their patterns of behaviour, nurses are in an excellent position to foster therapeutic ego splitting.

The examples given above (pp. 105–29) illustrated how we demarcated therapeutic tasks under the integrative model. Once the parameters of therapy have been set, nurses take on a caring and maternal role, enabling patients to enter into diatrophic (Spitz 1954, 1956/7) or facilitating relationships (see pp. 74–85). Problems of all kinds may be discussed with the nurses; they are there to tend to needs and can always be called upon outside hours. During scheduled rounds they are receptive to input from patients, encouraging them to verbalize their complaints and concerns; conflicts, dreams and worrying affects are ventilated and those involved encouraged to reflect upon them. In this capacity, the nurses act as receiving and accepting objects. They help to clarify issues and relationships and, if a patient seems to be avoiding something (e.g. by not attending individual therapy), this can be broached. Nurses also have occasion to interpret, basing themselves on insights gained during interaction with patients on the ward (see below). Their interpretations will normally relate to manifest behaviour. They are encouraged to ask questions and stimulate reflection, but are unlikely to address unconscious reactivation of past relational patterns.

Along with everyone else in the therapist team, nurses become involved in transference processes. In some cases (depending on pathogenic psychodynamics and level of regression) they will be confronted with the potent affects and strong desires of relived infantile relationships. A nurse in this situation needs to be able to endure the particular constellation, interpreting events in the here-and-now. The work of interpretation in our setting was done at team meetings or in groups of nurses known as Balint groups.

At one team meeting a young nurse who was new to the unit reported on the rejection she had met with from a woman of around 40; she wondered how best to handle the situation. The other nurses contributed to the discussion, as did the therapists. This input, together with various biographical details we already had about the patient, suggested to us that there was negative transference on to the nurse as daughter at work here. The patient's poor relationship with her mother had been reactivated and, in a reversal of roles, she was now turning her negative affects towards the 'new baby' in the therapy team. This put the young nurse on the defensive. The group thoroughly talked through the relational dynamics with her and made the following recommendation: Next time she went on her ward round she should put it to the patient that her rejecting attitude could be interpreted as negative transference towards herself, the nurse, as daughter. At a subsequent group therapy session the patient came forward with an emotional account of her relations with the nurse. The negative relationship with her mother was elucidated and discussed, and tension diminished in future interaction with the nurse.

This example proves how important it is for nurses to be allotted space at team meetings to speak about the subjective dimension of their relations with patients. Team discussion furthers their understanding of the unconscious underbelly of staff-patient interaction and strengthens their sense of therapeutic identity and worth. Regular team meetings reduce the risk of random acting out in the countertransference – although such action does sometimes trigger insight into what exactly a patient is re-enacting.

The nursing staff as a body has a pivotal therapeutic role to play, particularly in cases of structural ego disorder. We have seen the analyst's perception of the nursing remit; let us now look at how nurses themselves view their role. What follows is an authentic account by a nurse of a certain phase in a patient's treatment (Koch 1982):

> The night nurse reported that Mr X had returned to the unit in the evening in a state of inebriation. He even brought a bottle of wine back with him, drinking it up with some fellow patients in the common room. The night nurse did not stop him, although she was very annoyed and thought his conduct outrageous. When they heard about this, the day nurses could no longer contain themselves.

> *Ms A:*   That is really the end; he has gone too far. His behaviour was jolly provocative and I ask myself why he is so bent on angering us. He often gets on my nerves during the daytime, too, with his loud mouth and 'look at me' manner – he seems to think he's King of the ward. He has to be told once and for all what is what. Let's just hope his therapist will now talk to him about his behaviour.

> *Ms B:*   (*tries to pacify her*): Calm down, we don't know what caused him to do it – he probably had his reasons. He doesn't seem very happy at the moment; perhaps he was trying to wash something away. Somehow I feel sorry for him; he doesn't come across to me as all that pleased with himself.

> *Ms A:*   That is not how tension should be resolved in our setting. Alcohol is not allowed anyway. I don't get the feeling that Mr X takes us or our therapy seriously.

> *Ms D:*   OK, alcohol is not allowed, but I can't see that Mr X can change a habit just like that. I don't think drink is the answer either, but he needs time to find other ways of managing. If he still feels unable to talk about his inner conflict, then he's going to keep drinking.

> *Ms A:*   I cannot understand why you are all so keen to protect him. Apparently I am the only person on the ward who is prepared to see that the rules we all set are obeyed. I

intend to go and ask him right out what is up. It will be interesting to hear what he has to say. We can meet again in the nurses' lounge when I get back.

After the encounter:

Ms A: I am very annoyed. Mr X is impossible. He just laughed in my face and said that he needed to get sloshed now and then. When I tried to explain that that was simply not acceptable here, he got even more cocky. I had to shut up, otherwise I would have exploded.

Ms B: You've got youself well and truly involved now – I think you'd better bring the matter up at a ward meeting.

Mr X's individual therapist reported on what he knew of the man's past. His childhood seemed to have been fairly traumatic; he was separated from his parents at an early age and spent a short while in a children's home before going back temporarily to his grandmother. He then went to foster parents, where he stayed until he was grown up, although they constantly threatened to return him to the children's home.

His life from then on was very unstable. He started out with an office job, but was pensioned out early because he was always sick. After that he had to make do with temporary work here and there. He was frequently caught up in rows and fights and, when he was drunk, would often beat his wife, much as he reproached himself afterwards.

The group therapist's impression of Mr X was of a rather timid, anxious figure. The very fact of being in a group worried and disturbed him, since issues such as separation inevitably cropped up; he told on one occasion of how, as a small boy, he had gone off in search of his real mother. The consultant psychiatrist acting as our group adviser believed that Mr X behaved as he did in order to attract our attention and convince us that we should look after him, helpless and threatened as he was. Further incidents occurred over the ensuing weeks and the nurses found themselves in a very delicate situation. They were expected to uphold the rules (strictly avoiding falling prey to aggressive or punishing acting out); yet at the same time they were to view the patient's actions as an expression of his helplessness. Ms A went on being extremely angry at the shameless way in which the man behaved. She worked on coming to grips with her feelings in the Balint group, reporting to the other nurses on her talks with the patient. He had apparently spoken in a very deprecating and insulting way about his wife. Whenever she reminded him of the house rules, his anger came down on her and she was afraid he might even resort to physical violence. She saw him as a typical example of the kind of man who drives a woman into a refuge.

Ms B then gave her point of view. She saw Mr X as a cross little boy who smashes things up all around him and tries madly to fend off powerful women. She wanted to protect him. Discussion in the Balint group revealed how lacking in control Mr X was; he could not bear any kind of tension, but had to convert it immediately into action of some sort. He delegated the controlling function to us, yet at the same time fought against that control. He virtually had his back against the wall; he therefore behaved cockily and played hard-to-get. This made him feel big and strong, leaving his opposite number (in this case Ms A) to seethe at her powerlessness. Once she came to understand and accept this, Ms A cooled down. The better able she was to tolerate his behaviour and to talk to him about it, the less he needed to puff himself up. When he discovered he was not going to be punished, he gradually became more confident and was able to get through to his feelings and express them.

One day he was smitten with terrible stomach pains. Ms B took this seriously and really looked after him, calming his fears when he insisted that they were bound to want to cut him up; he could actually see himself on the operating table. He happily accepted all this care and concern and went to bed with a hot water bottle. He also had a nice cup of tea.

Since Ms B seemed to understand his desire for warmth and protection, he began to perceive in her the good and holding other. After a while he felt much more secure and began working through material with his individual therapist. He spoke increasingly of his memories, feelings and behaviour. Rather than acting out every time, he learnt to recount his experiences and ride out tension; it could always be talked about afterwards. He realized that Ms A was not all bad and dominant like his stepmother. He could see why she kept reminding him of the ward rules and felt able to talk to her about it. The learning process continued with Ms B too. Because she could not always be at his beck and call, he felt let down and abandoned. He grew angry, but eventually realized that he could be freer and more independent without her constant protection. Little by little he came to see us as real people for each one of whom he would feel differently.

The Registrar is not in quite the same position as the nurses. Although he may be acting as an individual therapist elsewhere, relations with patients on the ward for which he holds medical responsibility are confined to the strictly medical and somatic. He is free however to air his views about the psychodynamic dimension of his interaction with the patients. In this way he contributes towards a better understanding of transference processes.

The Registrar as boundary-setter is of considerable therapeutic significance for patients with structural ego disorders. If they are caught up in a negative transference bind, for example, they may push for certain drugs or request referral to another department for a second opinion. Extending the parameters of therapeutic interaction to take in neighbouring medical departments can bring with it considerable problems; patients are liable to insist on further physical tests, or even surgery. If agreement to pursue psychotherapy is secured in such instances, despite the patient's acting out, it is largely thanks to the Registrar. He has the job of convincing the Consultant to whom he has referred the patient that the psychodynamic approach should be given another chance.

The Registrar cannot however afford to view a patient's somatic symptoms solely in terms of transference; he must check whether there is in fact a need for medical intervention. The manner in which the Registrar deals with patients' somatic crises (e.g. weight loss in anorexia sufferers) to some extent determines how the nurses respond in their daily care. Where death fears and phantasies are aroused, the physician's perceived reliability is paramount. Where the integrative process is truly working, Registrar and nurses are together able to exercise a physical holding function for patients.

The Registrar holds ultimate responsibility for matters of medication. Perhaps I should pause to explain this further, as people might find such demarcation contrary to integrative principles. Most patients admitted for inpatient therapy are taking some kind of psychopharmacological drug. Some are substance dependent.

Patients with organic complaints (e.g. ulcerative colitis, bronchial asthma) continue to receive their medication, either under the charge of the Department's clinical adviser, or by referral back to the physician who treated them prior to admission. The main problem lies with those patients who have previously been on extremely high doses of psychoactive drugs or analgesics for functional and psychical disturbances; they generally expect to go on as before during inpatient psychotherapy. Our motto for drug administration was that substance intake should progressively be reduced, provided no psychical or somatic decompensation occurred (e.g. acute anxiety attacks, suicidal ideation, psychotic episodes, psychosomatic crises). Yet the prime goal of any psychotherapeutic inpatient undertaking is to keep patients in therapy; this may well entail dispensing psychoactive drugs (cf. Fürstenau *et al.* 1970; Zauner 1974; Danckwardt 1979). 'Demonizing' drugs helps no one in our experience, since patients and therapists alike finish up avoiding the unconscious motivation underlying drug intake.

Sound reasons led to the decision to place medical and medicinal 'holding functions' in the hands of the Registrar, delegating him to represent the team in this area vis-à-vis patients. We realized that leaving issues of psychopharmacology to the patient's individual therapist complicated the therapeutic relationship and risked overburdening the therapist. In analytical terms drugs figure as 'objects' for patients; in order to defend themselves against loss anxiety, they cling to surrogates. Structural ego disorder patients are particularly prone to this pattern of psychodynamic functioning. They crave a reliable anaclitic and diatrophic therapeutic relationship beyond the frame of the working alliance. Yet if drugs enter into the patient-therapist relationship it soon becomes a patient-drug relationship. Because he dispenses the drug, the therapist is seen as 'all good' and negative transference is excluded from the therapeutic process. Unworked through latent negative transference upholds pathogenic dynamics and the patient remains dependent on those objects or surrogates perceived as all good (Danckwardt 1978, 1979). Drug dispensing should therefore be the province of a therapist who does not directly interpret patient interaction. If transference splitting occurs, it can be discussed at team meetings, where the relational dynamics will receive due examination. Contrary to what happens when an outside practitioner is brought in to advise on drugs, relations with the Registrar are not split off from the rest of the interactive process.

However important it is to differentiate between therapeutic tasks, the real key to therapeutic success lies in the therapist team's integrative capacities. The team as an entity takes on board all aspects of transference and regression. At an individual level, each member of the professional staff is called upon to apprehend reactivated infantile object relations and adopt the appropriate therapeutic stance. Behind him however stands the whole team with its capacity to integrate the many variegated patterns of interaction.

THE INDIVIDUAL AND THE THERAPEUTIC PROCESS

Understanding transference

At the beginning of this chapter I spoke of what I termed the psychoanalytical essentials, one of these being a willingness to view the therapeutic process from the vantage point of transference and countertransference. How transference is conceived of and put to use is crucial for inpatient psychotherapy, so maybe it is time for me to elucidate my own particular understanding of the processes involved.

Freudian theory states that, in transference, individuals experience re-actualization of the drive-defence dichotomy that characterized relations with their parents; the reappearance of these primitive constellations allows for interpretation and working through (cf. Chapter 2). The psychoanalytic situation has been described as a therapeutic setting liable to promote regressive transference neurosis. Transference is 'illusory apperception of another person' (Sandler *et al.* 1973: 48). Ideas, feelings and desires are directed on to the person of the analyst in a repetition of the past in the present (Greenson 1967). Equally characteristic of transference are the 'unconscious (and often subtle) attempts to manipulate or to provoke situations with others which are a concealed repetition of earlier experiences and relationships' (Sandler ibid.) 'Restoration' might perhaps be a more appropriate term than 'repetition', but what matters is that these are *interactional* definitions of transference; they highlight the element of object relationship – which is so important in the hospital setting.

This perspective on the dynamics of transference has been shared by analysts whose whole therapeutic practice was structured around the notion of object relationships (Balint 1968; Winnicott 1965, 1971; Loch 1974; Kernberg 1975a, 1976a, 1981). Object relations theory concerns itself with the trajectory of object relationships from the beginning of infantile development onwards. At every stage specific relational configurations take shape and are internalized. Kernberg (1981) took his lead from Glover in describing the analysis of transference as involving not only 'the analysis of instinctual impulses and their warding-off'; it equally signalled 'a special object relationship within which instinctual and defence processes are played out'. Understood in this way, transference always expresses a particular object relationship 'under the influence of' a particular drive derivative. Take the example of the internalization of primitive *self and object images*. By allowing primitive object relationships to be externalized, the transference process uncovers the trace of infantile relational structures – still present even though the initial configuration has undergone subsequent transformation.

Transference in inpatient psychotherapy can perhaps best be described as the manifestation of infantile object relationships in the multipersonal social environment of the hospital – and I include under the heading 'transference' the recurring patterns of primitive infantile object-relating (e.g. symbiotic, merger-seeking, oral-aggressive, incorporative) characteristic of patients with disorders of early onset. This vision of the transference process does justice to the fact that it is possible to find within one and the same individual a whole spectrum of primitive behavioural patterns, ranging from the very immature to the mature. Infantile configurations become pathogenic when psychic equilibrium is lost, e.g. in regressive states; where trauma attaches to specific infantile object relations; or where the infantile patterns are actually blocking growth.

Admission into hospital

Patients react in different ways to the large-group environment of the hospital. Some find reassurance in the protective, nurturing atmosphere, whereas others become edgy and intimidated, maybe feeling annoyed at the restrictions on their time and movements. Admission is voluntary, but when a patient enters a residential unit he at the most enjoys a working relationship with his individual therapist and has yet to forge a therapeutic alliance with the whole staff team. People become inpatients for all sorts of reasons (e.g. a desire for care and consolation) and a run-in period is usually required before they feel ready to launch wholeheartedly into the process of self-exploration.

I now propose to describe in more detail the way in which our integrative unit operated. Responsibility for welcoming patients lay with the nurses, who helped people to familiarize themselves with the new situation etc. The various treatment and organizational arrangements were explained and everyone was handed a timetable, together with what we called a 'patient's manual', laying down the house rules. All this enabled new arrivals to overcome their initial nerves and cope with the sense of disorientation they experienced on leaving their everyday environment. The nurses also tried to instil in the new patient a feeling that he was accepted and that his problems, both physical and mental, would be thoroughly addressed.

New patients took part in group-analytic psychotherapy as of the first week. They were free to see their individual therapist if they so wished and received regular visits from the nurses. Dance movement sessions were joined right away and contact was made with art and music therapists. After a week or so, having been in touch with everyone involved in his treatment, the new arrival was effectively a patient of the whole team. Ten days or so into therapy, the team met to discuss what we termed the *arrival scene*. Account was taken of the psychodynamic diagnosis drawn up by the outpatient therapist and views were exchanged on future priorities in all areas of treatment. We always endeavoured to keep our therapeutic options open, not wishing to dig ourselves in prematurely.

Being in the unit considerably loosened a patient's ties with his social environment, cutting him off from everyday relationships. This encouraged regression, with all the attendant therapeutic advantages and disadvantages (cf. Tarachow 1963; Zauner 1978; Ziese 1978). The positive side was that infantile behavioural patterns came relatively quickly and fully to the fore, revealing what needed working on therapeutically. The downside was that patients risked losing touch with the real world; it would then no longer be possible to work on regression satisfactorily. This pitfall could usually be avoided if patients maintained contact with their social environment at weekends (cf. pp. 105–12), although there were patients who obtained so much gratification from relationships outside the hospital that their weekends away undermined the whole therapeutic process.

> One young obsessive-compulsive patient presented with a high level of libidinal fixation. For a brief spell this energy was transferred on to a particular nurse. At home the man had managed to recruit his mother into his toilet and hygiene ritual. He would wake her up in the middle of the night and demand that she serve him food and drinks on the lavatory. He sometimes remained 'enthroned' for between two and three days. His mother was his love object and he hers. Despite the efforts of her husband and other children, she would not pull away. On the contrary, she let it be known that if need be she would leave her husband in order to help her son. Because the patient returned home at weekends, this pattern was continually resumed and his libidinal relationship with his mother was consequently never challenged.

Taking individuals out of their everyday environment and plunging them into a large-group setting generally does impact on established interpersonal relationships with family and/or partner. Patients unconsciously negotiate arrangements with those close to them, either to shore up neurotic defence mechanisms, or to provide surrogate gratification of repudiated infantile needs. Individual psychodynamic imperatives find an outlet in social interaction (Richter 1967, 1970; Mentzos 1976). Removing a patient from this interpersonal framework destabilizes his defence structures and interferes with his private matrix; therapeutic contact with his family or partner may then prove necessary. The prime focus of inpatient psychotherapy is nevertheless the individual and there should not in my view be any slide into family or marital therapy.

Transference in action

Let me once again underscore the multifaceted nature of the inpatient setting, with all its organizational parameters and therapeutic fields. Patients enter a *large group* and, as with any community environment, there is potential for regression to earlier stages of psychical development. Ohlmeier (1976, 1979) puts this down to the very structure of the psychical apparatus, which bears the imprint of infantile internalization of the entire family group as object. Triggered by the large-group situation, past patterns of interaction with parental objects are set in motion over again.

The hospital environment offers patients a whole range of opportunities for making relationships and they set about seeking new interpersonal configurations for the re-enactment of internalized object relationships. The team allows this process to unfold, although therapists must not be drawn into actually fulfilling repetition wishes; their remit is to encourage verbalization and observe the indicators of re-enacted object relationships: behaviour, object choice, social intercourse. The importance of interactional replay for inpatient psychotherapy cannot be overstated. In outpatient analysis, free association provides the material for processing (Lorenzer 1970), whereas the institutional setting favours observation of social behaviour as well as attention to verbally communicated representations. The particular quality of inpatient psychotherapy is that it allows for interactional replay in the here-and-now (cf. Wittich 1977; Becker and Lüdeke 1978; Trimborn 1983).

According to the tenets of classical psychoanalysis, re-enactment is acting out, i.e. resistance. For Freud (1914), acting out involved repetition rather than remembering (Fenichel 1945). Acting out is certainly more prevalent in an inpatient than an outpatient setting; yet our unit's approach was not to view it as primarily signalling resistance. Acting out in the institutional context is 'a dramatization of an intrapsychic problem' (Tarachow 1963: 72). Therapists working with inpatients should not stop at verbalization, but need equally to direct their therapeutic gaze to interactive group behaviour. Close observation is of the essence. The team must empathize with patients as they weave patterns of interrelations, yet it must also be alert to the countertransference responses of its own members to the scenes being played out. Interpretation can then begin.

Vignette 1

A 35-year-old man was admitted to the unit suffering from severe depressive moods. He went through periods of alcohol abuse, had a stomach ulcer and was now unable to work as a result of growing regressive and passive tendencies. 'Reserved', 'polite', 'aligned', 'submissive', 'goody-goody' were some of the terms used by his individual therapist and the group analyst to describe his intercourse with them. He had experienced his own father as a threat and behaved towards them rather like a clever schoolboy towards a strict and demanding father. His sensible attitude, prompted by fear of his aggressive impulses, translated in therapy into an apparent unwillingness to allow processes to unfold, much to the annoyance of the therapists. The nurses found him distant, intent on maintaining a 'buffer zone' and quite unselective in his object choice. He demonstrated clear regressive-passive traits in dance movement therapy, e.g. he liked to make the mats into a couch and then ensconce himself like a teddy bear. His defensive position and passive-regressive desires emerged unequivocally from such behaviour. He paid frequent visits to the Registrar, complaining to her of bodily discomfort. This suggested a fragile body-self, but the true pathogenic dynamics involved were only uncovered when we came to consider his relationship with the music therapist.

He started out behaving in rigid and retentive fashion towards her and was manifestly anxious. He said he was afraid that something might prevent him from holding out for the whole session. He would sit at the piano, play a few notes, then curse and bang down the lid as if needing to protect himself against a sudden upsurge of anxiety. The therapist suspected that he held back for a specific cause, so she allowed him to take the musical lead in the hope that this might diminish his anxiety.

The team agreed with her that the patient's conduct signalled a fear of something specific. This reassured her and she decided to tell him how she felt about his interaction with her. A dialogue ensued and at one point he recalled having had a positive relationship with an elder sister; they used to play piano duets together. When their mother was away, as she frequently was, his sister would take charge and therefore became a significant object for him. This relationship was clearly being reactivated in his transference to the music therapist and he was desperately afraid of losing control. He eventually admitted to a fear that he might be unable to resist touching her, risking the kind of reprimand ('a rap over the knuckles') he had received from his sister or father on similar occasions in the past.

Musical interaction with the therapist lessened his fear of such impulses. He felt able to tell her about his daydreams of having a 'giant penis' capable of 'killing' or 'stopping up'. Once these infantile memories and present-day phantasies had found an outlet, he grew freer and more relaxed in his other relationships. In both group and individual therapy he began to work on his feelings of guilt and to address the deep fear of his own phallic-aggressive tendencies.

This case is instructive on two accounts. We see how patients re-enact inner conflict, but we also learn how the central command of psychoanalysis – that conflict be worked through in transference – *can* be obeyed in inpatient therapy, provided the special nature of institutional transference is recognized. Transference processes in outpatient analysis usually unfold in consecutive stages; if any reactions develop outside the analytic situation, they are labelled secondary and interpreted in relation to primary transference to the analyst. In the hospital setting, more than one form of transference can occur simultaneously.

Analysis of the results of inpatient treatment (cf. pp. 93–103) confirms that inpatient transference is mainly multidimensional. Elsewhere I have described the process as involving simultaneous externalization of previously internalized (libidinally or aggressively cathected) family object relationships; interaction with therapists and patients sets off regressive re-enactment of the whole gamut of relational constellations experienced within the family. Where therapy is working properly, the structure of these internalized object relationships can be deduced from the various patterns of multidimensional transference. Because of the potential for choice, elements originating in different stages of infantile development attach to different therapists.

Vignette 1 offered a clinical demonstration of multidimensional transference in action, yet it will be clear from what follows that no advance conclusions should be drawn as to which object from within the team will be selected for any particular aspect of transference. Certain leads are admittedly given; the doctor-nurse configuration in group therapy tends to trigger oedipal or pre-oedipal transference, based respectively on paternal and maternal imagos (cf. Stephanos 1973, 1978a), but patients do not necessarily re-enact conflict according to pre-set patterns, e.g. therapist = father, nurse = mother. Nurses sometimes figure in transference as siblings or daughters, even as fathers; male therapists are idealized as mothers etc.

Psychosomatics and severely regressed patients may initially view the whole institution as a single orally dispensing mother; they are then liable to develop oral-passive tendencies in all their relationships. Here we are confronted with a symbiotic, idealizing transference reaction which, like other primitive forms of transference, is one-dimensional.

Vignette 2

A 38-year-old patient presented for inpatient therapy in a state of oral-passive regression. In the aftermath of withdrawal treatment for alcoholism he developed cardiac neurosis and began to suffer from polyphagia and vomiting. Gastro-intestinal problems followed and his sleep patterns became disturbed. He grew incapable of any kind of activity and could not go out of the house. At the start of hospitalization he recounted his phantasies freely, speaking of disembowelled animals and giant, all-devouring female genitals. This openness then ceased abruptly and he rarely said anything. Over the ensuing months he showed signs of oral-passive dependence in all fields of therapy. In every relational configuration (with nurses, his individual therapist, the group) he felt pathetic and helpless – 'a little squirt'. There was no question of confronting fellow patients in the group and working things through. He did cautiously warm to music, however, and began to express his regressive state in homophonic musical interaction with the music therapist. These sessions brought him some relief. For several months the team stood supportively by, bearing with his regression, anxiety and phantasies. Interpretation was of no avail; his state remained unchanged. Then, spurred on by romantic interest in a nurse, he tentatively branched out. He took up cooking and the guitar, activities he had enjoyed in the past. His love feelings for the nurse were transferred to a seductive and flirtatious fellow patient and this new constellation gave him new momentum. He now took an active part in group sessions and started to emerge from his passive-regressive state. He began to idealize the unit and the group therapist, in this way acquiring a positively cathected object. He also engaged actively with other male patients and fought for his love object. On leaving the unit he found it hard to part from the 'ideal object' the hospital had by then become, but he remained stable, keeping up his newly rediscovered creative activities and managing a satisfactory emotional life.

This is an example of how the one-dimensional transference of regression can develop multiple dimensions as therapy proceeds. If multidimensional transference is the (oedipally driven) re-enactment of internalized family object relationships, one-dimensional transference signals regressive resistance to that re-enactment.

In that it reflects the oedipal side of human relations, multidimensional transference differs from *transference splitting* – or what in inpatient psychotherapy is known as *pathognomonic* transference. Attitudes towards splitting of the transference vary, depending on the type of inpatient strategy followed. Splits may be encouraged, in which case they are worked on therapeutically with a view to subsequent integration (Arfsten and Hoffmann 1978; Möhlen and Heising 1980). Alternatively, the phenomenon is seen as a deviant offshoot of multidimensional transference; efforts are then made to prevent its advent by clearly defining what is therapeutic space and what is not (Heigl and Nerenz 1975; König 1974; Beese 1978). Beneath these differences lie diverging conceptions of the nature of transference splitting. We go along with Kernberg (1975a) and Volkan (1976) in viewing it as a pathognomonic indicator of borderline personality structure. Because the ego lacks integrative capacity, the patient's various ego states cannot be reconciled with one another. His object representations, good and bad, are therefore projected on to separate individuals.

As we have seen, splitting of the transference is a challenge to the integrative capacities of the team. Patients in whom it occurs are in some ways the 'salt' of inpatient psychoanalytic therapy, as I hope to demonstrate with the following detailed extract from a case history.

Vignette 3

The patient, a 28-year-old social worker, enjoyed a high profile among the young people in his care and was generally viewed as outgoing and hardworking. His troubles began when his girl-friend left him; at that point he also had to seek medical treatment for a fungal infection of the penis. He subsequently fell victim to all sorts of bodily ailments: a burning sensation in the anus, pains in his joints, backache and impotence. Numerous urological tests were carried out. Deep down he was permanently ill-at-ease, suffering panic attacks accompanied by chest pains. He felt devastated and unable to control his life. If his new partner said the slightest thing to upset him, he was liable to break into a rage.

'Total exhaustion' led him to consent to inpatient treatment. He immediately began to behave in the same clinging way towards the therapists as he did towards his girlfriend; he was terrified of being abandoned or sent away. He hoped that hospital therapy would help him to recover his 'survival capability'. This for him meant restoration of his ideal representation of himself (narcissistic desire for reparation). He equated access to the unit with the doorway to salvation – and it should be noted in this context that patients with narcissistic disorders nearly always enter inpatient therapy in the wake of 'breakdown' of some kind; otherwise they tend to avoid what they see as the humiliation of admission to hospital.

The first phase of therapy was dominated by the unfolding of phantasies of narcissistic omnipotence. The patient put his desires directly into action, using the therapeutic objects at his disposal as self-objects; they were to be available whenever and wherever he wanted. He was continually asking his individual therapist for appointments and wanted the group therapist all to himself; he could not abide the other members of the group. Out of hours he expected the nurses to chat with him over coffee; they were also summoned to provide food outside set mealtimes. When they failed to comply he did a deal with the kitchen lady, who agreed to serve him at different times from the other patients. He presented the music therapist with a record so that she could get used to his taste. He asked the dance movement therapist out for a drive and announced that he would like a closer relationship with her. In other words, he was ruled by narcissism and wish fulfilment phantasies.

The team soon discovered that his difficulties in adjusting to the parameters of therapy were going to cause problems. He simply could not accept being a patient like any other. Mealtimes did not apply to him, nor did rules governing weekend leave (Saturday to Sunday evening). He would leave the unit on Friday and not return until Monday. Other patients were back at night by 10 p.m.; he showed up at midnight or even 1 a.m. This was perfectly in order in his view; after all, he had been visiting friends and having a good time.

The realities of the setting were nevertheless such that, sooner or later, something was going to happen to temper this narcissistic onslaught; institutional boundaries were being seriously overstepped. He had already managed to get the kitchen lady to keep his breakfast on one side so that he could get up later than everyone else. The time duly came when a particular nurse could take no more. She put it to him sardonically that his relations with the kitchen lady were unusually good, given that she was willing to break the rules on his behalf. This confrontation caused narcissistic hurt and he turned decidedly aggressive towards the 'evil' nurses. Meanwhile, in a clear demonstration of splitting transference, he sprang to the defence of the bountiful and pampering object 'kitchen lady'. His violation of the institutional parameters was then taken up on other fronts too, boosting his aggressive and destructive affects still further.

He now perceived the hospital as a separate object and this was reflected in transference. The object 'withholding mother' was reactivated, triggering outbreaks of fury. Whereas aggressive impulses are often somatized under such circumstances, this was only partly the case here. In the absence of intra-psychical control mechanisms, he looked outside and targeted the community.

His hatred of the hospital as maternal object led him to stir up an 'anti-therapist movement'. In the small group he engineered a personal dissection of the therapist, confronting her for an opinion on the way the unit was run. He accused us of running a 'fascist regime' and found allies in his fellow patients, whose memories of negative maternal objects were revived. The small group built up a phantasy of 'bad mother hospital' and expressed solidarity with its new 'Führer' in the hope of seeing the unit reorganized. We the therapists were 'bad' and quite incapable of helping our patients. They said we were arbitrary and destructive, interested only in tormenting them. The nurses on the other hand were nice and would see to it that the bad therapists were punished.

Most of the other patients were content to leave things at

that, following their new leader at phantasy level and projecting negative affects on to the unit. He however was intent on action. Allies were found in two male patients, who were also suffering from major narcissistic disorders. A veritable combat strategy was devised. The existence of a common enemy generated a sense of closeness (not without homosexual overtones); this complicity in turn provided a measure of security and warded off sibling rivalry. The 'triumvirate' set up an alternative kitchen and, in a bid to gain oral independence from bad, persecuting objects, openly flouted the ward's no alcohol rule. They hoped in this way to force the 'inhumane' therapist team into counteraction. The team did none the less contain one positively cathected object for our patient: his individual therapist, to whom he went for consolation, confident of finding a listening ear. Transference splitting was manifestly at work here and the therapist became his idealized maternal object. This was not enough in terms of care and attention, however. He was concerned that his body might disintegrate and asked for special physical examination by the Registrar. The latter did what he could, but was unable to match the patient's ever-increasing demands. Disappointment ensued and the patient decided to consult a doctor outside the hospital. Meanwhile he continued to test out his phantasies of narcissistic omnipotence on the other patients, telling them how he would organize the unit if he were in charge. If he were a therapist, he assured them, he would behave in much more friendly and reconciliatory fashion towards his patients, really making them a part of his life.

All this won him special status among fellow patients. Simultaneously he drew sustenance from the idealized relationship he had forged with his individual therapist. Other team members provided him with multiple targets on to which he could project his hate feelings; the clinical setting had activated splitting transference in highly affect-laden form. The reactions of the team towards this splitting, and their subsequent conduct, were determining factors in the future course of the therapeutic process. The patient's doings triggered a stormy and highly charged debate within the team as to his accessibility to therapy. More input came into the discussion and we grew to see his infringements of the house rules (e.g. the long weekends) as repetitions of an early childhood scene. When the patient was 6 years old, his father had mysteriously disappeared (whether through suicide or murder was never clarified). A year later he was faced with a stepfather, whom he described as strict and brutish. As a helpless young boy he had passively endured the absence of his deeply idealized father. Now the tables were turned; he was the one to be absent. Action had replaced passivity, yet his grandiose behaviour called into question our whole system of therapy. According to the rules of the institution, he had effectively discharged himself through his prolonged weekend absences.

After just such an extended weekend, we were confronted with an example of negative countertransference. On the patient's return to the unit, one of the nurses told him that he had brought about his own discharge; the administrative services had been informed and another patient had taken over his bed. We were interested in what led the nurse to take this step. Several team members had been wounded in their narcissism by deprecating and insulting remarks from the patient; this inevitably generated tension within the team and negative countertransference began to build up. Such sentiments initially remained unconscious, or else found a focus in arguments over therapeutic technique, but things eventually erupted in the discharge dramatization. The event constituted a form of psychosocial defence for those of the team members whose own aggressive self-aspects had become reactivated during interaction with the patient; others in the team were distressed by such non-integrated intervention.

This transference–countertransference scenario was an acid test for therapy; the team's integrative capacities faced a severe challenge. As for the patient, he was taken aback that his conduct could have any real consequences; he was totally mystified and very angry. Anger gave way to disappointment; disappointment to despair. He had formed therapeutic attachments and wished to return to the unit. He therefore decided to exploit the relationship with his two fellow-conspirators. They duly requested an interview with me as psychoanalytic consultant, endeavouring to win me over to their side with a view to getting their friend re-admitted. Here was a clear instance of narcissistic projection; I was being invested with some kind of power over the team. My counter-strategy was to have a long talk with the patient, explaining that, although re-admission was possible, the matter would have to be discussed beforehand in the team. I then went to the team and we thrashed out the meaning of all this positive and negative countertransference. One factor to emerge was how important negative counter-transference reactions are for the process of therapy; they should certainly not be brushed aside as anti-therapeutic. For the first time, the team as a body rallied round the patient. He no longer figured as 'that dreadful, untreatable case', but rather as a man needing to escape hate-objects – someone who had run away in an acute state of panic. We agreed to re-admit him and he later told of how important an experience this scene of discharge and re-admission had been.

Let me now try to summarize the process. Externalization of negative and positive object relationships on to the team led to regression and transference splitting. Teamwork as described above enabled the split to be overcome. The patient saw the team as a single object. This object turned out to have good and bad aspects, which he eventually learnt to reconcile with one another. After re-admission, he was integrated enough inside himself to be able to accept both his destructiveness and his need of help. He appeared to have overcome what Melanie Klein termed the *paranoid-schizoid position*.

His conspiratorial activities ceased and he began to fall in much better with our therapeutic arrangements. Eventually a stage came when we could jointly discuss a discharge date. As to his relations with the patient group, he managed to get two mass meetings off the ground. This signalled a move away from *destructive collective illusions* to *constructive collective aspirations*. The patients as a group suggested talks with the psycho-analytic adviser; they were not fully satisfied with the therapy on offer and felt that the unit should be more nurturing and accommodating. This group initiative reflected the patients' insatiable longing for a bountiful and caring object. The discovery that we were willing to discuss their requirements with them opened the way for future therapeutic cooperation.

In the case of this particular patient, the large group became a locus for new experience. The 'glass partition' that had stood between himself and us was breached and we became real, tangible objects for him.

This case exemplifies the effects of inpatient psychoanalytic treatment on a certain kind of narcissistic patient; similar patterns also emerge when dealing with borderline personality structure (as defined by Kernberg, cf. Ahrens *et al.* 1983). In order to restore their illusion of omnipotence, patients use the multipersonal matrix of the hospital to seek out objects that they can dispose of according to their desires. What we in fact witness is the unfolding of narcissistic needs inside an institutional frame; therapeutic objects are manipulated within the temporal and spatial parameters of the setting in a re-creation of the infantile scene. The group climate induces regression and in this way generates narcissistic visions of omnipotence.

The narcissistic patient described above tried to engineer a state of unlimited, passive, conflict-free satisfaction in all areas of therapy. Disillusionment inevitably followed, for he came up against the limits inherent in the therapeutic setting and had to face the realities of coexistence with fellow patients and the therapy team. He broke into fits of destructive rage, carefully targeting the institution which presumed to set such boundaries. As a result he became trapped in a malign and regressive spiral, reliving memories of a frustrating and negative maternal object.

Experience with the psychoanalytic treatment of borderline patients in an inpatient setting led Trimborn (1983) to the conclusion that the institutional framework disrupted the unfolding of omnipotence phantasies at too early a stage; patients are deprived of the world of transitional objects – or subjective objects – which the presence of the analyst in a traditional psychoanalytic setting guarantees. Trimborn doubted that a comparable *intermediate area* could develop in the hospital environment and believed outpatient analysis to be indicated in such cases. The model he described (Arfsten and Hoffmann 1978) was strictly oriented towards group-analytic psychotherapy, whereas our approach involved a two-pronged therapeutic thrust, with attention to extraverbal interaction as well as analytic groupwork. The integrative model is underpinned by the principles of ego psychology and object relations theory. In group therapy, ego functions are exercised under the monitoring guidance of the team, whilst in the extra-verbal field (art therapy, music therapy), and in relations with their individual therapist and the nurses, patients are freer to phantasize and can cast themselves in the role of strong and ideal objects (cf. pp. 174–8).

Green (1975) pinpointed four recurring mechanisms in borderline patients: somatic consummation, acting out, splitting and withdrawal of cathexis. All led to a feeling of emptiness. Our experience generally corroborated this, although a further element came to play in the case reported above, namely what is termed 'grouping' by Denford (1983) and 'gang organization' by Hartocollis (1980). In the hospital setting, gangs are experienced as a threat to the survival of the therapist team – and even of the institution as a whole. The hallmark of grouping behaviour is that patients with like personality structures form alliances and act rebelliously in a bid to demarcate themselves from the psychoanalytic team. Exchange of self-aspects, the search for a common hate-object and 'brother/sisterhood' are relevant factors. Therapists are idealized until their withholding and disciplining functions become apparent; at which point they are transformed into Aunt Sallys against whom the group targets its operations. Projective mechanisms of this kind forestall conflict among the parties to the grouping. Eventually the aggressive charge of the constellation in question penetrates both small-group and large-group processes; true political-style operations are then launched.

It is the growth of transference splitting, sparking off as it does countertransference reactions in the therapists, that constitutes the biggest challenge to the integrative capabilities of an inpatient therapist team. Yet a team crisis like that surrounding the discharge incident recounted above can turn out to be a therapeutic watershed. A patient will only overcome the split inside himself once he is confident that the team can carry the burden of splitting and will not be torn apart by the embodiments of opposites it is called upon to sustain. He then feels able to identify with the therapeutic task and may well venture a glance into the chaos of his inner world.

It is of course difficult in real life to draw an absolute distinction between multidimensional and one-dimensional transference. Multidimensional relations develop as inpatient therapy progresses, i.e. we are dealing with a process. Neurotic patients tend to respond best and therapeutic outcome is generally good (cf. pp. 85–103). Some cases nevertheless straddle the line between one-dimensional and multidimensional transference. Depressive patients may remain under the sway of a rigid superego for prolonged periods – sometimes until termination of therapy. Throughout treatment they continue to complain and accuse; their abiding impression in all their relationships is that they are being bossed around, criticized and put down. Other patients are compliant and retiring, with a tendency to over-rationalize; they exist in isolation and show no sign of affective attachments. Given that the clinical environment induces labile states and regression, such defence mechanisms are not generally sustained for long. After a month or so, we expect affective object relating to develop. Other than in extreme cases of regression, with clear-cut patterns of object choice and response to setting, it is unlikely that a fixed transference constellation can be predicted from the very outset.

In our experience, multidimensional and one-dimensional transference generally occur in patients with neurotic disorders; splitting transference of the kind described above is more prevalent in borderline patients. Special types of splitting can also be observed in patients suffering from recognized psychosomatic disorders (e.g. ulcerative colitis, hypertension, peptic ulcer) and in cases of perversion. The therapeutic profile of such patients resembles that of those with borderline personality structure, although pathology and individual psychodynamics vary.

Vignette 4

The case of a 39-year-old patient should help to clarify this. The woman in question had begun to suffer from periodic bouts of ulcerative colitis eight years before admission to the unit. Hospitalization was required on several occasions. The first bout occurred following the death of her over-idealized mother, who figured in her recollections as 'spotless'. The patient was unable to overcome this loss through mourning. Unconscious feelings of guilt remained; she had not sufficiently stood by her mother and ought never to have parted from her. She accused her father of not having given her mother adequate support either, and found his re-marriage a year after her death 'shameless'. She had known a variety of men, but always broke off the relationship because they were not 'good enough'. She could not even bring herself to marry the father of her 6-year-old daughter. The relationship with this child was symbiotic and she justified the closeness of the bond by her wish to be a good mother. She effectively used the girl as a replacement mother; any separation from her made her ill.

The patient was a very sober, orderly, no-nonsense woman (alexithymic?), yet her instant desire for acceptance at the very first therapeutic interview betrayed her need for a replacement object to idealize. This explained her willingness to be separated from her daughter, who spent the weekdays in the good care of relatives. For about six weeks the therapeutic process bore the imprint of her idealization of the unit and the therapists in it. She was solicitous towards fellow patients and anxious that they share her idealized picture of her childhood and family life. Music therapy was dominated over this period by her insistence on homophony, reflecting her desire for merger. She and another two women patients in the group formed a kind of symbiotic triad; they were always together and undertook joint activities outside the hospital. When the group therapist broached this with the patient, she was hurt and visibly annoyed. Unlike the borderline patients described above, she did not have the ability to put her affects into words or deeds; instead she grew even more silent and withdrawn and the colitis came back. Submitting to the necessary medical treatment and nursing care was not at all easy for her. She tried to mask her need of help by running errands for other patients etc.; yet deep down she enjoyed the expressions of concern from nurses and fellow patients. Her somatic symptoms receded and she took an interest in dancing and finding a new partner. By now she had reached a stage where she could allow herself to give vent to aggressive affects towards others. She admitted to being irritated by the restrictive nature of the setting; she told the group therapist that she found him lacking in understanding; she made it clear that she thought a particular nurse was being bossy and off-hand. Negative affects no longer needed to be somatized since she had now learnt to project them on to us. She was beginning to ease herself away from symbiotic objects (the nurses and the two other patients) and parted from them without tears when the time came to leave the unit. For over a year she continued to attend as an outpatient. We discovered that her relationship with her daughter was now on a new footing and both were willing to admit a 'third party' in the shape of a new male acquaintance.

We also came across splitting of the transference when treating cases of perversion (paedophilia, exhibitionism, transsexualism). Although our experience in this area has been limited, the results are worth reporting for the light they shed on the nature of transference.

Vignette 5

The 40-year-old patient presented complaining of a series of problems: paedophile homosexual tendencies, a failed marriage, conflict at work, severe inner turmoil. Therapy began and a particular object configuration soon took shape. Some patients and staff members were positively cathected; to these he talked freely, especially about his perversion. Other were negatively cathected and 'bad'; they despised and punished him, so he believed. He sought out the former and avoided the latter. The first group included his individual therapist, the music therapist and a nurse (all one-to-one relationships). He seemed confident that they would not discuss his problem with other team members. The forms of musical expression he used in his interaction with the music therapist, and his inability to see her as a separate object, pointed unequivocally to a symbiotic relationship. The rhythms he produced were regular and lulling, designed to restore his narcissistic equilibrium.

At a certain point he decided to broach his problem with a patient from the 'bad' group. Much to his 'horror', disclosure met with comprehension, not rejection. He was completely thrown and broke down. A nurse later raised the incident with him and he voiced his bewilderment that avowal could herald such a sense of emptiness and abandonment. He had clearly derived a degree of inner security from splitting his object world into 'good and comprehending' and 'rejecting and contemptuous'. No longer able to maintain this defensive strategy, he was forced to acknowledge the breadth of feelings he had inside himself; negative and aggressive affects had previously clustered around his perversion. Structural defect was sustained by splitting. Working through the transference process enabled him to overcome the divide between tolerant objects, which protected and understood him, and persecuting objects, which despised him for his deviant behaviour.

Perhaps I might now venture a general description of the processes involved in the treatment of inpatients with structural ego disorder, particularly the psychosomatic group. Common patterns do emerge, even if each individual case is unique (cf. Janssen and Quint 1987). Unless they are in a regressed state on admission, these patients normally adapt well to the practical implications of the inpatient setting, but cut themselves off emotionally.

Psychosomatic patients are happy to have the Registrar around, for there is always the hope that he will confirm their own view of their illness. In his capacity as departmental physician, he examines them, gives advice, and possibly drugs, where necessary making referrals to a specialist.

Some patients are unable to enter into affective relationships for weeks on end; they remain aloof, describing events in terms of bare facts and offering no personal or emotional input. Their longing for an idealized object usually leads them to transfer affects on to one of the therapists, bringing the first phase of therapy to a close. Idealized relationships, based as they are on need and desire, boost the patient's motivation and ability to bond with the therapist. Allowing this process to unfold is vital for the patient's future progress.

During the second phase of treatment, patients learn about boundaries and absence. They realize that they cannot be united with the longed-for, idealized object. It will not always be at their disposal. Objects must be shared with fellow patients and other therapists. Patients with structural ego disorders find this knowledge hard to bear. Archaic fears and aggressive impulses are reactivated; veritable narcissistic crises often ensue. Borderline personalities act out their disappointment and anger, or else project them defensively on to the therapist (*Vignette 3*). Psychosomatics abreact physically (*Vignette 4*), discharging split-off negative affects in a 'somatic creation' (McDougall 1974). Physical complaints gain in intensity and somatic treatment may be necessary. In this way psychosomatic patients obtain the object relationships they need to survive, engineering for themselves the services of a good, nurturing mother.

Although patients with psychosomatic disorders react primarily with their bodies during the early stages of therapy, they may develop borderline-style transference splitting as the process advances. This rarely leads to serious acting out, but is important therapeutically in that they learn to distinguish between good objects, which spoil and pamper, and bad objects, which threaten and disturb. They may maintain a symbiotic and incorporative relationship with one therapist, while feeling threatened, wounded and constricted by another; the 'bad' therapist will then become negatively cathected. The therapeutic goal is to induce patients to make a leap away from established psychical routines. We always encouraged them to project their archaic aggression on to the therapist group. For this to work, it is essential that team members sustain a holding function. They do this by by offering care, nurture and diatrophic support. The shift from somatic discharge to psychical projection is a watershed in the process of working through negative object experiences. The team accepts these projections and patients are in a position to reformulate their affects in more mature form: verbally (in group therapy) and pictorially (in art therapy).

The next step is to overcome splitting. This cannot happen until team members have acknowledged and overcome certain things within themselves. Fear, death anxiety, loss anxiety, aggressive countertransference – all these things can be set off by the behaviour, somatic state and projections of patients. The countertransference triggered by swings from symbiotic/incorporative to aggressive/destructive conduct is particularly difficult to handle (cf. pp. 124–5). Therapists experience narcissistic hurt and are tempted to stand off and reject the patient. Signs of this happening include efforts to have patients transferred, refusal to abide by the rules of the setting and suggestions that the patient is beyond the reach of therapy. The team faces a serious challenge. It must demonstrate its ability to sustain a nurturing role – in feeling and action, as well as in words. It is called upon to contain and carry a whole network of seemingly irreconcilable behavioural constellations. If it is successful, the climate created will allow patients to experience the kind of succour they never received from their mother. They will introject this new world and retain it within themselves as a positive maternal imago. The primary layer of structural ego damage is in this way repaired. These new patterns of relating can then be repeated in future interaction with fellow patients and therapists.

A crucial phase follows: weaning from the therapists. Impending separation reactivates loss anxiety and symptoms may well intensify. The hope is that disappointment and anger will be expressed verbally; memories of past crises, together with the therapy team's management of them, should ideally serve as a model for coping with separation. Provided patients are able to mourn the loss of their new, positively cathected objects, they can generally say goodbye without resorting to decompensation, or deciding to break off relations altogether. As part of the process of mourning, patients take into their own ego structure certain aspects of the therapist; the intrapsychical transformation brought about leads to greater ego autonomy. This leaves them better equipped for life and relationships in the real world.

Now that we have looked at the processes involved in the management of structural ego disorder, let us turn to a key question: what are the curative and healing powers of inpatient psychoanalytic therapy?

The effectiveness and limits of inpatient psychoanalytic therapy

Inpatient psychoanalytic therapy aims to facilitate repetition or restoration of infantile scenes within the multipersonal matrix of the hospital. That is the first step, yet repetition alone does not constitute healing. Patients must not be left abandoned with an 'open wound', deprived of access to therapeutic help. This is precisely what many a psychoanalyst fears. Traditional psychoanalytical wisdom holds that patients with structural ego disorders require prolonged therapy; the relatively short, albeit intensive, treatment available in a hospital is totally inadequate. Such assumptions are frequently based on insufficient knowledge of the way inpatient psychotherapy operates. Critics are apt to focus on where things go wrong – and therapy can fail to achieve its goals in any setting. It none the less behoves analysts working in an inpatient environment to be vigilant; pitfalls do exist.

How does inpatient psychoanalytic therapy *cure* people? Not an easy question; even non-hospital analysts are hard put to deliver a clear-cut answer in respect of their practice, however convinced of its merits they – and many of their patients – may be. Psychoanalysis has always been understood as a form of therapy, from its inception until the present day, yet few have ventured a commitment on its healing dimension (cf. Kächele 1981). Opinions vary as to the true goals and the means to be deployed. Freud and his successors work on the basis of an intact ego (cf. Chapter 2); a person is neurotic if his ego is unable to handle unconscious drive-defence conflict. The aim of therapy is to bring about structural change by promoting ego insight and mellowing the punitive tendencies of the superego. Interpretation is the key instrument in any such process (Sandler *et al*. 1973).

The Kleinian approach is somewhat different in its thrust. Melanie Klein was interested in how object relations develop in early childhood and stressed the active role of projective identification in structuring the ego; the purpose of the psychoanalytic setting is to provide a space which will facilitate ego development. Klein and her followers no longer presuppose an intact ego, capable of viable, integrated object relations. They instead work on the assumption of a structurally damaged ego, which relates to objects in a pre-oedipal way. Modern therapeutic strategies grounded in Kleinian theory are above all associated with the names Balint and Winnicott (cf. Chapter 2). 'Emotional experience' (Cremerius 1979b), not interpretation, emerges as the prime tool of psychoanalysis. Spitz (1956/7) was one of the first to call for the analyst to approach his patients in a maternal, diatrophic manner; Loch (1974) spoke of the therapist 'taking on a nurturing role'. For Fürstenau (1977a, b), what really counted in the analytical process was the dynamic interweaving of experience and insight. My belief is that the healing dimension of inpatient therapy derives from the fact that patients enter a world where they can make up for what has been lacking in their lives to date, namely proper nurturing mothering. The hospital functions as an enabling matrix, facilitating insight into behaviour and helping to resolve inner conflicts.

In our setting, therapeutic space was created by the structuring influence of both institution and team. Patients were offered an environment which was both *holding* and *facilitating* (Winnicott 1965); therapeutic objects were *reliable* (Balint 1968) and acted as receptacles for split-off components of the self, furthering insight into psychical structure. Individuals discovered that rejected and split-off self aspects could after all be accepted. They experienced in the team a viable unit, capable of sustaining their projections (cf. *Vignette 3*, pp. 161–6), and began to process the negative carry-over of infantile object relationships.

A holding, facilitating and diatrophic environment also encourages symbiotic relations, e.g. with individual therapists, nurses, or fellow patients. Homophonic interaction in music therapy is the clearest indicator of symbiosis, yet finding a focus for regressive desires is not an end in itself. Change will not come about until symbiotic configurations yield to more mature patterns of object relating. The 'oedipalization' of relationships should not be hindered by ill-timed interpretation (Blanck and Blanck 1974). As *Vignette 2* demonstrated (see pp. 160–1), oedipal-style relations rekindle patients' motivation to act and ability to love.

Inherent in any symbiotic and idealized relationship is the potential for 'interference'; contact may be limited in time, the other person may be absent etc. Aggressive affects are then reactivated and somatization or acting out may well ensue. The distress experienced can however facilitate the process of separation from maternal objects; patients learn to stand on their own feet and gain autonomy (Blanck and Blanck 1974). Because the setting and the relationships established within it can no longer be taken for granted, the word 'no' takes on real meaning (Spitz 1956/7). Contrary to commonly held beliefs, autonomy is not fostered by preventing regression. Regression engenders the very affects which lead patients to assert independence; it equips them to bid farewell to both hospital and therapists. Their strivings, aggressive as they may be, must be given therapeutic support.

Fürstenau (1977a, b) has written of how a psychoanalyst actually *causes something to happen*. It is the therapist group as a whole which exerts active influence in an institutional setting. Group members provide care and nurture; they also show insight and understanding, inducing patients to work problems through. The very structure of the inpatient environment is an active element in the treatment of borderline patients, who have an abiding tendency to act out. They urgently need stability if they are instead to verbalize narcissistic hurt, anger and emptiness (see pp. 121–2). Psychosomatic patients on the other hand draw greatest benefit from the nurturing dimension of the residential setting.

New experience is not in other words the only factor involved in healing; verbalization is an integral part of the curative process. We have seen how insight can be gained from talking through re-enacted scenes. Speaking about what happens in art and dance movement therapy is also important; inner reality is given plastic form or bodily expression and needs elaboration. Verbalization is especially helpful for patients who are prone to acting out. Talking through the things they do and their interaction with others uncovers infantile distortion of object perception (cf. Rosenfeld 1978). Every therapist, whatever his field, should engage patients in verbalization, allowing insights gained from analysis of his own countertransference to inform his observations. Patients gain a new perspective on their behaviour and begin to re-assess their image of themselves. Translating feelings, actions and affects – in particular negative affects – into words and images boosts the ego's capacity for symbolization (Green 1975). Patients tentatively undertake the difficult task of distinguishing between different categories of objects: phantasized, infantile, primitive and real.

Insight into transference in the here-and-now enhances self-awareness and improves ego achievement; the individual's own needs move to the surface and he is better able to adjust to the realities of the world outside. If he can then make a further leap and perceive the infantile aspect of his relationships and conduct, he will start to comprehend the past through its impact on the present. This is not to claim that inpatient therapy allows the depth of reconstruction of infantile events found in outpatient analysis. Once the process of recollection has been sparked off, however, individual patients may well decide to embark on full outpatient analysis at a later stage.

The expertise of the psychoanalytic adviser is called upon by the team in both areas of healing: the experiential and the insight-oriented. He exercises a holding function and puts what he sees into words. Throughout the therapeutic process he acts as an 'observer' (Devereux 1967), watching what people do, how they interact and what they say about it (verbalization). His analysis of countertransference ensures that maximum benefit is drawn from all therapeutic relationships.

The psychoanalytic adviser's integrating – and regulating – capacities are particularly needed in cases where borderline patients are acting out (*Vignette 3*); the dynamics of splitting can easily end up dividing the team. It strikes me as improbable that a patient's individual therapist could perform the integrative feat referred to by Kernberg (1976b) all on his own; ultimate responsibility for the integrating and regulating side of therapy should rest with the team as a whole, backed by its adviser. Regression leads to externalization of object relations and transference splitting; mutual support among therapists is of the essence. Pulling together is the way to help a structurally damaged ego along the road to repair.

A patient's ability to reconcile contradictory and disruptive elements within himself will improve if he can identify with the integrative approach of the therapy team, or a positively cathected member of it. Take the case of the man mentioned on papes 134–5. He offers a shining example of positive cathexis. Despite projective distortion in other areas of therapy and a general lack of psychical cohesion, the relationship he established with his individual therapist held up well, even surviving his discharge from the unit. Our meeting with him three years later confirmed that introjection of this positive therapeutic relationship had been sufficient to stabilize his ego boundaries. The good, reliable object lived on in his phantasy; the therapist did not need to be physically present, although at the time she had been indispensable. The experience of this relationship, and the insight it granted, left him better equipped to assess people; he no longer burst into fits of rage or fell back on psychotic transference reactions (Kernberg 1975a).

Inpatient psychoanalytic therapy does trigger change and help to make patients' lives more worthwhile. Supported by the therapist team with its integrative skills, they experience what it means to forge positive relations with others and gain insight into the infantile patterns informing their world. The limits of treatment ultimately lie with the individual; not everyone is accessible to therapeutic outreach. Frontiers are also marked out by the many limitations inherent in the hospital setting. Yet the real issue remains how well team and patients work together, as we have seen in so many examples. The deciding factor is whether the patient can find a way into therapy; or, from another vantage point, whether the therapist team can get through to the patient. It is a two-way process and, if it works, the patient enters a libidinally cathected relationship with the therapist team and relives infantile patterns of object relating. Successful rapprochement – and our surveys (cf. pp. 85–103) revealed a rate of 50 per cent in terms of good or satisfactory outcome – opens up the prospect of a whole new world of activities and relationships beyond the hospital.

Appendix

Tables

Table 1 Inpatient psychotherapy: survey of results (N = 87)

No.	Age	Sex	Marital status	Occupation	Symptoms and their duration	Diagnosis	Duration of therapy	Score at 2–6 mths	Score for outcome
1	37	M	Married	Civil servant	Cardiac symptoms, mild compulsion, agitation, anxiety, sweating 9 years	Cardiac neurosis, obsessive-compulsive personality disorder	3 mths inpatient	0	16 mths 0
2	20	F	Single	Trainee nurse	Bulimia, anorexia, self-induced vomiting, laxative abuse, dysmenorrhoea and oligomenorrhoea, sleep disorder, agitation, mild compulsion, aggressive outbreaks, suicide attempts 4 years	Anorexia nervosa, hysterical neurosis	3 mths inpatient	2	15 mths 1
3	42	F	Married	Housewife	Agoraphobia, compulsive ideation, headaches, sleep disorder, nervousness, erythrophobia, fainting fits, depressive moods, frigidity 25 years	Hysterical neurosis	3 mths inpatient	1	15 mths 1
4	27	F	2 × divorced	Office employee	Severe depression, 3 suicide attempts, frigidity 10 years	Depressive neurosis	3 mths inpatient	0	–
5	27	F	Single	Secretary	Agoraphobia, depressive moods, sleep disorder, vomiting, diarrhoea 4 years	Neurosis with depressive, anxious and hysterical traits	3 mths inpatient	1	16 mths 0

No.	Age	Sex	Marital status	Occupation	Symptoms and their duration	Diagnosis	Duration of therapy	Score at 2–6 mths	Score for outcome
6	26	F	Single	Nursery teacher	Compulsive controlling, depressive moods, poor rapport, headaches, nausea, vomiting 2 years	Obsessional/counter-depressive neurosis	3 mths inpatient	2	19 mths 2
7	36	F	Married	Housewife	Depressive moods, obsessional brooding over marital problems 1 year	Hysterical neurosis	3 mths inpatient	1	14 mths 1
8	42	M	Married	Electrician	Heart problems, dizziness, nausea, vomiting, abdominal problems, fear of death, agoraphobia, depressive moods 5 years	Cardiac neurosis, personality disorder	3 mths inpatient	0	14 mths 0
9	26	F	Single	Student	Overpowering examination nerves, difficulty sustaining study 2 mths	Hysterical neurosis	3 mths inpatient	2	18 mths 2
10	20	F	Single	Assistant pharmacist	Anxiety attacks, paroxysmal tachycardia, sweating 1.5 years	Anxiety neurosis	3 mths inpatient	3	13 mths 3
11	29	M	Married	Personnel clerk	Heart pain, shortage of breath, facial neuralgia, headaches, visual disturbance, impotence, agoraphobia, anxiety attacks 3 years	Hysterical neurosis, with anxious traits	3 mths inpatient	2	14 mths 2
12	22	F	Single	Telex operator	Suicide attempts, frigidity 2 years	Hysterical neurosis	3 mths inpatient	2	9 mths 2

	Age	Sex	Marital status	Occupation	Symptoms / duration	Diagnosis	Treatment		Follow-up	
13	21	F	Single	Technical draftswoman	Depressive moods, anxiety episodes, 1 suicide attempt, periodic drug abuse, heart problems, sweating, nausea, headaches, frigidity 3 years	Depressive neurosis	3 mths inpatient	1	8 mths	1
14	33	M	Married	Teacher	Periodic cardiac pain, fear of death, difficulty sustaining work 7 years	Cardiac neurosis, personality disorder	3 mths inpatient	1	15 mths	2
15	23	M	Single	Student	Depressive moods, poor rapport, impotence 5 years	Hysterical neurosis	3 mths inpatient	1	15 mths	1
16	24	M	Married	Administrative employee	Abdominal pain, headaches, muscular tension, fainting fits, constipation, diarrhoea, impotence, depressive moods, suicidal ideation 9 years	Narcissistic personality disorder	3 mths inpatient	1	36 mths	1
17	24	M	Single	Student	Anxiety states, sleep disorder, poor rapport, abdominal problems, potency difficulties, periodic drug abuse, tendency towards self-neglect Many years	Borderline personality disorder	4.5 mths inpatient 1 yr outpatient	0	14 mths	0
18	22	M	Married	Technical draftsman	Cardiac pain, paroxysmal tachycardia, shortage of breath, dizziness, nausea, headaches, stomach cramps, diarrhoea, fear of death, agoraphobia 2 years	Cardiac neurosis, anxious and hysterical traits	4.5 mths inpatient 1 yr outpatient	1	24 mths	0
19	21	F	Married	Special needs teacher	Ulcerative colitis, vomiting, frigidity, depressive moods 6 years	Narcissistic personality disorder	4.5 mths inpatient 1 yr outpatient	2	24 mths	2

No.	Age	Sex	Marital status	Occupation	Symptoms and their duration	Diagnosis	Duration of therapy	Score at 2–6 mths	Score for outcome
20	31	F	Single	Administrative employee	Migraine, frigidity, agoraphobia, severe depressive moods, 1 suicide attempt 6 years	Depressive-hysterical neurosis	4.5 mths inpatient 1 yr out-patient	2	12 mths 2
21	22	M	Single	Student	Poor rapport, problems sustaining work, depressive moods 3 years	Narcissistic personality disorder	4.5 mths inpatient	1	23 mths 2
22	31	M	Married	Technician	Itching, abdominal problems, depressive moods, hyperactivity, alcohol and pharmacological substance abuse 5 years	Depressive-narcissistic personality disorder	2.5 mths inpatient	0	–
23	20	F	Single	Doctor's assistant	Compulsive controlling, obsessional ideation, depressive moods, frigidity 4 years	Obsessional neurosis	4.5 mths inpatient 1 yr out-patient	2	24 mths 3
24	22	F	Single	Insurance clerk	Anorexia, amenorrhoea, vomiting 5 years	Hysterical-depressive neurosis	4 mths inpatient	0	24 mths 1
25	23	M	Single	Student	Searing pains in face and neck, concentration difficulties, memory disturbance, depressive moods 3 years	Hysterical neurosis	4 mths inpatient 1 yr out-patient	3	30 mths 3

No.	Age	Sex	Marital status	Occupation	Symptoms / duration	Diagnosis	Treatment		Follow-up	
26	20	F	Single	Technical draftswoman	Agoraphobia, erythrophobia, fear of fainting, contact anxiety, headaches 8 years	Borderline personality	4 mths inpatient 1 yr outpatient	0	36 mths	0
27	35	F	Married	Housewife	Panic attacks, obsessional ideation, depressive moods, suicide attempts, psychogenic attacks, derealization episodes, anorgasmia, aggressive instinctual outbursts, tendency towards self-neglect 19 years	Borderline personality	4 mths inpatient 1 yr outpatient	1	24 mths	1
28	19	M	Single	Administrative trainee	Depressive moods, suicide attempts, poor rapport, erythrophobia, stuttering, impotence, periodic alcohol abuse 10 years	Depressive neurosis	4 mths inpatient 1 yr outpatient	1	30 mths	2
29	22	M	Single	Student	Concentration difficulties when studying, depressive moods, abdominal problems 2 years	Obsessive-compulsive personality disorder	4 mths inpatient 1 yr outpatient	1	18 mths	1
30	22	M	Single	Student	Heart problems, paroxysmal tachycardia, tendency to sweat, concentration difficulties, impotence, anxiety 1 year	Cardiac neurosis, obsessive-compulsive personality disorder	4 mths inpatient 1 yr outpatient	1	15 mths	1
31	24	F	Single	Student	Severe depressive moods, several suicide attempts, stuttering 8 years	Depressive-hysterical neurosis, pronounced narcissistic traits	4 mths inpatient 1 yr outpatient	2	30 mths	2

No.	Age	Sex	Marital status	Occupation	Symptoms and their duration	Diagnosis	Duration of therapy	Score at 2–6 mths	Score for outcome
32	46	F	Married	Housewife	Depressive moods, suicidal tendencies 26 years	Depressive neurosis	3.5 mths inpatient	2	48 mths 2
33	38	M	Married	Civil servant	Heart problems, anxiety attacks, vomiting, abdominal problems, polyphagia, trembling, periodic alcohol abuse 3 years	Cardiac neurosis, personality disorder	8 mths inpatient	2	48 mths 3
34	42	F	Married	Weaver, crane driver, auxiliary teacher	Back pain (4 spinal operations), headaches, gynaecological problems, aggressive and paranoid reactions, general inner unrest, depressive moods, disturbances of memory and concentration 9 years	Borderline personality	4 mths inpatient	2	36 mths 1
35	40	F	Married	Housewife	Depressive moods, obsessional brooding, dysmenorrhoea Indeterminate duration	Depressive neurosis	3 mths inpatient	1	–
36	29	M	Married	Skilled chemical worker	Compulsive controlling, fear of failure, abdominal pain, diarrhoea 7 years	Obsessional neurosis	8 mths	0	36 mths 0
37	21	F	Married	Housewife	Headaches 1 year	Depressive-hysterical neurosis	2 mths	2	–
38	31	M	Divorced	Metalworker	Stuttering (17 years), erythrophobia, difficulties sustaining work, sweating 2 years	Obsessive-compulsive personality disorder	6 mths inpatient	0	–

No.	Age	Sex	Marital status	Occupation	Symptoms / duration	Diagnosis	Treatment		Follow-up	
39	40	M	Married	Engineering inspector	Depressive moods, sleep disorder, obsessional brooding, abdominal problems, impotence, cardiac pain, inner unrest, paranoid reactions 1.5 years	Borderline personality	1.5 mths inpatient	1	–	
40	23	F	Married	Dental assistant	Migraine, vaginismus, analgesic substance abuse, suicide attempts 9 years	Hysterical neurosis, underlying dysfunction	8 mths inpatient	1	–	
41	25	M	Single	Student	Duodenal ulcer, poor rapport, depressive moods 2 mths	Narcissistic personality disorder	7 mths inpatient	3	96 mths	3
42	23	F	Married	Housewife	Heart problems, dizziness, frigidity, abdominal problems, anxiety attacks, agoraphobia 4 years	Depressive-hysterical neurosis, underlying dysfunction	4 mths inpatient	2	48 mths	2
43	22	F	Single	Housekeeper	Polyphagia, anorexia, vomiting, amenorrhoea, alcohol-, laxative- and appetite suppressant abuse, periodic narcotic drug abuse, tendency towards self-neglect 7 years	Borderline personality	9.5 mths inpatient	2	84 mths	3
44	24	M	Single	Bank clerk	Swallowing difficulties, headaches, premature ejaculation, sexual phobia, concentration disorder 1 year	Obsessive-compulsive personality disorder	8.5 mths inpatient	2	12 mths	2
45	31	F	Married	Commercial clerk	Recurring ulcerative colitis 5 years	Borderline personality disorder, mainly narcissistic	4 mths inpatient	1	84 mths	2

No.	Age	Sex	Marital status	Occupation	Symptoms and their duration	Diagnosis	Duration of therapy	Score at 2–6 mths	Score for outcome
46	23	F	Single	Administrative employee	Obsessional suicidal ideation, considerable motor unrest, trichotillomania, poor rapport 10 years	Borderline personality	7 mths inpatient	2	48 mths 2
47	39	F	Single	Commercial clerk	Recurring ulcerative colitis 8 years	Depressive personality disorder	3 mths inpatient	2	–
48	22	M	Single	Student	Heart problems, headaches, muscular tension, apraxia 2 years	Narcissistic personality disorder	9 mths inpatient	1	60 mths 2
49	33	F	Single	Hairdresser	Ulcerative colitis, up to 20 diarrhoea attacks per day, alcohol abuse, depressive moods, lack of social contact 12 years	Infantile hysterical personality disorder	5.5 mths inpatient	2	84 mths 0
50	23	M	Single	Nurse	Swallowing difficulties, irritable cough, choking fits, diarrhoea, anxiety states, homosexual tendencies 3 years	Narcissistic personality disorder	2 mths inpatient	0	48 mths 2
51	25	F	Single	Student	Anorexia, vomiting, amenorrhoea 4 years	Hysterical and narcissistic personality disorder	9 mths inpatient	1	12 mths 1
52	30	F	Divorced	Employee	Anxiety attacks, heart problems, shortage of breath 1 year	Anxiety neurosis	3 mths inpatient	2	12 mths 2
53	38	F	Married	Housewife	Paroxysmal tachycardia, sleep disorder, inner unrest, trembling 1 year	Hysterical-depressive neurosis	3 mths inpatient	2	12 mths 3

No.	Age	Sex	Marital status	Occupation	Symptoms	Diagnosis	Treatment			
54	25	M	Married	Machine operator	Spasmodic heart problems, fear of death, shortage of breath, sweating, eating disorder 1 year	Borderline personality	8.5 mths inpatient	1	36 mths	0
55	39	F	Married	Housewife	Depressive moods, suicidal 7 years	Depressive-hysterical neurosis, with narcissistic traits	5 mths inpatient	1	36 mths	2
56	25	M	Single	Taxi driver	Nocturnal enuresis 20 years	Impulsive personality disorder	2 mths inpatient	0	84 mths	0
57	21	F	Single	Student	Anorexia, self-induced vomiting, amenorrhoea, constipation, laxative abuse, depressive moods, suicide attempts, impulsive kleptomaniac behaviour 4 years	Narcissistic personality disorder	8.5 mths inpatient (3.5 + 5)	2	48 mths	3
58	36	F	Married	Housewife	Gynaecological and abdominal problems, severe nausea, headaches, anorgasmia, cancer phobia, depressive moods. Ever since she was a young woman, but intensification over 2 years prior to therapy	Depressive neurosis	6 mths inpatient	3	–	
59	30	M	Married	Commercial clerk	Acute breakdowns, obsessional ideation, paedophile tendencies (?), 1 suicide attempt ca. 16 years	Borderline personality	7.5 mths inpatient	0	48 mths	0
60	34	F	Divorced	Secretary	Heart problems, fear of death, shortage of breath, paroxysmal tachycardia, agoraphobia, obesity 20 years	Cardiac neurosis, personality disorder	1.5 mths inpatient	0	94 mths	1

No.	Age	Sex	Marital status	Occupation	Symptoms and their duration	Diagnosis	Duration of therapy	Score at 2–6 mths	Score for outcome
61	39	F	Married	Housewife	Migraine (18 years), dyspepsia, hypochondriasis 4 years	Borderline personality	3 mths inpatient	0	84 mths 0
62	31	M	Married	Engineer	Depressive moods; suicidal ideation, fear of failure, cardiac pain, increase in alcohol consumption 3 mths	Obsessive-compulsive personality disorder, with depressive traits	1 mth inpatient (broken off)	1	–
63	20	M	Single	Student	Depressive moods, fear of failure, loss of motivation, difficulty sustaining study, suicidal ideation, headaches 2 years	Depressive neurosis	7.5 mths inpatient	3	12 mths 3
64	19	F	Single	Employee	Homosexuality, depressive moods, suicide attempts, vomiting, nausea, headaches, obesity, periodic alcohol and pharmacological substance abuse ca. 4 years	Borderline personality	7 mths inpatient	2	12 mths 2
65	40	F	Married	Housewife	Migraine, dyspareunia, anorgasmia, depressive moods, suicidal ideation 16 years	Depressive-hysterical neurosis	2 mths inpatient (broken off)	0	–
66	23	F	Single	Student	Swallowing difficulties, loss of appetite, weight loss, allergic asthma (pollen allergy), sleep disorder, heart problems 1.5 years	Obsessional-counter-depressive neurosis	8.5 mths inpatient	3	–

67	43	M	Married	Skilled worker	Nocturnal ejaculation, severe sleep disorder, impotence, prostatitis, paranoid reactions 36 years	Borderline personality	3 mths inpatient	0	60 mths	0
68	35	M	Married	Policeman	Depression accompanied by agitation, weeping fits, diffuse anxiety and panic states, aggressive and paranoid reactions, suicidal ideation, abdominal pain, heart problems, sleep disorder, homosexuality 2 years	Borderline personality	7 mths inpatient	1	36 mths	1
69	27	M	Married	Skilled worker	Swallowing difficulties, vomiting, abdominal pain, headaches, weight loss, eczema, depressive moods 7 years	Obsessive-compulsive narcissistic personality disorder	8 mths inpatient	1	36 mths	2
70	33	F	Married	Housewife	Hypochondriasis, depressive moods, anxiety-induced agitation 8 years	Depressive-hysterical neurosis, with obsessional traits	8 mths inpatient	2	84 mths	2
71	25	M	Single	Fitter	Compulsive controlling, fear of failure, examination nerves, claustrophobia, tendency to sweat 15 years	Obsessional neurosis	9 mths inpatient	2	–	
72	22	F	Single	Administrative employee	Eating problems, headaches, dizziness, back pain, loss of libido, depressive moods 2 years	Borderline personality	4.5 mths inpatient	1	–	

No.	Age	Sex	Marital status	Occupation	Symptoms and their duration	Diagnosis	Duration of therapy	Score at 2–6 mths	Score for outcome
73	20	F	Married	Administrative employee	Ulcerative colitis, anorgasmia, depressive moods 4 years	Narcissistic personality disorder	5 mths inpatient	3	–
74	45	F	Married	Housewife	Vertigo, headaches 9 years	Hysterical neurosis	7 mths inpatient	2	84 mths 1
75	27	F	Divorced	Secretary	Polyphagia, self-induced vomiting, amenorrhoea, periodic alcohol abuse 1.5 years	Infantile hysterical personality disorder, with narcissitic traits	9 mths inpatient	1	–
76	26	F	Married	Housewife	Anxiety attacks, shortage of breath, derealization episodes, suicide attempts, headaches, psychogenic paralysis of one arm, periodic alcohol and pharmacological substance abuse, tendency towards self-neglect 14 years	Borderline personality	6 mths inpatient	0	–
77	42	F	Married	Housewife	Cardiac pain, depressive moods, anxiety states, inner unrest 15 years	Depressive-hysterical neurosis	5 mths inpatient	2	84 mths 3
78	26	F	Single	Commercial clerk	Uterine problems (chronic), 8 gynaecological procedures for endometriosis, nausea, back pain, headaches 2 years	Depressive, mainly masochistic, personality disorder	6.5 mths inpatient	1	–

No.	Age	Sex	Marital status	Occupation	Symptoms	Diagnosis	Treatment		Follow-up	
79	25	F	Married	Housewife	Claustrophobia, agoraphobia, problems sustaining work, eating phobia, weight loss 0.5 years	Narcissistic personality disorder	9.5 mths inpatient	2	48 mths	0
80	31	M	Married	Civil servant	Recurring duodenal ulcer (8 years), anxiety attacks, agoraphobia, impotence, heart problems, trembling 2 years	Obsessive-compulsive personality disorder	3 mths inpatient	1	84 mths	1
81	49	M	Married	Painter and decorator	Heart problems, headaches, sweating, dizziness, shortness of breath, anxiety attacks, agoraphobia, apraxia 6 years	Cardiac neurosis, narcissistic personality disorder	4.5 mths inpatient	1	84 mths	1
82	19	M	Single	Skilled worker	Obsessional ideation, compulsion, paranoid reactions, hand trembling (1 year); nocturnal enuresis, stuttering (since childhood)	Borderline personality, with obsessive-compulsive traits	12.5 mths + 7.5 mths inpatient	2	12 mths	2
83	32	M	Married	Skilled worker	Heart problems, visual disorder, muscle pain, anxiety attacks 4 years	Anxiety neurosis	5 mths inpatient	2	–	
84	19	F	Single	School student	Compulsive controlling, anxiety attacks, self-destructive tendencies, suicide attempts, screaming and crying fits, derealization episodes 5 years	Obsessional neurosis, with borderline traits	8.5 mths inpatient	2	84 mths	2
85	31	W	Married	Housewife	Compulsive controlling, obsessional ideation 4 years	Obsessional counter-depressive neurosis	8.5 mths inpatient	2	–	

No.	Age	Sex	Marital status	Occupation	Symptoms and their duration	Diagnosis	Duration of therapy	Score at 2–6 mths	Score for outcome
86	22	F	Single	Trainee commercial clerk	Washing compulsion, fear of contamination through touch, fear of soiling (ca. 10 years), anorexia, amenorrhoea 1 year	Most probably, psychotic personality structure, obsessive-neurotic compensation	6 mths inpatient	0	–
87	31	M	Divorced	Manual worker	Heart problems, fear of heart attack, cancer phobia, headaches, stuttering, poor rapport 5 years	Cardiac neurosis, narcissistic personality disorder	6 mths inpatient	2	84 mths 2

Table 1a Survey of the results of inpatient psychotherapy

No.	Authors	N	Diagnosis	Sex M (%)	Sex F (%)	Age (yrs)	Type of therapy	Duration	Method of assessment	Results
1	Amds et al. (1967)	289	Neuroses; functional organic disorders	61.2	38.8	~32	Bipolar model (Enke et al. 1964; Hau 1969)	~69.5 days	Evaluation by therapy team	48.7%: improvement in the symptom and human relations
2	Baerwolff (1958)	82	Organic neuroses	–	–	–	Inpatient psychotherapy	67.8 days	Evaluation by treatment team + outside assessment, including by health insurance company medical expert	79%: therapeutic success; also structural change
3	Balzer et al. (1980)	41	Psychoneuroses; psychosomatic complaints	–	–	–	Bipolar inpatient/ outpatient group therapy model (Bräutigam 1974)	3mths inpatient; 2 yrs outpatient	Bales Interaction Profile; interviews, Rorschach Test	44%: satisfactory or very satisfactory improvement
4	Beckmann et al. (1976/7)	13	Psychosomatic complaints; psychoneuroses	–	–	–	Integrative model (Stephanos 1973)	4 mths inpatient; up to 4 yrs outpatient	Gießen Test	Good results in respect of therapeutic goal set (internalization of the libidinal object); stable for over 4 yrs

No.	Authors	N	Diagnosis	Sex M (%)	F (%)	Age (yrs)	Type of therapy	Duration	Method of assessment	Results
5	Degler et al. (1967)	107	Neuroses; functional organic disorders	66	41	~32	Bipolar model (Enke et al. 1964; Hau 1969)	59.7 days	Tests by outside therapists and hospital therapists; questionnaire	45.2%: improvement maintained after 5 yrs
6	Denford et al. (1983)	28	Severe personality disorders; borderline syndromes; alcoholism	18	10	~27	Therapeutic community + individual analytic psychotherapy	6 mths–2 yrs	In-house clinical rating scale	Fair and satisfactory results for neuroses and florid depression in high IQ patients with no previous treatment history
7	Deter (1981)	31	Anorexia nervosa	–	–	–	Medicopsychosomatic model (Hahn et al. 1974; Petzold 1979)	3 mths inpatient	30 assessment forms giving somatic, psychic and social data	Improvements, e.g. weight gain
8	Ermann (1974)	50	Neuroses; functional organic disorders	31	19	18–47	Bipolar model; inpatient individual and group therapy (Beese 1977)	100–200 days	Gießen Complaints List	Level of symptomatic improvement during therapy dependent on length of treatment

9	Göllner et al. (1978)	94	Neuroses; personality disorders; psychosomatic complaints	67	33	18–38	Bipolar model; inpatient individual and group therapy (Beese 1977)	av. 4 mths inpatient	FPI, Complaints List, Malan method (1963)	45.6%: clear improvement, i.e. initial therapeutic goal achieved; 59%: improvement in the symptom
10	Heigl-Evers (1969)	443	Neuroses; organic neuroses; psychosomatic complaints	214	229	21–55	Bipolar model; limited inpatient group therapy (24–30 double sessions)	8–10 wks	Questionnaire	76% M, 72% F: symptomatic relief or sub-stantial improvement; 15% M, 13% F: complete loss of symptom; 57% M, 47% F: career promotion; 63% M, 64% F: improvement in human relations
11	Kind and Rotach-Fuchs (1968)	98	Neuroses; psychosomatic complaints	–	–	–	⅓: psychotherapy; ⅔: psychopharma-cotherapy	–	Check-up in form of medical examination	Upon discharge: 70% substantial improvement; follow-up 10 yrs later: 65% improvement or cure (30%). Greater stability in *improved* category in wake of psychotherapy

No.	Authors	N	Diagnosis	Sex M (%)	Sex F (%)	Age (yrs)	Type of therapy	Duration	Method of assessment	Results
12	Köndgen and Überla (1962)	150	Neuroses; personality disorders; functional organic disorders	100	50	15–61 ~31	Bipolar model with group therapy (Enke et al. 1964)	~61.2 days	Evaluation by members of therapy group not directly involved in treatment	60%: improvement; 23% slight improvement; 17%: no improvement
13	Kordy et al. (1983)	98	Psychoneuroses; psychosomatic complaints	–	–	–	Bipolar inpatient/ outpatient model with group therapy (Bräutigam 1974; Von Rad and Rüppell 1975)	3 mths inpatient; 2 yrs outpatient	Therapist evaluation; rating by independent assessors; self-reports	~50% improvement on assessor rating; 53%: self-reports; 80%: therapist evaluation
14	Langen (1956)	66	Neuroses; personality disorders	–	–	–	Multidimensional inpatient psychotherapy (Langen 1956)	av. 7.5 wks	Evaluation by hospital therapists	55.5%: improvement; 26% satisfactory improvement; 23%: no improvement

15	Mentzel and Mentzel (1977)	247	Neuroses; functional organic disorders (some chronic)	–	–	–	Psychosomatic *Kurklinik* + group therapy	6–8 wks	Questionnaire	Initial symptomatic improvement; recurrence of symptom after 1 yr. Enhanced post-discharge stability with group therapy; also less sick leave, reduced reliance on drugs, fewer visits to doctor
16	Pohlen and Bautz (1974)	54	Schizophrenia; hysterias; depression; obsessional neuroses etc.	28	26	~30	Integrative inpatient model, with closed and open groups (Pohlen 1972)	4 mths inpatient	Gießen Test; 16 PF Test; Complaints List	No difference between closed and open groups
17	Pohlen and Bautz (1978)	40	Schizophrenia; hysterias; depression; obsessional neuroses etc.	–	–	–	Integrative model (Pohlen 1972)	4 mths inpatient	Gießen Test; 16PF Test; Complaints List	Same results in same setting with different therapists

No.	Authors	N	Diagnosis	Sex M (%)	F (%)	Age (yrs)	Type of therapy	Duration	Method of assessment	Results
18	Von Rad and Werner (1981)	52	Neuroses; psychosomatic complaints	26	26	30	Bipolar inpatient/ outpatient model with group therapy (Von Rad and Rüppell 1975)	3 mths inpatient/ 2 yrs outpatient	Gießen Test	Reduction in depressive symptoms and increase in stable couple relationships (neurotics). Improved self-esteem and greater independence (psychosomatic patients)
19	Rüger (1981)	24	Severe neuroses; borderline syndromes; non-florid psychoses	12	12	~28	Inpatient/ outpatient group therapy (Rüger 1981)	3 mths inpatient/ 2 yrs outpatient	Psychometric tests; interviews	Reduction in depressive symptoms, psychosomatic disturbances and complaints. Enhanced self-confidence. Improvement in human relations and communication

No.	Study	N	Diagnosis			Age	Model	Duration	Assessment	Results
20	Schwarz (1979)	32	Depressive neuroses (N 20); obsessional neuroses (N 12)	19	13	~31	Integrative model 4 mths inpatient with inpatient group therapy and outpatient psychotherapy (Pohlen 1972)		Interviews; 16 PF Test, Complaints List	72%: improvement in the symptom; 43%: structural change (higher self-esteem, better rapport); 80%: improvement in human relations
21	Sellschopp-Rüppell (1977)	45	Neuroses; psychosomatic complaints	–	–	–	Bipolar inpatient/ outpatient model with group therapy (Von Rad and Rüppell 1975)	3 mths inpatient	Questionnaire and clinical rating	Good therapeutic results (psychosomatic patients included)
22	Wiegmann (1955)	459	Organic neuroses	–	–	–	Inpatient psychotherapy (Wiegmann 1968)	~42 days	Evaluation by hospital therapists	Only 17% with no improvement
23	Zauner (1969)	473	Neuroses; functional organic disorders (some patients on invalidity pensions; limited social mobility)	224	249	21–55; 35 yrs	Brief bipolar inpatient therapy	Min. 4 wks	Questionnaire	On discharge: 81% (384) symptomatic relief or improvement. After 5 yrs: 65% (308) symptomatic improvement or relief + career enhancement

Table 2: Data on the 87 patients surveyed

	Bipolar model	Integrative model	Total
Age	19–42 ~26.2	19–49 ~30	
Sex:			
Female	17	34	51
Male	14	22	36
Marital status:			
Married	11	31	42
Single	19	19	38
Divorced	1	6	7
Occupation:			
In training (e.g.student)	10	8	18
Unskilled worker/employee	–	3	3
Skilled worker	5	13	18
Executive employee/ civil servant	12	16	28
Administrative employee/ civil servant	1	1	2
Self employed	–	–	–
Housewife	3	15	18

Table 3 Results of therapy

| | Follow-up after 2–6 months (N = 87) | | | | Outcome studies | | | |
| | Bipolar model (Patient nos 1–31) N = 31 | | Integrative model (Patient nos 32–87) N = 56 | | Bipolar model (Patient nos 1–31) N = 29 | | Integrative model (Provisional results) N = 37 | |
	N	(%)	N	(%)	N	(%)	N	(%)
Score 3 Good therapeutic result; substantial improvement in the symptom; considerable structural change	2	6.5	5	8.9	3	10.3	7	19
Score 2 Satisfactory therapeutic result; improvement in the symptom; noticeable structural change	9	29.0	24	42.9	10	34.5	14	38
Score 1 Fair therapeutic result; valuable false solution; loss of symptom or symptomatic improvement; mild improvement; no appreciable changes in the problems of human relations	13	42.0	16	28.6	10	34.5	7	19
Score 0 Therapeutic failures; no symptomatic change, or deterioration in the symptom; no structural change	7	22.6	11	19.6	6	20.7	9	24

Table 4 Statistical breakdown of psychodynamic characteristics

	Model 1 (N = 31)			Model 2 (N = 56)		
	Total	Score 3 + 2	Score 1 + 0	Total	Score 3 + 2	Score 1 + 0
Oedipal object relating patterns	16	9	7	18	13	4
Pre-oedipal object relating patterns	15	2	13	38	16	22
Neurotic ego disorders	24	9	15	37	23	14
Structural ego disorders	7	2	5	19	6	13
Anxiety level:						
Castration/superego	13	6	7	14	9	5
Object loss/loss of love	16	5	11	32	17	15
Annihilation	2	0	2	10	3	7
Defence level:						
Hysterical	4	2	2	3	2	1
Obsessional-phobic	21	7	14	20	12	8
Depressive	4	2	2	16	9	7
Borderline/narcissistic	2	0	2	17	6	11

Bibliography

Ahlbrecht, W. (1969) 'Großgruppen in einer psychosomatischen Kuranstalt', *Gruppenpsychotherapie und Gruppendynamik* 3: 109–11.

Ahlbrecht, W., Ermann, M. and Mentzel, G. (1972) 'Patienten-Mitverwaltung in einer psychosomatischen Kurklinik', *Zeitschrift für Psychotherapie und medizinische Psychologie* 22: 54–65.

Ahrens, S., Freiwald, M. and Rath H. (1983) 'Psychoanalytische stationäre Gruppentherapie bei narzißtisch gestörten Patienten', *Gruppenpsychotherapie und Gruppendynamik* 18: 341–9.

Arfsten, A.J., Auchter, T., Hoffmann, S.O., Kindt, H. and Stemmer, T. (1975) 'Zur stationären Behandlung psychotherapeutischer Problempatienten oder: Noch ein Modell stationärer Psychotherapie', *Gruppenpsychotherapie und Gruppendynamik* 9: 212–20.

Arfsten, A.J. and Hoffmann, S.O. (1978) 'Stationäre psychoanalytische Psychotherapie als eigenständige Behandlungsform', *Praxis der Psychotherapie* 23: 233–45.

Argelander, H. (1963/4) 'Die Analyse psychischer Prozesse in der Gruppe', *Psyche* 17: 450–70, 481–515.

—— (1968) 'Gruppenanalyse unter Anwendung des Strukturmodells', *Psyche* 22: 913–33.

—— (1972) *Gruppenprozesse, Wege zur Anwendung der Psychoanalyse in Behandlung, Lehre und Forschung*, Reinbek: Rowohlt.

Arnds, H.G., Hillenbrand, D. and Studt, H.H. (1967) 'Stationäre psychotherapeutische Behandlungen', *Münchener medizinische Wochenschrift* 109: 467–71.

Arnds, H.G. and Studt, H.H. (1973) 'Zur Durchführung stationärer Psychotherapie', in T.F. Hau (ed.) (1975) *Psychosomatische Medizin in ihren Grundzügen*, Stuttgart: Hippokrates.

Baerwolff, H. (1958) 'Katamnestische Ergebnisse stationärer analytischer Psychotherapie', *Zeitschrift für psychosomatische Medizin* 5: 80–91.

Balint, M. (1968) *The Basic Fault: Therapeutic Aspects of Regression*, London: Tavistock Publications.

Balint, E. and Norell, J.S. (eds) (1975) *Six Minutes for the Patient*, London: Tavistock.

Balint, M., Ornstein, P.H. and Balint, E. (1972) *Focal Psychotherapy: An*

Example of Applied Psychoanalysis, London: Tavistock.

Balzer, W., Kuchenhoff, B., Ranch, H. and Sellschopp-Rüppell, A. (1980) 'Kurzzeitergebnisse und prognostische Gesichtspunkte bei stationären analytischen Psychotherapiegruppen', *Gruppenpsychotherapie und Gruppendynamik* 16: 268–86.

Bartemeier, L.H. (1978) 'An historical note on the psychoanalytic hospitals', *The Psychiatric Journal of the University of Ottawa* 3: 77–9.

Battegay, R. (1971) 'Gruppenpsychotherapie als Behandlungsmethode im psychiatrischen Spital', in S. de Schill (ed.) *Psychoanalytische Therapie in Gruppen*, Stuttgart: Klett.

Baumann, U., Barbalk, H. and Seidenstücker, G. (eds) *Klinische Psychologie: Trends in der Forschung und Praxis* 4, Bern: Huber.

Beck, D. (1974) *Die Kurzpsychotherapie*, Berne: Huber.

Beck, D. and Lambelet, L. (1972) 'Resultate der psychoanalytisch orientierten Kurztherapie bei 30 psychosomatisch Kranken', *Psyche* 26: 265–85.

Becker, H. (1981) *Konzentrative Bewegungstherapie*, Stuttgart: Thieme.

Becker, H. and Lüdeke, H. (1978) 'Erfahrung mit der stationären Anwendung psychoanalytischer Therapie', *Psyche* 32: 1–20.

Beckmann, D., Berger, F., Leister, G. and Stephanos, S.A. (1976/7) '4 year follow-up study of inpatient psychosomatic patients', *Psychotherapy and Psychosomatics*, 27: 168–78.

Beese, F. (1971a) 'Indikation zur klinischen Psychotherapie', *Fortschritte der Medizin* 89: 208–10; 234–8.

—— (1971b) 'Das Modell der therapeutischen Gemeinschaft und seine Anwendung auf psychotherapeutische Kliniken', *Gruppenpsychotherapie und Gruppendynamik*, 4: 282–94.

—— (1977) 'Klinische Psychotherapie', in *Die Psychologie des 20. Jahrhunderts, 3*, Zurich: Kindler.

—— (ed.) (1978) *Stationäre Psychotherapie*, Göttingen: Vandenhoeck & Ruprecht.

Begemann, H. (1976) *Patient und Krankenhaus*, Munich: Urban & Schwarzenberg.

Bellak, L. and Small, L. (1965) *Emergency Psychotherapy and Brief Psychotherapy*, New York: Grune and Stratton.

Benedetti, G. (1964) *Klinische Psychotherapie*, Berne: Huber.

Bepperling, W. (1974) 'Modell einer psychosomatischen Krankenhausabteilung', *Deutsches Ärzteblatt* 71: 3496–502.

—— (1981) 'Integration psychosomatischer Versorgung in das Allgemeinkrankenhaus', in Von Uexküll, T. (ed.) *Integrierte Psychosomatische Medizin*, Stuttgart: Schattauer.

Bergin, A.E. (1971) 'The evaluation of therapeutic outcomes', in A.E. Bergin and S.L. Garfield (eds) *Handbook of Psychotherapy and Behaviour Change*, New York: John Wiley.

Bericht zur Lage der Psychiatrie in der Bundesrepublik Deutschland (1975): 'Zur psychiatrischen und psychotherapeutischen/psychosomatischen Versorgung der Bevölkerung', Survey, Deutscher Bundestag, 7. Wahlperiode, Drucksache 7/4200/4201.

Biermann, C. (1975) 'Probleme der Beendigung stationärer Psychotherapie', *Psychotherapie medizinische Psychologie* 25: 149–59.

Bion, W.R. (1961) *Experiences in Groups*, London: Tavistock.

Bister, W. (1977) 'Psychodynamisch orientierte psychiatrische Gruppenarbeit – Möglichkeit und Grenzen', *Gruppenpsychotherapie und Gruppendynamik* 11: 244–55.

Blanck, G. and Blanck, R. (1974) *Ego Psychology: Theory and Practice*, New York: Columbia University Press.

—— (1979) *Ego Psychology II: Psychoanalytic Developmental Psychology*, New York: Columbia University Press.

Borens, R. and Wittich, G. (1976) 'Klinische Rehabilitation von psychosomatischen Patienten – eine Rehabilitation zu Verhaltensgestörten', *Therapiewoche* 26: 950–4.

Bräutigam, W. (1974) 'Pathogenetische Theorien und Wege der Behandlung in der Psychosomatik', *Der Nervenarzt* 45: 354–63.

—— (1978a) 'Verbale und präverbale Methoden in der stationären Therapie', *Zeitschrift für psychosomatische Medizin und Psychoanalyse* 24: 146–55.

—— (1978b) 'Die stationäre Psychotherapie in der Versorgung psychisch Kranker', in F. Beese (ed.) *Stationäre Psychotherapie*, Göttingen: Vandenhoeck & Ruprecht.

Braütigam, W. and Von Rad, M. (eds) (1977) *Towards a Theory of Psychosomatic Disorders, Alexithymia, Pensée opératoire, Psychosomatische Phänomene*, Basle: Karger.

Bräutigam, W., Von Rad, M. and Engel, K. (1980) 'Erfolgs- und Therapieforschung bei psychoanalytischen Behandlungen', *Zeitschrift für psychosomatische Medizin und Psychoanalyse* 26: 101–18.

Brenner, C. (1968) 'Psychoanalysis and science', *Journal of the American Psychoanalytic Association* 16: 675.

—— (1976) *Praxis der Psychoanalyse. Psychischer Konflikt und Behandlungstechnik*, Frankfurt: Fischer (1979).

Brown, D. and Pedder, J. (1979) *Introduction to Psychotherapy*, London: Tavistock.

Chapman, G.E. (1984) 'A therapeutic community. Psychosocial nursing and the nursing process', *International Journal of Therapeutic Communities* 5: 68–76.

Christie, G. (1984) Personal communication.

Cohn, R.C. (1975) *Von der Psychoanalyse zur themenzentrierten Interaktion*, Stuttgart: Klett.

Cremerius, J. (1962) 'Die Beurteilung des Behandlungserfolgs in der Psychotherapie', *Monographie aus dem Gesamtgebiet der Neurologie und Psychiatrie, 99*, Berlin: Springer.

—— (1968) *Die Prognose funktioneller Syndrome*, Stuttgart: Enke.

—— (1977a) 'Über-Ich-Störung und ihre Therapie', *Psyche* 31: 593–636.

—— (1977b) 'Kritik des Konzepts der psychosomatischen Struktur', *Psyche* 31: 293–317.

—— (1979a) 'Die Entwicklung der psychoanalytischen Technik' in *Theorie und Praxis der Psychoanalyse*, Fellbach: Bonz.

—— (1979b) 'Gibt es zwei psychoanalytische Techniken?' *Psyche* 33:

577–96.

Cumming, J. and Cumming, E. (1962) *Ego and Milieu*, New York: Atherton Press.

Danckwardt, J.F. (1976)'Stationäre Behandlung. Katamnese und sekundäre Prävention neurotischer Störungen', *Der Nervenarzt* 47: 225–31.

—— (1978) 'Zur Interaktion von Psychotherapie und Psychopharmakotherapie', *Psyche* 32: 111–54.

—— (1979) 'Psychotherapie und Psychopharmakotherapie in Kombination', *Psyche* 33: 528–50.

De Board, R. (1978), *The Psychoanalysis of Organisations*, London: Tavistock.

De Boor, C. and Künzler, E. (1963) *Die psychosomatische Klinik und ihre Patienten*, Stuttgart: Klett.

Degler, R., Diedrich, R. Enke, H. and Studt, H.H. (1967) '5–Jahres-Katamnesen stationär psychotherapeutisch behandelter Patienten', Doc. III, *Münchener medizinische Wochenschau* 109: 925–34.

Dehe, W., Kontos, J., Markert, F., Mentzos, S. and Rothe, H.J. (1979) 'Abgebrochene psychotherapeutische Behandlungen', *Praxis der Psychotherapie und Psychosomatik* 24: 165–83.

Denford, J. (1983) 'Some in-patient groupings and their effects', Unpublished paper, Cassel Hospital, London.

Denford, J., Schachter, J., Temple, N., Kind, P. and Rosser, R. (1983) 'Selection and outcome in in-patient psychotherapy', *British Journal of Medical Psychology* 56: 225–43.

De Schill, S. (ed.) *Psychoanalytische Therapie in Gruppen*, Stuggart: Klett.

De Schwaan, A. (1978) 'Zur Soziogenese des psychoanalytischen 'Settings'', *Psyche* 32: 793–826.

Deter, H.C. (1981) 'Zur Methodik von katamnestischen Untersuchungen bei psychosomatischen Patienten am Beispiel einer Gruppe von 31 Anorexiepatienten', *Psychotherapie medizinische Psychologie* 31: 48–52.

Deter, H.C. and Allert, G. (1983) 'Group therapy of asthma patients: a concept for the psychosomatic treatment of patients in a medical clinic – a controlled study', *Psychotherapy and Psychosomatics* 40: 95–105.

Deter, H.C., Leukeit, S., Becker-von Rose, P. and Rapp, W. (1979) 'Die Bedeutung des psychosozialen Hintergrunds für Diagnose und Therapie von Patienten einer allgemein- internistischen Station', *Praxis der Psychotherapie und Psychosomatik* 24: 213–30.

Deter, H.C. and Reindell, A. (1981) 'Gruppenbehandlung in der klinischen Psychosomatik', *Gruppenpsychotherapie und Gruppendynamik*, 17: 193–204.

Devereux, G. (1967) *From Anxiety to Method in the Behavioral Sciences*, The Hague-Paris: Mouton & Co.

Drees, A. (1981) 'Alexithymie auf einer psychosomatischen Station', in F. Heigl and H. Neun (eds) *Psychotherapie im Krankenhaus*, Göttingen: Vandenhoeck & Ruprecht.

Drees, A., Künsebeck, H-W., Otte, H. and Ritter, J. (1978) 'Die Psychosomatische Station der Medizinischen Hochschule Hannover',

Der Krankenhausarzt 51: 628–34.

Dührssen, A. (1962) 'Katamnestische Ergebnisse bei 1004 Patienten nach analytischer Psychotherapie', *Zeitschrift für psychosomatische Medizin* 2: 94–113.

—— (1972) *Analytische Psychotherapie in Theorie, Praxis und Ergebnisse*, Göttingen: Vandenhoeck & Ruprecht.

Dührssen, A. and Jorswieck E. (1965) 'Eine empirisch-statistische Untersuchung zur Leistungsfähigkeit psychoanalytischer Behandlungen', *Der Nervenarzt* 36: 166–9.

Eicke, D. (ed.) (1976) *Die Psychologie des 20. Jahrhunderts 2*, Zurich: Kindler.

Engel, K., Haas, E., Von Rad, M., Senf, W. and Becker, H. (1979a) 'Zur Einschätzung von Behandlungen mit Hilfe psychoanalytischer Konzepte ('Heidelberger Rating')', *Medizinische Psychologie* 5: 253–68.

Engel, K., Von Rad, M., Becker, H. and Bräutigam, W. (1979b) 'Das Heidelberger Katamneseprojekt', *Medizinische Psychologie* 5: 124–37.

Enke, H. (1965) 'Bipolare Gruppenpsychotherapie als Möglichkeit psychoanalytischer Arbeit in der stationären Psychotherapie', *Zeitschrift für Psychotherapie und medizinische Psychologie* 15: 116–21.

—— (1968) 'Analytisch orientierte stationäre Gruppenpsychotherapie und das psychoanalytische Abstinenzprinzip', *Gruppenpsychotherapie und Gruppendynamik* 1: 28–40.

Enke, H., Houben, A., Ferchland, E., Maass, G., Rotas, P. and Wittich, G.H. (1964) 'Gruppenpsychotherapie – ihre Bedeutung für die stationäre Psychotherapie in der inneren Klinik', in W. Keiderling (ed.) *Beiträge zur Inneren Medizin*, Stuttgart.

Enke, H. and Wittich, G.H. (1965) 'Moderne Formen aktiver Bewegungstherapie in der psychosomatischen Medizin', *Therapiewoche* 15: 688.

Erikson, E.H. (1956) 'The problem of ego identity', in *Identity: Youth and Crisis*, New York: Norton.

Ermann, M. (1974) 'Verlaufsbeobachtung zur körperlichen Symptomatik bei stationär behandelten Neurotikern', *Zeitschrift für psychosomatische Medizin und Psychoanalyse* 20: 378–83.

—— (1979) 'Gemeinsame Funktionen therapeutischer Beziehungen bei stationärer Anwendung der Psychoanalyse', *Zeitschrift für psychosomatische Medizin und Psychoanalyse* 25: 333–41.

—— (1982) 'Regression in der stationär-analytischen Psychotherapie', *Zeitschrift für psychosomatische Medizin und Psychoanalyse* 28: 176–88.

—— (1983) 'Psychovegetative Störungen und stationäre Psychotherapie', *Praxis der Psychotherapie und Psychosomatik* 28: 131–8.

—— (1985) 'Die stationäre Langzeitpsychotherapie als psychoanalytischer Prozeß', in H. Schepank and W. Tress (eds) (1988) *Die stationäre Psychotherapie und ihr Rahmen*, Berlin: Springer.

Ermann, M., Gaitzsh, U. and Schepank, H. (1981) 'Erfahrungen mit einem mehrstufigen stationären Psychotherapiekonzept', in F. Heigl and H. Neun (eds) *Psychotherapie im Krankenhaus*, Göttingen:

Vandenhoeck & Ruprecht.
Ernst, K., Kind, H. and Rotach-Fuchs, M. (eds) (1968) *Ergebnisse der Verlaufsbeobachtungen bei Neurosen*, Berlin: Springer.
Feiereis, H. (1982) 'Integrierte psychosomatische Diagnostik und Therapie', *Schleswig-Holsteinisches Ärzteblatt*, 823–38.
Fenichel, O. (1941) *Problems of Psychoanalytic Technique*, Albany, NY: The Psychoanalytic Quarterly Inc.
—— (1945) *The Psychoanalytic Theory of Neurosis*, New York: Norton.
Filter, P., Wesemann, H.G., Kahley, M., Bayerl, P., Demmering, M., Franz, J., Kettner, W., Korenberg, H., Reim, W. and Schmidt, S. (1981) 'Patientenzentrierte Medizin an einer internistischen Fachklinik', in T. von Uexküll (ed.) *Integrierte psychosomatische Medizin*, Stuttgart: Schattauer.
Foulkes, S.H. (1964) *Therapeutic Group Analysis*, London: Allen & Unwin. (Maresfield Reprints 1984).
—— (1975) *Group-Analytic Psychotherapy*, London: Gordon & Breach (Maresfield Reprints 1986).
Freud, S. (1910) 'The future prospects of psycho-analytic therapy', in Standard Edition of the *Complete Psychological Works* of Sigmund Freud (SE) 11, London: Hogarth Press and the Institute of Psycho-analysis.
—— (1912) 'The dynamics of transference', in SE 12.
—— (1913) 'On beginning the treatment', in SE 12.
—— (1914) 'Remembering, repeating and working through', in SE 12.
—— (1919 [1918]) 'Lines of advance in psycho-analytic therapy', in SE 17.
—— (1921) *Group Psychology and the Analysis of the Ego*, in SE 18.
—— (1923) 'Two encyclopaedia articles', in SE 18.
—— (1937) 'Constructions in analysis', in SE 23.
Freyberger, H. (1977) 'Psychosomatik der erwachsenen Patienten', in H. Freyberger (ed.) *Psychosomatik des Kinderalters und des erwachsenen Patienten. Klinik der Gegenwart, 11*, Munich: Urban & Schwarzenberg.
—— (1978) 'Klinisch-psychosomatische Praxis: Grundlagen und Effektivitätskriterien', *Der Krankenhausarzt* 51: 645–58.
Fromm-Reichmann, F. (1947) 'Probleme der Durchführung der Behandlung in einer psychoanalytischen Klinik', in *Psychoanalyse und Psychotherapie*, Stuttgart: Klett.
—— (1950) *Principles of Intensive Psychotherapy*, Chicago: University Press.
Fürstenau, P. (1974) 'Zur Problematik von Psychotherapiekombinationen aus der Sicht der vergleichenden Psychotherapieforschung und der Organisationssoziologie', *Gruppenpsychologie und Gruppendynamik* 8: 131–40.
—— (1977a) 'Die beiden Dimensionen des psychoanalytischen Umgangs mit strukturell Ich-gestörten Patienten', *Psyche* 31: 197–207.
—— (1977b) 'Praxeologische Grundlagen der Psychoanalyse', in L.J. Pongratz (ed.) *Handbuch der Psychologie, Klinische Psychologie 8*, Göttingen: Verlag für Psychologie.
—— (1977c) 'Über die politische Relevanz psychoanalytischer Praxis',

Gruppendynamik 8: 49–65.

Fürstenau, P., Stephanos, S.F. and Zenz, H. (1970) 'Erfahrungen mit einer gruppentherapeutisch geführten Neurotikerstation', *Psychotherapie medizinische Psychologie* 20: 95–104.

Göllner, R. and Deter, H.C. (1979) 'Bemerkungen zu Verlaufs- und Erfolgskontrollen', in P. Hahn (ed.) *Psychologie des 20. Jahrhunderts 9*, Zurich: Kindler.

Göllner, R., Langen, D. and Streeck, U. (1981) 'Psychotherapeutische Kliniken im überregionalen Vergleich', *Psychotherapie medizinische Psychologie* 31: 42–7.

Göllner, R., Volk, W. and Ermann, M. (1978) 'Analyse von Behandlungsergebnissen eines zehnjährigen Katamneseprogrammes', in F. Beese (ed.) *Stationäre Psychotherapie*, Göttingen: Vandenhoeck & Ruprecht.

Goffman, E. (1967) *Stigma. Über Techniken der Bewältigung beschädigter Identität*, Frankfurt: Suhrkamp.

Graupe, S-R. (1975) 'Ergebnisse und Probleme der quantitativen Erforschung traditioneller Psychotherapie-Verfahren', in H. Strotzka (ed.) *Psychotherapie: Grundlagen, Verfahren, Indikation*, Munich: Urban & Schwarzenberg.

Green, A. (1975) 'Analytiker, Symbolisierung und Abwesenheit im Rahmen der psychoanalytischen Situation', *Psyche* 29: 503–41.

Greenacre, P. (1976) 'Rekonstruktionen', *Psyche* 30: 703–22.

Greenson R. R. (1967) *The Technique and Practice of Psychoanalysis*, London: Hogarth Press.

Häfner, H. (1975) 'Sondervotum', in Bericht zur Lage der Psychiatrie in der Bundesrepublik Deutschland (1975), Deutscher Bundestag, 7. Wahlperiode, Drucksache 7/4200/4201.

Hahn, P. (ed.) (1979) *Die Psychologie des 20. Jahrhunderts 9*, Zurich: Kindler.

Hahn, P., Vollrath, P. and Petzold, E. (1974) 'Aus der Arbeit einer klinisch-psychosomatischen Station', *Praxis der Psychotherapie* 2: 66.

Harrach, A., Hauser, R., Lössberg, K. and Nadler, H. (1981) 'Gruppentherapie kombiniert mit nonverbalen Therapiemethoden', in G. Mentzel (ed.) *Die psychosomatische Kurklinik*, Göttingen: Vandenhoeck & Ruprecht.

Hartocollis, P. (1980) 'Long-term hospital treatment for adult patients with borderline and narcissistic disorders', *Bulletin of the Menninger Clinic* 44: 212–26.

Hau, T.F. (1968) 'Stationäre Psychotherapie: ihre Indikation und ihre Anforderungen an die psychoanalytische Technik', *Zeitschrift für psychosomatische Medizin und Psychoanalyse* 14: 25.

—— (1970) 'Die Abhängigkeit der Psychotherapieform von Struktur und Gruppendynamik der Klinik', *Gruppenpsychotherapie und Gruppendynamik* 3: 199–206.

—— (1973) 'Prinzipien stationärer Psychotherapie', in T.F. Hau (ed.) (1975) *Psychosomatische Medizin in ihren Grundzügen*, Stuttgart: Hippokrates.

—— (ed.) (1975) *Psychosomatische Medizin in ihren Grundzügen*,

Stuttgart, Hippokrates.

Heigl, F. (1972) *Indikation und Prognose in Psychoanalyse und Psychotherapie*, Göttingen: Verlag für Medizinische Psychologie.

Heigl, F. and Nerenz, K. (1975) 'Gruppenarbeit in der Neurosenklinik', *Gruppenpsychotherapie und Gruppendynamik* 9: 96–117.

Heigl, F. and Neun, H. (1981) *Psycotherapie im Krankenhaus*, Göttingen: Vandenhoeck & Ruprecht.

Heigl-Evers, A. (1969) 'Zum sozialen Effekt klinischer analytischer Gruppenpsychotherapie', *Psychotherapy and Psychosomatics* 17: 50–62.

Heigl-Evers, A. and Heigl, F. (1973a) 'Die themenzentrierte interaktionelle Gruppenmethode (R. C. Cohn): Erfahrungen, Überlegungen, Modifikationen', *Gruppenpsychotherapie und Gruppendynamik* 7: 237–55.

—— (1973b) 'Gruppentherapie: interaktionell – tiefenpsychologisch fundiert (analytisch orientiert) – psychoanalytisch', *Gruppenpsychotherapie und Gruppendynamik* 7: 132–57.

—— (1975) 'Zur tiefenpsychologisch fundierten oder analytisch orientierten Gruppenpsychotherapie des Göttinger Modells', *Gruppenpsychotherapie und Gruppendynamik* 9: 237–66.

—— (1976) 'Zum Konzept der unbewußten Phantasie in der psychoanalytischen Gruppentherapie des Göttinger Modells', *Gruppenpsychotherapie und Gruppendynamik* 11: 6–22.

—— (ed.) (1979) *Die Psychologie des 20. Jahrhunderts 8*, Zurich: Kindler.

Heigl-Evers, A., Heigl, F. and Münch, J. (1976) 'Die therapeutische Kleingruppe in der Institution Klinik', *Gruppenpsychotherapie und Gruppendynamik* 10: 50–63.

Heim, E. (ed.) (1978) *Milieu-Therapie. Erlernen sozialer Verhaltensmuster in der psychiatrischen Klinik*, Bern: Huber.

Heimann, P. (1960) 'Bemerkungen zur Gegenübertragung', *Psyche* 18: 483–93.

Heising, G., Brieskorn, M. and Rost, W-D. (1982) *Sozialschicht und Gruppenpsychotherapie*, Göttingen: Vandenhoeck & Ruprecht.

Heising, G. and Möhlen, K. (1980) 'Die "Spaltungsübertragung" in der klinischen Psychotherapie', *Psychotherapie Medizinische Psychologie* 30: 70–6.

Hilpert, H. (1979) 'Therapeutische Gemeinschaft in einer psychotherapeutischen Klinik. Zum Behandlungskonzept des Cassel-Hospitals in London', *Psychotherapie medizinische Psychologie* 29: 46–53.

—— (1983) 'Über den Beitrag der therapeutischen Gemeinschaft zur stationären Psychotherapie', *Zeitschrift für psychosomatische Medizin und Psychoanalyse* 29: 28–36.

Hilpert, H. and Schwarz, R. (1981) 'Entwicklung und Kritik des Konzepts der therapeutischen Gemeinschaft', in H. Hilpert, R. Schwarz and F. Beese (eds) *Psychotherapie in der Klinik*, Berlin: Springer.

Hilpert, H., Schwarz, R. and Beese, F. (eds) (1981) *Psychotherapie in der Klinik. Von der therapeutischen Gemeinschaft zur stationären Psychotherapie*, Berlin: Springer.

Hinshelwood, R.D. and Manning, N. (eds) (1979) *Therapeutic Communities. Reflections and Progress*, London: Routledge & Kegan Paul.

Hoffmann, S.O., Brodthage, H., Trimborn, W. and Stemmer, T. (1981) 'Stationäre psychoanalytische Psychotherapie als eigenständige Behandlungsform', in F. Heigl and H. Neun (eds) *Psychotherapie im Krankenhaus*, Göttingen: Vandenhoeck & Ruprecht.

Jakab, J. (1968) 'Coordination of verbal psychotherapy and art therapy', *Psychiatry and Art* 1: 92–101.

James, O. (1984) 'The role of the nurse-therapist relationship in the therapeutic communities', *International Review of Psycho-Analysis* 11: 151–9.

Janssen, P.L. (1978) 'Zu einigen psychotherapeutischen Aspekten der Beschäftigungstherapie in einer psychiatrischen Klinik', *Psychotherapie medizinische Psychologie* 28: 183–93.

—— (1979) 'Zur Identität verschiedener Berufsgruppen in einer stationären psychoanalytischen Therapie', in *Theorie und Praxis der Psychoanalyse*, Fellbach: Bonz.

—— (1980) 'Stationäre Psychotherapie als angewandte Psychoanalyse', doctoral dissertation, University of Essen.

—— (1981a) 'Zur Vermittlung von Erfahrung und Einsicht in der stationären psychoanalytischen Therapie', in F. Heigl and H. Neun (eds) *Methoden stationärer Psychotherapie*, Göttingen: Vandenhoeck & Ruprecht.

—— (1981b) 'Sind psychosomatische Kliniken überflüssig?' *Deutsches Ärzteblatt* 78: 2353–8.

—— (1982) 'Psychoanalytisch orientierte Mal- und Musiktherapie im Rahmen stationärer Psychotherapie', *Psyche* 36: 541–70.

—— (1983) 'Behandlungsmodelle der stationären Psychosomatik und Psychotherapie', *Praxis der Psychotherapie und Psychosomatik* 28: 1–8.

—— (1985) 'Auf dem Wege zu einer integrativen analytisch-psychotherapeutischen Krankenhausbehandlung', *Forum der Psychoanalyse* 1: 293–307.

—— (1986) 'On integrative analytic-psychotherapeutic hospital treatment', *International Journal of Therapeutic Communities* 7: 225–41.

—— (1987) 'Zum Verstehen psycho-somatischer und somato-psychischer Vorgänge', *Zeitschrift für medizinische Psychologie, Psychopathologie und Psychotherapie* 36: 62–73.

Janssen, P.L. and Hekele, W. (1986) 'Die therapeutische Bedeutung des Malens im Gruppenprozeß stationärer psychoanalytischer Behandlungen', *Gruppenpsychotherapie und Gruppendynamik* 22: 151–65.

Janssen, P.L. and Quint, H. (1977) 'Stationäre analytische Gruppenpsychotherapie im Rahmen einer neuropsychiatrischen Klinik', *Gruppenpsychotherapie und Gruppendynamik* 11: 221–43.

—— (1987) 'Zur stationären analytischen Psychotherapie psychosomatisch erkrankter Patienten', in H. Quint and P.L. Janssen (eds) *Psychotherapie in der psychosomatischen Medizin*, Heidelberg: Springer.

Janssen, P.L. and Wienen, G. (1985) 'Narzißmus und Aggression in stationären Behandlungen', in *Narzißmus und Aggression*, Collected Congress Papers of the Deutsche Psychoanalytische Vereinigung, Wiesbaden.

Jonasch, K. (1978) 'Stationäre Psychotherapie als Einstieg in den psychotherapeutischen Prozeß', in F. Beese (ed.) (1978) *Stationäre Psychotherapie*, Göttingen: Vandenhoeck & Ruprecht.

Jones, M. (1953) *The Therapeutic Community: a New Treatment Method in Psychiatry*, New York: Basic Books.

Kächele, H., in cooperation with R. Schors (1981) 'Ansätze und Ergebnisse psychoanalytischer Therapieforschung', in U. Baumann, H. Berbalk and G. Seidenstücker (eds) *Klinische Psychologie: Trends in der Forschung und Praxis* 4, Bern: Huber.

Kauss, E.L. (1981) 'Das Prinzip der Re-Formierbarkeit im therapeutischen Raum. Ein Beitrag zur Indikation für stationäre Psychotherapie', in F. Heigl and H. Neun (eds) *Psychotherapie im Krankenhaus*, Göttingen: Vandenhoeck & Ruprecht.

Kayser, H. (1974) 'Die verschiedenen Formen der therapeutischen Gemeinschaft und ihre Indikation für die Praxis', *Psychotherapie medizinische Psychologie* 24: 80–94.

Kayser, H., Krüger, H., Mävers, W., Petersen, P., Rohde, M., Rose, H.K., Veltin, A. and Zumpe, V. (1973) *Gruppenarbeit in der Psychiatrie. Erfahrungen mit der therapeutischen Gemeinschaft*, Stuttgart: Thieme.

Keiderling, W. (ed.) (1964) *Beiträge zur Inneren Medizin*, Stuttgart.

Kemper, W.W. (1958) 'Psychoanalytische Gruppenpsychotherapie', *Zeitschrift für psychosomatische Medizin* 4: 221–3.

—— (1969) 'Übertragung und Gegenübertragung als funktionelle Einheit', *Jahrbuch der Psychoanalyse* 6: 35–68.

Kernberg, O.F. (1975a) *Borderline Conditions and Pathological Narcissism*, New York: Jason Aronson.

—— (1975b) 'Zur Behandlung narzißtischer Persönlichkeitsstörungen', *Psyche* 29: 890–905.

—— (1976a) *Object-Relations Theory and Clinical Psychoanalysis*, New York: Jason Aronson.

—— (1976b) 'Toward an integrative theory of hospital treatment', in *Object-Relations Theory and Clinical Psychoanalysis*, New York: Jason Aronson.

—— (1981) 'Zur Theorie der psychoanalytischen Psychotherapie', *Psyche* 35: 673–704.

Kernberg, O.F., Bierstein, E.D., Coyne, L., Appelbaum, A., Horwitz, L. and Voth, H. (1972) 'Psychotherapy and Psychoanalysis. Final Report of the Menninger Foundation Psychotherapy Research Project', *Bulletin of the Menninger Clinic* (1/2).

Kind, H. (1972) 'Die "Allgemeine" Psychotherapie des Nervenarztes', in K.P. Kinsker, J.E. Meyer, M. Müller and E. Stromgren (eds) *Psychiatrie der Gegenwart* 2 (1), Berlin: Springer.

Kind, H. and Rotach-Fuchs, M. (1968) 'Die Bedeutung der psychotherapeutischen und medikamentösen stationären Behandlung im langen Verlauf neurotischer Syndrome', in K. Ernst, H. Kind and M. Rotach-

Fuchs (eds) *Ergebnisse der Verlaufsbeobachtungen bei Neurosen*, Berlin: Springer.

Klausmeier, K. (1976) 'Musik-Erleben in der Pubertät', *Psyche* 30: 1113–36.

Koch, B. (1982) 'Die Schwester als Bezugsperson in der stationären Psychotherapie', *Die Schwester/Der Pfleger* 21: 578–81.

Köhle, K. (1979) 'Klinisch-Psychosomatische Krankenstation', in T. von Uexküll (ed.) *Lehrbuch der Psychosomatischen Medizin*, Munich: Urban & Schwarzenberg.

Köhle, K., Böck, D. and Grauhan, A. (1977) 'Die internistisch-psychosomatische Krankenstation'. A Workshop Report, Basle: Rocom.

Köhle, K., Bosch, H., Gaus, E., Joraschky, P., Gingelmaier, M., Kubanek, B., Simons, C., Paar, G., Rassek, M., Scheytt, C., Schultheis, K.H., Urban, H. and Jens, J. (1976) 'Klinische Psychosomatik', in H. Begemann (ed.) *Patient und Krankenhaus*, Munich: Urban & Schwarzenberg.

Köhle, K. and Kubanek, B. (1981) 'Zur Zusammenarbeit von Psychosomatikern und Internisten. Erfahrung aus zwölf Jahren', in T. von Uexküll (ed.) *Integrierte Psychosomatische Medizin*, Stuttgart: Schattauer.

Kohut, H. (1957) 'Observations on the psychological functions of music', *Journal of the American Psychoanalytic Association* 5: 389–407.

Kohut, H. and Levarie, S. (1950) 'On the enjoyment of listening to music', *Psychoanalytic Quarterly* 19: 64–87.

Köndgen, R. and Überla, K. (1962) 'Einjahreskatamnesen von 150 stationären psychotherapeutisch behandelten Patienten', *Psychotherapie medizinische Psychologie* 12: 246–52.

König, K. (1974) 'Analytische Gruppenpsychotherapie in der Klinik', *Gruppenpsychotherapie und Gruppendynamik* 8: 260–79.

—— (1975) 'Der Einfluß des klinisch-therapeutischen Settings auf die konfliktorientierte Behandlungsmotivation der Patienten', *Psychotherapie medizinische Psychologie* 25: 103–8.

König, K. and Neun, H. (1979) 'Psychotherapeutische Heilverfahren', in P. Hahn (ed.) *Die Psychologie des 20. Jahrhunderts 9*, Zurich: Kindler.

König, K. and Sachsse, U. (1981) 'Die zeitliche Limitierung in der klinischen Psychotherapie', in F. Heigl and H. Neun (eds) *Psychotherapie im Krankenhaus*, Göttingen: Vandenhoeck & Ruprecht.

Kordy, H., Von Rad, M. and Senf, W. (1983) 'Success and failure in psychotherapy: hypotheses and results from the Heidelberg follow-up project', *Psychotherapy and Psychosomatics* 40: 211–27.

Kramer, E. (1971) *Art as Therapy with Children*, New York: Schocken Books.

Krappmann, L. (1969) *Soziologische Dimensionen der Identität*, Stuttgart: Klett.

Kreeger, L. (ed.) (1975) *The Large Group*, London: Constable.

Krüger, H. (1979) *Therapeutische Gemeinschaft, ein sozialpsychiatrisches Prinzip*, Stuttgart: Enke.

Künsebeck, H.W., Otte, H., Ritter, J., Liebicher-Rawohl, J. and Drees, A. (1978) 'Erste Arbeitserfahrungen der psychosomatisch-psychotherapeutischen Station der Medizinischen Hochschule Hannover', *Therapiewoche* 28: 8079–94.

Kuiper, P.C. (1969) 'Zur Metapsychologie von Übertragung und Gegenübertragung', *Psyche* 23: 95–120.

Kutter, P. (1976) *Elemente der Gruppentherapie*, Göttingen: Vandenhoeck & Ruprecht.

—— (1977) 'Konzentrierte Psychotherapie auf psychoanalytischer Grundlage', *Psyche* 31: 957–74.

—— (1978) 'Modelle psychoanalytischer Gruppenpsychotherapie und das Verhältnis von Individuum und Gruppe', *Gruppenpsychotherapie und Gruppendynamik* 13: 134–51.

Lachauer, R., Neun, H. and Dahlmann, W. (1992) 'Psychosomatische Einrichtungen in Deutschland – eine Bestandsaufnahme', *Psychotherapie – Psychosomatik – medizinische Psychologie* 42: 1–10.

Lampl-De Groot, J. (1967) 'Die Zusammenarbeit von Patient und Analytiker in der psychoanalytischen Behandlung', *Psyche* 21: 73–83.

Langen, D. (1956) *Methodische Probleme der klinischen Psychotherapie*, Stuttgart: Thieme.

—— (1978) 'Mehrdimensionale stationäre Psychotherapie', in F. Beese (ed.) *Stationäre Psychotherapie*, Göttingen: Vandenhoeck & Ruprecht.

Langer, S.K. (1965) *Philosophie auf neuem Wege. Das Symbol im Denken, im Ritus und in der Kunst*, Frankfurt: Suhrkamp.

Lehrmann, C., Lempa, W. and Freyberger, H. (1987) 'Supportive Psychotherapie – eigenständig und als Vorstufe konfliktbearbeitender Therapie (einschließlich familientherapeutischer Manahmen) – mit besonderer Berücksichtigung des studentischen Hilfstherapeuten', in H. Quint and P.L. Janssen (eds) *Psychotherapie in der Psychosomatischen Medizin*, Berlin: Springer.

Levita, J.D. de (1971) *Der Begriff der Identität*, Frankfurt: Suhrkamp.

Loch, W. (1965a) *Voraussetzungen, Mechanismen und Grenzen des psychoanalytischen Prozesses*, Bern: Huber.

—— (1965b) 'Übertragung – Gegenübertragung', *Psyche* 19: 1–23.

—— (1974) 'Der Analytiker als Gesetzgeber und Lehrer', *Psyche* 28: 432–60.

—— (1975) 'Ärztliche Psychotherapie auf psychoanalytischer Grundlage', *Psyche* 29: 383–98.

Lorenzer, A. (1970) *Sprachzerstörung und Rekonstruktion*, Frankfurt: Suhrkamp.

McDougall, J. (1974) 'The psychosoma and the psychoanalytic process', *International Review of Psycho-Analysis* 1: 437–59.

Mahler, M.S., Pine, F. and Bergmann, A. (1975) *The Psychological Birth of the Human Infant*, London: Hutchinson.

Main, T.F. (1946) 'The hospital as a therapeutic institution', *Bulletin of the Menninger Clinic* 10: 66–70.

—— (1957) 'The ailment', *British Journal of Medical Psychology* 30: 129–45.

—— (1977) 'The concept of the therapeutic community: variations and vicissitudes', in *The Evolution of Group Analysis*, London: Routledge & Kegan Paul (1983) and in *Group Analysis*, 10 (2).

Malan, D.H. (1963) *A Study of Brief Psychotherapy*, London: Tavistock.

—— (1973) 'The outcome problem in psychotherapy research. A historical review', *Archives of General Psychiatry* 29: 719–29.

—— (1976) *Towards the Validation of Psychotherapy*, New York: Plenum Press.

Menninger, W. (1936) 'Psychoanalytic principles applied to the treatment of hospitalized patients', *Bulletin of the Menninger Clinic* 1: 35.

Mentzel, G. (1969) 'Zur gezielten Kurztherapie bei funktionellen Erkrankungen', *Zeitschrift für psychosomatische Medizin und Psychoanalyse* 1: 37.

—— (1976) 'Die Gruppenvisite', *Gruppenpsychotherapie und Gruppendynamik* 10: 233–48.

—— (1981) 'Das therapeutische Netz der psychosomatischen Kurklinik', in G. Mentzel (ed.) *Die psychosomatische Kurklinik*, Göttingen: Vandenhoeck & Ruprecht.

Mentzel, G. and Mentzel, C. (1977) 'Die Patienten der psychosomatischen Kurklinik', *Zeitschrift für psychosomatische Medizin und Psychoanalyse* 23: 56–72.

Mentzos, S. (1976) *Interpersonale und institutionalisierte Abwehr*, Frankfurt: Suhrkamp.

Meyer, A-E., Richter, R., Graw, K., von der Schulenburg, J.M. and Schulte, B. (1991) *Forschungsgutachten zu Fragen eines Psychotherapeutengesetzes*.

Meyer, R. (1978) 'Der psychosomatisch Kranke in der analytischen Kurzpsychotherapie', *Psyche* 32: 881–928.

Mitscherlich, A. (1969) *Krankheit als Konflikt*. Studien zur psychosomatischen Medizin 2, Frankfurt: Suhrkamp.

Modell, A.H. (1976) 'Die "bewahrende Umwelt" und die therapeutische Funktion der Psychoanalyse', *Psyche* 35: 788–808.

Möhlen, K. and Heising, G. (1980) 'Integrative stationäre Psychotherapie', *Gruppenpsychotherapie und Gruppendynamik* 15: 16–31.

Möller, M.L. (1977) 'Zur Theorie der Gegenübertragung', *Psyche* 31: 142–66.

Morgenthaler, F. (1978) *Technik. Zur Dialektik der psychoanalytischen Praxis*, Frankfurt: Syndikat Autoren- und Verlagsgesellschaft.

Morrice, J.K.W. (1972) 'Myth and the democratic process', *British Journal of Medical Psychology* 45: 327–31.

Müller-Braunschweig, H. (1974) 'Psychopathologie und Kreativität', *Psyche* 28: 600–34.

—— (1977) 'Aspekte einer psychoanalytischen Kreativitätstheorie', *Psyche* 31: 821–43.

Müller-Braunschweig, H. and Möhlen, K. (1980) 'Averbale Therapieformen bei Anfallsleiden', *Psyche* 34: 1073–91.

Muir, B.J. (1980) 'Is in-patient psychotherapy a valid concept?', Lecture, Cassel Hospital Diamond Jubilee Conference. Unpublished.

Naumburg, M. (1966) *Dynamically Oriented Art Therapy: Its Principles and Practices*, New York: Grune & Stratton.

Nemiah, J.C. and Sifneos, P.P. (1970) 'Affect and fantasy in patients with psychosomatic disorders', in O.W. Hill (ed.) *Modern Trends in Psychosomatic Medicine – 2*, London: Butterworth.

Nerenz, K. (1977) 'Die Bedeutung der äußeren Realität für die psychoanalytische Situation', *Zeitschrift für psychosomatische Medizin und Psychoanalyse* 23: 152–69.

Neun, H. and Arbeitskreis Klinischer Psychosomatik in dem DKPM (1981) 'Stationäre Behandlungsmöglichkeiten für psychosomatisch Kranke in der BRD'. Paper delivered at the DKPM Conference, March 1981.

Novotny, P.C. (1973) 'The pseudopsychoanalytic hospital', *Bulletin of the Menninger Clinic* 37: 193–210.

Ohlmeier, D. (1976) 'Gruppeneigenschaften des psychischen Apparates', in D. Eicke (ed.) *Psychologie des 20. Jahrhunderts 2*, Zurich: Kindler.

—— (1979) 'Bemerkungen zur gruppentherapeutischen Anwendung der Psychoanalyse', in *Theorie und Praxis der Psychoanalyse*, Fellbach: Bonz.

Petzold, E. (1979) 'Aktiv-Klinische Verfahren', in P. Hahn (ed.) *Psychologie des 20. Jahrhunderts 9*, Zurich: Kindler.

Pines, M. (1975) Overview, in L. Kreeger (ed.) *The Large Group*, London: Constable.

Ploeger, A. (1972) *Die therapeutische Gemeinschaft in der Psychotherapie und Sozialpsychiatrie*, Stuttgart: Thieme.

Plojé, P.M. (1977) 'Über einige Schwierigkeiten bei der psychoanalytisch orientierten Einzeltherapie von Klinikpatienten', in H. Hilpert, R. Schwarz and F. Beese (eds) *Psychotherapie in der Klinik*, Berlin: Springer.

Pohlen, M. (1972) *Gruppenanalyse. Eine methodenkritische Studie und empirische Untersuchung im klinischen Feld*, Göttingen: Vandenhoeck & Ruprecht.

—— (1973) 'Das Münchener Kooperationsmodell. Gruppentherapie in einem neuen klinischen Organisationsmodell', *Der Nervenarzt* 44: 476–83.

Pohlen, M. and Bautz, M. (1972) 'Eine empirische Untersuchung über die therapeutische Funktion des Schwesternpersonals in einem neuen klinischen Organisationsmodell', *Psychotherapie medizinische Psychologie* 22: 161–76.

—— (1974) 'Gruppenanalyse als Kurzpsychotherapie', *Der Nervenarzt* 45: 514–33.

—— (1978) 'Die Rolle des Therapeuten im Münchener Kooperationsmodell', *Gruppenpsychotherapie und Gruppendynamik* 13: 1–24.

Pohlen, M., Kauß, E. and Wittmann, L. (1979) 'Der therapeutische Raum als psychotherapeutisches Behandlungsprinzip im klinischen Feld', in A. Heigl-Evers (ed.) *Die Psychologie des 20. Jahrhunderts 8*, Zurich: Kindler.

Pongratz, L.J. (ed.) (1977) *Handbuch der Psychologie, Klinishe Psychologie 8*, Göttingen: Verlag für Psychologie.

Quint, H. (1969) 'Über analytische Psychotherapie im Rahmen der

Klinik', *Medizinisch Welt* 20: 2722–7.

—— (1972) 'Psychoanalytische Aspekte klinischer Gruppenpsycho-therapie', in *Sozialpsychiatrie und Psychopharmakologie in ihrer Verflechtung*, Janssen Symposium 10.

Quint, H. and Janssen, P.L. (eds) (1987) *Psychotherapie in der psychosomatischen Medizin*, Heidelberg: Springer.

Rapoport, R.N. (1960) *Community as Doctor*, London: Tavistock.

Reindell, A. and Petzold, E. (1976) 'Formen und Kriterien für eine Behandlung auf einer klinisch-psychosomatischen Station', *Zeitschrift für Psychotherapie und medizinische Psychologie* 26: 191–9.

Reindell, A., Petzold, E., Deter, C., Stindl, E. and Hahn, P. (1977) 'Simultandiagnostik und Simultantherapie auf einer klinisch-psychosomatischen Station', *Zeitschrift für psychosomatische Medizin und Psychoanalyse* 23: 387–96.

Remplein, S. (1977) *Therapieforschung in der Psychoanalyse*, Munich: Reinhardt.

Rice, A.K. (1965) *Learning for Leadership*, London: Tavistock.

—— (1969) 'Individual, group and intergroup processes', *Human Relations* 22: 565–84.

Rice, C.A. and Rutan, J.S. (eds) (1987) *Inpatient Group Psychotherapy: A Psychodynamic Perspective*, New York: Basic Books.

Richter, H-E. (1967) *Eltern, Kind und Neurose*, Reinbek: Rowohlt.

—— (1970) *Patient Familie. Entstehung, Struktur und Therapie von Konflikten in Ehe und Familie*, Reinbek: Rowohlt.

Rosenfeld, H. (1978) 'Some therapeutic factors in psychoanalysis', *International Journal of Psychoanalytic Psychotherapy*, 7: 152–64.

Rotmann, M. (1978) 'Über die Bedeutung des Vaters in der "Wiederannäherungs-Phase"', *Psyche* 32: 1105–47.

Rüger, U. (1980) 'Various regressive processes and their prognostic value in inpatient group psychotherapy', *International Journal of Group Psychotherapy* 30: 95–105.

—— (1981) *Stationär-ambulante Gruppenpsychotherapie*, Berlin: Springer.

—— (1982) 'Die stationär-ambulante Gruppenpsychotherapie – Ergebnisse im Hinblick auf Änderung im Bereich von Symptomatik und Persönlichkeitsstruktur', *Zeitschrift für psychosomatische Medizin und Psychoanalyse* 28: 189–99.

Sandler, J., Dare, C. and Holder, A. (1973) *The Patient and the Analyst: The Basis of the Psychoanalytic Process*, London: George Allen & Unwin.

Sandner, D. (1978) *Psychodynamik in Kleingruppen*, Munich: Reinhardt.

Schepank, H. and Studt, H.H. (1976) 'Die psychosomatische Klinik am Zentralinstitut für seelische Gesundheit', *Medizin Mannheim* 1: 30–4.

Schepank, H. and Tress, W. (eds) (1988) *Die stationäre Psychotherapie und ihr Rahmen*, Berlin: Springer.

Schmölz, A. (1976) 'Motivation und Methode aktiver Musiktherapie', *Musik und Medizin* 7: 43–6.

Schulz, U. and Hermanns, L.M. (1987) 'Das Sanatorium Schloß Tegel Ernst Simmels – Zur Geschichte und Konzeption der ersten

Psychoanalytischen Klinik', *Psychotherapie medizinische Psychologie* 37: 58–67.
Schwarz, F. (1979) 'Ergebnisse nach stationärer Gruppenpsychotherapie neurotisch depressiver und zwangsneurotischer Patienten', *Der Nervenarzt* 50: 379–86.
Schwennbeck, R. (1992) 'Langzeiteffekte stationärer psychoanalytischer Therapie', Inaug. Dissertation, Ruhr-Universität Bochum: .
Sellschopp, A. and Vollrath, P. (1979) 'Psychoanalytisch-klinische Therapie', in P. Hahn (ed.) *Die Psychologie des 20. Jahrhunderts 9*, Zurich: Kindler.
Sellschopp-Rüppell, A. (1977) 'Behavioural characteristics in in-patient group psychotherapy with psychosomatic patients', in W. Bräutigam and M. Von Rad (eds) *Towards a Theory of Psychosomatic Disorders, Alexithymia, Pensée opératoire, Psychosomatische Phänomene*, Basle: Karger.
Simmel, E. (1928) 'Die psychoanalytische Behandlung in der Klinik', *Internationale Zeitung der Psychoanalyse* 14: 352–70.
Spitz, R.A. (1954) *Die Entstehung der ersten Objektbeziehungen*, Stuttgart: Klett (1978).
—— (1956/7) 'Übertragung und Gegenübertragung', *Psyche* 10: 63–81.
—— (1957) *No and Yes: On the Genesis of Human Communication*, New York: International Universities Press.
Stanton, A.H. and Schwarz, M.S. (1954) *The Mental Hospital*, New York: Basic Books.
Stephanos, S. (1973) 'Analytisch-psychosomatische Therapie', *Jahrbuch der Psychoanalyse*, Supplement 1, Berne: Huber.
—— (1978a) 'Therapiebezogene Forschung in der psychosomatischen Medizin', *Zeitschrift für psychosomatische Medizin und Psychoanalyse* 24: 180–6.
—— (1978b) 'Sexualobjekt, libidinöses Objekt und Übertragungsprozeß', *Jahrbuch der Psychoanalyse* 10: 111–34.
—— (1979) 'Theorie und Praxis der analytisch-psychosomatischen Therapie', in T. von Uexküll (ed.) *Lehrbuch der psychosomatischen Medizin*, Munich: Urban & Schwarzenberg.
Stephanos, S. and Zens, J. (1974) 'Die Krankenschwester als therapeutische Bezugsperson und das Nachbehandlungsarrangement im Stationsmodell der Psychosomatischen Klinik Gießen', *Zeitschrift für Psychotherapie und medizinische Psychologie* 24: 117–31.
Stierlin, H. (1975) *Von der Psychoanalyse zur Familientherapie*, Stuttgart: Klett.
Strobel, W. and Huppmann, G. (1978) *Musiktherapie. Grundlagen – Formen – Möglichkeiten*, Göttingen: Verlag für Psychologie Hogrefe.
Strotzka, H. (1975) 'Stationäre Psychotherapie', in H. Strotzka (ed.) *Psychotherapie: Grundlagen, Verfahren, Indikation*, Munich: Urban & Schwarzenberg.
Tarachow, S. (1963) *An Introduction to Psychotherapy*, London: Hogarth Press.
Thomä, H. (1977) 'Identität und Selbstverständnis des Psychoanalytikers', *Psyche* 31: 1–42.

Trimborn, W. (1983) 'Die Zerstörung des therapeutischen Raumes. Das Dilemma stationärer Psychotherapie bei Borderline-Patienten', *Psyche* 37: 204–36.

Trimborn, W., Brodthage, H., Hoffmann, S.O. and Stemmer, T. (1981) 'Die Bearbeitung von Trennung und Entlassung im Rahmen der stationären Psychotherapie', in F. Heigl and H. Neun (eds) *Psychotherapie im Krankenhaus*, Göttingen: Vandenhoeck & Ruprecht.

Tyson, R.L. and Sandler, J. (1974) 'Probleme der Auswahl von Patienten für eine Psychoanalyse', *Psyche* 28: 530–59.

Van Eck, L.A.J.M. (1972) 'Transference in relation to the hospital', *Psychotherapy and Psychosomatics* 20: 135–8.

Volkan, V.D. (1976) *Primitive Internalized Object Relations*, New York: International Universities Press.

Von Rad, M. (1983) *Alexithymie*, Berlin: Springer.

Von Rad, M. and Rüppell, A. (1975) 'Combined inpatient and outpatient group psychotherapy: a therapeutic model of psychosomatics', *Psychotherapy and Psychosomatics* 26: 237–43.

Von Rad, M. and Werner, K.H. (1981) 'Kombinierte analytische Gruppentherapie bei psychosomatischen und psychoneurotischen Patienten. Eine Nachuntersuchung', *Gruppenpsychotherapie und Gruppendynamik* 16: 321–34.

Von Uexküll, T. (1973) 'Psychosomatic medicine. Subspeciality or integrated discipline?', *Psychotherapy and Psychosomatics* 22: 185–8.

—— (1979) *Lehrbuch der psychosomatischen Medizin*, Munich: Urban & Schwarzenberg.

—— (1981a) 'Psychosomatische Medizin gestern, heute und morgen', *Therapiewoche* 31: 838–52.

—— (ed.) (1981b) *Integrierte psychosomatische Medizin*, Stuttgart Schattauer.

Von Weizsäcker, V. (1948) *Grundfragen medizinischer Anthropologie*, Tübingen: Furche.

Wälder, R. (1930) 'Das Prinzip der mehrfachen Funktion', *Internationale Zeitung der Psychoanalyse* 16: 285–300.

Weiner, H. (1977) *Psychobiology and Human Disease*, New York: Elsevier.

Whiteley, J.S. (1978) 'Die heikle Position des Leiters in therapeutischer Gemeinschaft und Großgruppe', in H. Hilpert, R. Schwarz and F. Beese (eds) (1981) *Psychotherapie in der Klinik*, Berlin: Springer.

Widok, W. (1981) 'Institutionalisierte psychoanalytisch begründete Psychotherapie', in F. Heigl and H. Neun (eds) *Psychotherapie im Krankenhaus*, Göttingen: Vandenhoeck & Ruprecht.

—— (1983) 'Stationäre psychosomatische Psychotherapie auf der Basis eines psychoanalytischen Konzeptes', *Praxis der Psychotherapie und Psychosomatik* 28: 103–6.

Wiegmann, H. (1955) *Medizinische Wochenschau 2*: 14 and 91, quoted in R. Köndgen and K. Überla (1962) 'Einjahreskatamnesen von 150 stationären psychotherapeutisch behandelten Patienten', *Psychotherapie medizinische Psychologie* 12: 246–52.

—— (1968) *Der Neurotiker in der Klinik. Einführung in die Theorie und*

Praxis stationärer Psychotherapie, Göttingen: Vandenhoeck & Ruprecht.

Willi, J. (1975) *Die Zweierbeziehung*, Reinbek: Rowohlt.

—— (1978) *Therapie der Zweierbeziehung*, Reinbek: Rowohlt.

Willms, H. (1975) *Musiktherapie bei psychotischen Erkrankungen*, Stuttgart: Fischer.

Wilson, G. (1984) Personal communication.

Winnicott, D.W. (1951) 'Transitional objects and transitional phenomena', in D.W. Winnicott (1958) *Through Paediatrics to Psycho-Analysis*, London: Hogarth Press.

—— (1958) *Through Paediatrics to Psycho-Analysis*, London: Hogarth Press.

—— (1960a) 'The theory of the parent-infant relationship', in D.W. Winnicott (1965) *The Maturational Processes and the Facilitating Environment*, London: Hogarth Press.

—— (1960b) 'Counter-transference', in D.W. Winnicott (1965) *The Maturational Processes and the Facilitating Environment*, London: Hogarth Press.

—— (1962) 'Ego integration in child development', in D.W. Winnicott (1965) *The Maturational Processes and the Facilitating Environment*, London: Hogarth Press.

—— (1965) *The Maturational Processes and the Facilitating Environment*, London: Hogarth Press.

—— (1971) *Playing and Reality*, London: Tavistock.

Wittich, G.H. (1967) 'Psychosomatische Rehabilitation', *Arbeitsmedizin, Sozialmedizin und Arbeitshygiene* 2: 73–5.

—— (1975) 'Therapy in psychosomatic hospitals. Strategy and management', in Antonelli, F. (ed.) *Therapy in Psychosomatic Medicine*. Third Congress of the International College of Psychosomatic Medicine, Rome: Pozzi.

—— (1977) 'The integrated psychosomatic hospital – its contribution to theory and treatment of psychosomatic disorders'. Paper given at the International Congress for Psychotherapy Research, Heidelberg.

Wittich, G.H. and Buchmüller, J. (1981) 'The psychosomatic hospital as a facilitating setting for the psychotherapeutic and psychoanalytic process'. Lecture at ICPM Congress in Montreal.

Wittich, G.H. and Enke-Ferchland, E. (1968) 'Mehrdimensionale integrierte Gruppentherapie in der psychosomatischen Rehabilitation', *Psychotherapy and Psychosomatics* 16: 261–70.

Yalom, I.D. (1983) *Inpatient Group Psychotherapy*, New York: Basic Books.

Zauner, J. (1969) 'Berufliche Wiedereingliederung durch klinische Psychotherapie', *Psychotherapy and Psychosomatics* 17: 63–72.

—— (1972) 'Analytische Psychotherapie und soziales Lernen in Klinik und Heim', *Praxis der Kinderpsychologie und Kinderpsychiatrie* 21: 166–70.

—— (1974) 'Psychopharmaka und klinische Psychotherapie', *Zeitschrift für psychosomatische Medizin und Psychoanalyse* 20: 138–47.

—— (1978) 'Das Problem der Regression und die Rolle des

Durcharbeitens im Realitätsraum der psychotherapeutischen Klinik', in F. Beese (ed.) *Stationäre Psychotherapie*, Göttingen: Vandenhoeck & Ruprecht.

Ziese, P. (1978) 'Steuerungsinstrumente in dem komplexen Mechanismus der stationären analytisch orientierten Psychotherapie', *Praxis der Psychotherapie* 23: 133–40.

Index